No One Ever

No One Ever Asked Me

The World War II Memoirs of an Omaha Indian Soldier

HOLLIS D. STABLER

Edited by VICTORIA SMITH

University of Nebraska Press   Lincoln and London

Library of Congress
Cataloging-in-Publication Data
Stabler, Hollis Dorion.
No one ever asked me : the World
War II memoirs of an Omaha
Indian soldier / Hollis D. Stabler,
edited by Victoria Smith.
p. cm.—(American Indian lives)
Includes bibliographical refer-
ences and index.
ISBN-13: 978-0-8032-4324-8
(cloth : alk. paper)
ISBN-10: 0-8032-4324-3 (cloth :
alk. paper)
ISBN-13: 978-0-8032-2083-6
(paper : alk. paper)
1. Stabler, Hollis Dorion.
2. Omaha Indians—Biography.
3. Army—Biography.   4. Indians
in military service—Biography.
5. Operation Torch.   6. Operation Husky, 1943.   7. Operation
Dragoon, 1944.   8. World War,
1939–1945—Participation, Indian.
9. United States—Armed Forces—
Indians.
I. Title: World War II memoirs of
an Omaha Indian soldier.   II. Smith,
Victoria, 1963–   .   III. Title.
IV. Series.
E99.04S837 2005
940.54′03′092—dc22

In memory of my mother and father,
and Marcella and Bob,
and my comrades, and their mothers . . .
Lest we forget . . .

H.D.S.

CONTENTS

ILLUSTRATIONS

Following page . . . 98

MAPS

INTRODUCTION

Victoria Smith

"Look!"

The tall, elderly man who opened the door to anthropologist Mark Awakuni-Swetland and me pushed a folded newspaper in my face as we stepped into his home in Walthill, on the Omaha Indian Reservation bordering the Missouri River in northeastern Nebraska. A little dog, no taller than the wheels on his master's aluminum walker, yapped an enthusiastic greeting from the floor.

"Hush up, Rambo!" he scolded jokingly in a loud, deep voice. "Look! Look what my horoscope says for today!" A gnarled finger jabbed the appropriate column. Not knowing what else to do, I read out loud . . .

"Today you might get to know someone better who is also eager to learn more about you. Do something constructive about developing this relationship." I glanced up to see him beaming down at me expectantly.

"Pleased to meet you, Mr. Stabler," I yelled at him, laughing as we shook hands. Hollis was almost deaf. "That's my horoscope, too."

So began my friendship with Noⁿzhíⁿthia, Mr. Hollis Stabler, much beloved and popular elder of the Omaha Nation—and with his dog, Rambo, and cat, Sweet Pea—in December 2001. As it turned out, Hollis and I didn't share an *exact* birth date, but we were cut out of the same bolt. I soon met Hollis's grandson, Redwing, a student at the Haskell Indian Institute in Kansas, and Redwing's mother, Wehnona, who is Hollis's daughter. As CEO of the nearby Winnebago Hospital and of the Carl T. Curtis Health Education Center, Nonie leads crusades for Native American healthcare. Her husband, Terry St. Cyr, a business manager for the neighboring Winnebago tribe, has been helping guide his Ho-chunk nation to financial solvency for several years.

Hollis had been a soldier in World War II, and he needed someone to help him write his war memoirs for publication. He had already made a film for the Omaha schoolchildren, and several of his anecdotes had been published in local newspapers, and in the newsletters of veterans' associations. Even the Smithsonian had videotaped a portion of his experiences, he told me. But now, Hollis wanted to write a book.

"Spirit is calling me home," Hollis had told his good friend Mark just a week earlier, in mid-December 2001. Adopted by Omahas many years ago, Mark was now a specialist in Omaha language and culture at the University of Nebraska, where we both teach. "I need you to help me get this book together before I go."

"I can't, Grampa," Mark yelled into the phone. "I'm sick. I have to go to the hospital. I have cancer, I told you. But Victoria will help you. I'll bring her so you can meet," Mark had told him.

Being a starwatcher myself, and coming from a long line of Indian soldiers, I should have known our friendship was destined. My great-great-great-great-great grandfather, a Delaware Indian named Archibald Oxendine, fought for General Jackson at the Natchez Tower in 1812. Another grandfather from that generation, a Delaware named Daniel Harmon, had fought the Creeks with Jackson the following year. During the Civil War, one of my Cherokee grandfathers, John Anderson Smith, served in the Confederate Army and another, Tom Smith, served the Union. My Cherokee uncles were in World War II, and my Cherokee father served twenty years as an enlisted man, including two tours of duty in Vietnam.

Furthermore, as the child of an Indian serviceman and a British mother, I had been born in a military field hospital near Verdun, France, scene of the bloodiest battle of World War I. A trip to the solemn burial ground at Flanders is among my first impressions of Europe. My sister was born in Bittburg, Germany, soon after. We spent several years of our childhood stationed in southern Spain, where time was measured in terms of the annual, world-famous Lenten processions through the streets of Seville—and the *feria* that followed, with its gypsies and dance—and trips to the mythical beach at Cadiz. Morocco beckoned, but at the time of our travels in the region, political tensions had closed the port at Tangiers. My parents settled on a trip to Gibraltar, where troops of friendly apes that inhabited the Rock were more interesting to my sister and I than the impressive view of the British naval station spread out on the shoreline far below. Later, our brother was born when we were assigned to a military installation in Lincoln, Nebraska.

Here, at the age of ten, I read a story about Cochise, inaugurating a lifelong passion for the history of the Apaches, and of Arizona. As if in answer to my silent prayer, my father's next assignment transported us from the Great Plains to Tucson in 1966. I spent the following thirty-five years exploring Arizona.

As a graduate student at the University of Arizona I studied under Tom Holm, a Creek-Cherokee scholar who knows the hearts of Indian veterans. At Arizona State University I wrote my dissertation on an Apache captive and scout, Mickey Free—with the very patient help of just about every recognized specialist in the field and under the oft-times bemused watch of my mentors, Peter Iverson, Bob Trennert, and Arturo Rosales. Currently, as a tenure-track faculty member at the University of Nebraska, Lincoln, (yes, life is a circle) it is my pleasure to work and consult with Pete Maslowski, among the foremost of military historians.

I had been revising my Apache work for publication when Mark called to see if I would help Hollis. I suspect that my friend and colleague, John Wunder, had a hand in the negotiations, as well. Time was of the essence, but with the help of Mark, as well as my research assistant, Frederick Grizzard (my thanks to the McNair Fellows Program), I felt I could meet the challenge. Cindy Hilsabek provided very welcome and capable clerical support, as well.

Unfortunately, another friend and mentor who might have lent much to the project did not get that opportunity. The incomparable Tom Dunlay—who knew everything about anything western, Indian, and army—passed away in March 2003. How I will miss him, now that he's gone—even if we didn't exactly agree on Kit Carson.

"I'm not a hero, you know," Hollis said as he explained why he wanted to leave a book for posterity. "I was just a guy in the army, part of a team. But we had so many things happen to us, unbelievable things. I don't want those stories forgotten. I don't want those men forgotten."

I promised I would not make him a hero, and then we began, audio-taping his memoirs in ninety-minute sessions, as my schedule would allow. (It is exactly one hundred miles from my home to Hollis's.) Most of our "interviews" were held via scrap-paper notes—due to Hollis's hearing—and those only in the vaguest of terms: "prior to your birth," and "1918–1928," and so on, in ten-year increments, at least in theory. In between my visits, Hollis wrote his anecdotes, and sorted out his voluminous documents, photographs, and artifacts, or sketched in his sketchbook. One year and some months later we were finished. Mark spent that year confronting unspeakable horrors in the hospital in Omaha while his wife, Donna, managed their home and two young sons in Lincoln. He survived, only to fall sick again, and faced another round of therapeutic hell. Occasionally, when he felt well enough, Mark would type up Hollis's handwritten stories, in between chapters of his own dissertation-in-progress.

I spun the colorful threads of Hollis's memories into a tale throughout the summer, fall, and winter of 2003, and on into the summer of 2004. Meanwhile, Redwing left Haskell and joined the Job Corps at a camp in Montana. Nonie was nominated for the Annual Siouxlander's Woman of Excellence Award, in the category of Women Striving to Improve the Quality of Life. Mark beat back death once again and will live to read this work. He received his doctorate from the University of Oklahoma and a tenure-track position at the University of Nebraska, Lincoln, and our mutual graduate student, Elaine Nelson, completed a fine thesis on Hollis's mother, Eunice Woodhull Stabler.[1]

In the end, Hollis's life-story bears many characteristics of the Native American autobiographical genre, as well as some distinctions. Autobiography is described by scholars as a Western literary genre characterized by a "comprehensive and continuous" narrative inscribed in chronological order. But as those who study Native American literature have recognized, this definition does not fully incorporate the process and description of Native American autobiography.[2]

For example, the frequent presence of an "editor-collector," such as myself, in the composition of Native American autobiographies has prompted literary theorist Kathleen Sands to redefine this particular subset of the genre as "collaborative biography," an idea I'm sure Hollis would have no quarrel with, could I sufficiently explain it to him, which I can't because of his diminished hearing and eyesight.[3]

Another deviation of Native American autobiography from genre norms is the propensity for Indians to tell circular (technically, "nonlinear") stories. Some theorists devote their careers to searching for layers of meaning (technically, "metatexts") in this nonlinear approach to personal narrative. If I could ask Hollis why his narrative as dictated to me is nonlinear (which it frequently is), he would probably attribute it to his advanced age and a tendency for his mind to wander. "Now where was I, before I started talking about . . . ?" he often asked me during the course of our interviews, though whether this was from a deliberate desire on his part to narrate chronologically, or because he thought I wanted him to, I never thought to ask. "I know you can straighten this all out later," he assured me many times. Consequently, I felt at liberty to hammer Hollis's circular, sometimes rambling, stories into linear ones. Chronology is the historians' temporal yardstick, and Hollis had a big story to tell. [4]

Fortunately, Hollis's recollection of names and dates proved almost flawless. Using his handwritten anecdotes, which relay the bulk of the "set pieces" in his oral repertoire, as foundations, and referring to the variants on these stories as revealed in his taped sessions, I doggedly gathered the usually scattered details of each anecdote and pieced them together to form a comprehensive (and chronological) presentation. I believe Hollis would have been sorely disappointed had I not. As I completed each draft of the book, Hollis would equally doggedly read it, making notes in the margins, or on a separate sheet of paper where he wanted revisions, usually clarifying names and dates. [5]

Theorists also say that chances are good that as the "collector-editor" in Hollis's collaborative biography I have given my voice a "pervasive authorial function" that is in danger of relegating Hollis's voice to the "role of the source," vulnerable to quotation and paraphrase. Maybe so, but I have tried to honor the responsibility entrusted me by Hollis to relate his stories as he remembered them in the intimacy of our collaboration. Such editorial interjections that do appear are intended simply to contextualize Hollis's story. [6]

Hollis's life span parallels those of three other recently published Native American collaborative autobiographies. Like Ted Rios, the Tohono O'Odham object of literary critic Kathleen Sands' Telling A Good One (a highly unconventional Indian "autobiography," the subject of which is how not to create a collaborative biography), Hollis was confident he had a "good one" to tell. Furthermore, he had the verbal skills to deliver an interesting story, as well as one he could personally live with, thus his repeated admonition that I not portray him as a war hero, befitting his modest nature. Hollis's childhood stories, like Ted's, are "vivid images of his youth that defined his identity." In Hollis's case, they lay a foundation for his "lifelong drive" for multicultural adventure, and a springboard for his wartime experiences. [7]

Though Rios was a native of Arizona, and Hollis of Nebraska, their lives intersected, at least experientially if not in actuality. Both men hopped trains to Oregon in their youth; both worked for Boeing, though Rios's employment was of much shorter duration than Hollis's. They differ in that Rios avoided service during the war, while Hollis embraced it. Additionally, while Rios never places himself as a central figure in the welfare of his "kin group," Hollis's story is rooted in the notion of service to community and family. Whereas Sands describes Rios as reluctant to narrate extensively on his family history, Hollis does so at length, and with pride.[8]

But, like Rios's memories, Hollis's stories have a point. As Sands describes it, this is to illustrate that, given ability and a willingness to "get along," life can be "manageable and rewarding"; Rios and Hollis have demonstrated that Indians of the 1920s-30s can "go anywhere and adjust to new conditions." And, like Rios, Hollis's narrative also demonstrates that Indian country is where he is *most* at home. Furthermore, to paraphrase Sands, Hollis's stories illustrate that no matter where he is, he narrates himself as an Omaha Indian.[9]

Hollis's life also parallels that of Henry Mihesuah, the Comanche narrator of Devon Abbott Mihesuah's *First To Fight*. Like Henry, the descendant of a distinguished line of Comanche from the Quahada Band (Quanah Parker's), Hollis's stories reveal old guilt and unresolved discrepancies begging for resolution and centered on internal family relations. Both men grew up in close relation to their fathers, learning from them traditional crafts and skills—the making of bows and arrows, hunting and marksmanship—that served their interests throughout their lives, and carried forward traditional knowledge. Henry and Hollis both recount anecdotes featuring warm childhood friends, while Ted Rios does not. Unlike Rios, both served in World War II, though in different branches of the service, and for different reasons. Henry enlisted in the marines after Pearl Harbor with pride and a sense of patriotism. Hollis enlisted in the army prior to Pearl Harbor, out of hunger. Hollis didn't mind being called "Chief"; Henry detested it. Both married white women who embraced their husbands' heritage; both men sought careers in the larger society after the war, although Hollis had considerably more education than either Rios or Mihesuah. All three—Rios, Hollis, and Henry—retired to their reservations permanently.[10]

In terms of literary form rather than content, Hollis chose to feature his World War II memoirs in his narrative, comprising all but two chapters of the book (as I edited it), while Henry's war experiences form an all-too-brief portion of his story. Additionally, whereas Hollis is the sole oral contributor to his own narrative (I have also occasionally incorporated Eunice's voice through her writing), Devon Mihesuah has added dimension to her father-in-law Henry's story by eliciting and incorporating his wife Fern's recollections into the presentation, underscoring the notion of a "collaborative biography."[11]

The lives of Hollis, Henry, and Ted Rios all temporally parallel that of Alma Hogan Snell, the Crow Indian narrator of Becky Matthews's *Grandmother's Grandchild: My Crow Indian Life*. Snell's grandmother, Pretty Shield, had been the first Plains Indian woman to share her life story with an American male collaborator, Frank Linderman, in 1932. Like Hollis's, Henry's, and Ted's families, Snell's ancestors worked hard to adjust to life in the reservation era. Snell's narrative also adds an interesting dimension to Hollis's circumstances, in that Snell held a devotion to Christianity equal to that of Hollis's mother, Eunice Woodhull Stabler, the most influential figure in Hollis's life. Though Snell's Protestantism lay with the Baptists, while Eunice's went to the Presbyterians, both women were shaped and molded by their determination to merge a traditional heritage with the gospel of Jesus. Both women profoundly affected their descendants.[12]

As to whether this collaborative biography is the story of an Indian who was a soldier, or of a soldier who was an Indian, I will let the reader decide. Hollis would probably say he was both. I would call and ask him *right now*, but he can hardly hear my questions over the phone. (He calls to talk almost every day, but I can only listen, or respond with a vague yes or no.) I could email him, but his computer is down; he is waiting for his friend Pee-wee to fix it—again. I would drive out and ask, but at this moment, I am in Arizona and he is in Nebraska. But despite the complications, Hollis's story clearly relates to the genre of World War II personal narrative. As early readers have pointed out, Hollis's narrative comes late in the era, as it is said that only one-third of all World War II veterans are alive today, and they are passing away at the rate of one thousand a day, or so I've heard. Most veterans who had a story to tell have already done so.

Ironically, some of the last World War II memoirs to be collected have been shared by Native Americans. This belated, but most welcome, impulse can perhaps be attributed to Hollis's own reasons for his tardy entry into the genre: "No one ever asked me." In truth, Doris Paul and Tom Holm recognized the value of Indian veterans' experiences at least as far back as the 1970s, but most other scholars were slow to follow, perhaps because so many of us were born after the war was over. Though in our youth we fought an antiwar in the streets, and an unwilling war in Asia, only with maturity have we come to appreciate the awesomeness, and terribleness, of World War II in academic terms, and with that understanding, arrived at an appreciation for, and desire to collect, the stories of all those who fought it, regardless of race.[13]

It came as a surprise to many World War II historians that Native Americans had volunteered more than their share of people to World War II, let alone that some had been "code talkers" in the war, but recent scholarship has brought these facts to life by giving voice to those who were Talkers and veterans. Doris Paul's *The Navajo Code Talkers* (1973) first called war historians' attention to the topic, and several studies have followed. Roderick Red Elk, a Comanche code talker, had tried to capture historians' attention in the early 1990s, but not until William C. Meadows interviewed him for *The Comanche Code Talkers of World War II*—in what can only be termed a "collective collaborative biography"—did academics embrace his story as a welcome addition to the foundational works of Alison Bernstein's *American Indians and World War II: Towards a New Era in Indian Affairs* and Jeré Bishop Franco's *Crossing the Pond: The Native American Effort in World War II*. Though both clearly lay out the logistics of Indian involvement in World War II, both lack enough Native voices to classify as "collective biographies." Meadows, on the other hand, interviewed several Comanche code talkers and/or their descendants. Unfortunately, like Sands's Ted Rios, several of Meadows's primary narrators passed away prior to the completion of his book.[14]

The lives of the Comanche narrators featured in Meadows's book parallel that of Henry Mihesuah, also a Comanche and a marine, but not a code talker. One code talker, Morris Sunrise, was a close pal of Hollis's in their youth. Their memoirs are most welcome into the canon. But it is Mihesuah's singular story—the lone voice of an Indian war veteran—that makes it of a rare subgenre. It is also this same quality—and particularly because it is an *extended* narration of one Indian soldier's war experiences—that makes Hollis's contribution so important and unique. His is a rare voice, indeed.

Now, my disclaimers: for all my life experience, my formal training is in Indian history, not World War II. While Hollis can, of course, be forgiven for lapses of memory, any errors of fact are of necessity my own. To those who recognize them, my sincere apologies. Likewise, this book is not a history of the Omaha Nation, except where that history overlapped with Hollis's ancestors. To literary critics who suspect I have poked a bit of fun at their concerns, I confess I did so in Hollis's name. To those who might wish to further investigate the life of Hollis Stabler, copies of my taped and transcribed interviews with him, as well as his handwritten and typed anecdotes, as well as other materials, will be deposited with the Nebraska Historical Society upon completion of this work, as per Hollis's wishes. To those who might wonder about the relationship between Hollis and me, I can only say that I was surprised to find how closely it mirrors that between Linderman and Pretty Shield: "The two partners exhibited some strikingly similar character traits. Each had a strong sense of adventure, an abiding passion for nature, a desire to construct an authentic record of the past."[15]

As the final keystrokes conclude this work, Sweet Pea is ailing and Rambo still loses his balance when he barks and wags his tail at the same time. Hollis is a little deafer. His bad leg is worse, and his eyes aren't working to his satisfaction, ever since he banged his head when his van slid down an icy driveway and slammed into the neighbor's car. Nonie took the keys away for good.

Here, old soldier-friend, is your book from me. *Wibthaho^n, wano^{n}she.*

No One Ever Asked Me

Wanoⁿshe: **Soldier**

War. No other human activity is as pivotal to the course of history, as decisive in its manifestation, as inhumane in its execution, as war. Yet conflict between humans is as least as old as human memory.

To the Umoⁿhoⁿ, Omaha Indians, who had originated in the Great Lakes region of the North American continent, but had settled in eastern Nebraska by the eighteenth century, kikína (war) meant perpetual conflict with the Dakota Sioux, their formidable enemies to the north. The Omahas considered a núdoⁿ (warrior) known for his exceptional courage and personal integrity to be hethúshka (guarded by thunder). Even today, an Omaha soldier (wanoⁿshe) who has achieved distinction in the American armed services, man or woman, is honored as hethúshka and welcomed into the Omaha warrior society.[1]

When Hollis Dorion Stabler, a young Omaha Indian, stepped into the U.S. Marines recruiting center at Sioux City, Iowa, in September 1939, he was following but a contemporary version of a path ridden by his ancestors, though he had yet to prove his worth in battle. Despite his heritage, he might not have been so eager to enlist had he known how soon that worth would be tested. But in 1939, America's Pacific naval fleet still basked in the sun of Hawaii's Pearl Harbor, and twenty-one-year-old Hollis Stabler needed a job.[2]

"Come back when you gain weight," the medic administering his physical examination abruptly commanded the tall, lanky young man. Neither the marine recruiter nor the physician could have known they had just rejected the great-great-great-grandson of Pierre Dorion, a French trader who had founded Sioux City. Historians believe him to have been the first white trader to reside among the Yankton Sioux, or even in South Dakota. In 1804 Dorion had served as interpreter for

Lewis and Clark, and it was the Corps of Discovery's refusal to use him as their interpreter in conferences with the Teton Sioux that led to their failure to open diplomatic relations with the Teton, at that time the most powerful tribe on the Northern Plains. Dorion married a Yankton woman, and together they had born a son, Jean Baptiste Dorion (see Appendix).[3]

As an adult, Baptiste wed an Omaha woman and the two parented a daughter, Rosalie. Rosalie wed Omaha Chief Four Hands, and they had a son, Long Wing.

"Long Wing was an orphan here at the Presbyterian Mission," eighty-four-year-old Hollis recalled in 2002 from an easy chair that dominated a corner of the living room. He motioned in the direction of a memory that hovered just over his shoulder. "This lady, Victoria Woodhull—ever heard of her? Ran for president and all that?—she came through and adopted him, sent him money and gave her name to him: Spafford Woodhull. So that's how we got the name 'Woodhull.' These are not our real names. 'Stabler' is a German name. They just gave it to us."[4]

The Presbyterian Mission School to which Hollis referred—remembered in Francis La Flesche's bittersweet classic, *The Middle Five: Indian School Boys of the Omaha Tribe*—was distinguished as the first Protestant mission and school established in the Louisiana Purchase Territory. Though the school only operated from 1856–68, its influence lasted. Located near what was then the Omaha's upper village, which conservative Omahas derisively called "the village of the 'make-believe' white men," today the mission cemetery is acknowledged as an historic site in Thurston County. But in the late nineteenth century, the school loomed large in the lives of Omaha Indians.[5]

As an adult, Spafford Woodhull had married an Omaha woman, Lucy Harlan, and together in 1885 they had born Eunice Victoria Woodhull, destined to be an exceptionally progressive Omaha woman whose accomplishments have been historically overshadowed by those of another significant Omaha woman, Susan La Flesche Picotte, who in 1889 became the first Native American woman to earn a medical degree. Picotte, in fact, was the only Indian ever appointed as a medical missionary by the Presbyterian Board of Home Missions.[6]

"Now," Hollis remembered, "my mother, Eunice, was proud that she was related to Pierre Dorion. And she remembered *her* grandmother, Rosalie, the granddaughter of Pierre. Rosalie was one-fourth French. I don't speak much Omaha. I understand a little bit. I know more French than Omaha."[7]

"I think when my mother was about eleven years old, and my dad, too, about that age, they gathered up all the Omaha kids and took them to the railroad station in Emerson, Nebraska, just a little ways over here," Hollis waved across the Omaha Reservation's rolling bluffs, "other side of Winnebago. The railroad track goes through there. That railroad took them to the Genoa Indian School. And they left them and they were gone for about four years—just little kids! And she told us about how they were treated in the boarding school. She said the worst thing was, they were hungry all the time. Didn't have enough to eat, you know. They didn't have the kind of food that they were used to: meat, soup, corn. They didn't feed them like that over there.[8]

"When my mother came back from Genoa, her father, Spafford, Long Wing, was pretty well off. He had land at Macy. Well, he leased it out. At that time there were very few Omahas who could speak English like he did, so he was able to get his money's worth, and all that. She told her dad, 'I want to go back to school,' so he sent her to school in Omaha.[9]

"I told you my grandfather, Spafford Woodhull, spoke English. A lot of the Omahas didn't speak English. He'd tell me about different people, different things. He remembered when the Omahas had their last buffalo hunt. He and a friend, they were about the same age. They made that last buffalo hunt. I remember him telling us about it. One thing I will always remember is him telling about the horses and travois and wagons. They all went together, you know, the people. Grandfather said he and his friend rode horses. They had a job to do, just keeping track of the horses, you know, Taking them out to water and bringing them back. They used to talk about it."[10]

Modern research places the last traditional Omaha bison hunt during the year 1876. As with the other indigenous Nebraska Indian tribes—the Ponca, Pawnee, and Otoe-Missouria—access to the reduced herds on the western plains had been impeded by settlers and hostile Sioux. With the demise of the buffalo hunt, many Plains Indian ceremonies passed into history also, as demand for their function decreased, and circumstances for the transmission of certain knowledge—how to call the buffalo near, for example, or other specific rituals for buffalo hunt blessings—diminished.[11]

He brought his attention back to his mother. "That's where Mrs. Picotte came in. 'Why don't you go to school in Missouri?' she asked my mother. So my mother went down there to 'teaching' school [Teacher's College]. She went there, and she was the only Indian in the school. But she met several women that were part Indian. She went to teaching school and she learned to speak better French. She had a voice. She was a contralto. Do you know what a contralto is? She sang contralto with different people. And she came back and she got this job at the agency, working for Mr. Springer, a real estate agent. She knew all about everything. A lot of people said, 'Why did they ask *her*?' Why? Because she was educated and she was interesting and she was aggressive, you know. She went right ahead.[12]

"About Mrs. Picotte, she was a sort of mentor of my mother's, a person who encouraged my mother to go ahead. At that time, alcohol came on our reservation, and that was a bad thing. It is still a bad thing. It was against the law for the Indians to drink, or to sell liquor to the Indians, so it was illegal. But they bootlegged here anyway. Anytime the Indians had a payday, all those bootleggers from Sioux City all come out here. And that's where all those bootleggers got the Omahas' land. Because those Omaha guys would get drunk and draw up lease papers or sign a lease paper to sell their land. I still have my land. I have eighty acres out here, and I also have twenty acres out here that belonged to my grandmother on my mother's side, Lucy Harlan. And then I've got a lot of little pieces. I'm the only one left, otherwise I would have to divide it between my brother and sister."[13]

After she completed William Woods College, Eunice had returned to the Omaha reservation. In 1912 she married George Stabler. George had attended the Genoa Indian School with Eunice, and afterwards the Carlysle Indian Institute in Pennsylvania and the Sherman Institute in Riverside, California. "He always said that when he was at Riverside, they had an earthquake while he was there," Hollis relayed. When George returned to the reservation, he and Eunice wed.[14]

"The two young people have had more than ordinary advantages and are intelligent and capable," the local newspaper reported. "Mrs. Stabler attended the Wm. Woods College at Fulton, Mo., and last year Bellevue College. Since then she has been employed as stenographer for Wm. Springer. Mr. Stabler has just returned from Omaha, where he has taken a course in 'automobilogy.'"[15]

"My mother was well educated," Hollis continued. "She married my dad when he wasn't hardly educated, no college education. But he was a nice-looking guy, didn't drink or anything. I think it was because of the clans, she was thinking about the clans, because she belonged to a real good clan. The Omahas have ten clans, five of the Sky People and five of the Earth People. Through my father my clan is the Buffalo clan, an Earth clan. And my mother belonged to the Bird clan, also an Earth clan. If a person married someone from their own clan, well, they'd be marrying a relative, a cousin. They don't go by that anymore."[16]

Although Eunice had found employment on the Omaha Reservation, George could not. He enrolled at Hampton Indian Institute in Virginia, and he and Eunice moved east. "He took his training in carpentry, that's why he was a carpenter. My mother worked in the school office. She had a good friend, Mrs. Darling, a wealthy lady. In fact, she was one of the rich people that sponsored people, and she sponsored my mother. My dad went to school. It was something new for the Indians, because they didn't know how to go to school. But my mother was there. She poked my dad right on. I was born at Hampton in 1918, and I was baptized at the oldest church in the United States. My mother always said that's why I was a soldier, because on the day I was born, soldiers marched down Hampton road in front of the hospital, in uniforms, going off to war."[17]

Just as Hollis had remembered, the Hampton Indian School had initiated a "model families program" into their Indian education curriculum in the 1880s, through which many an Omaha couple and their children had passed by the first decade of the twentieth century. The planners intended that the Indian families who completed their program would "take civilization home to be the center of civilization among the tribes."[18]

As for Hollis's claim to have been baptized in the oldest church in the United States, he may not have been far off. A photograph from the collection of the Denver Public Library, created between 1880 and 1900, shows a Reverend Gravatt and a group of Native American men, teenagers, and boys in front of St. John's Church in Hampton, Virginia. The inscription on the reverse states, "One of the oldest churches, with Indian boys and Rev. Gravatt."[19]

Through his mother's line, Hollis Stabler identified himself as having 1/32 French blood, but his paternal heritage had been purely Omaha. His father, George Stabler, was the son of Hiⁿzízhⁿga, Sampson Stabler. Sampson had been born to Moⁿégahi, Jordan Stabler. Jordan and Sampson, father and son, were born to the Black Shoulder Buffalo clan of the Omaha, who were responsible for the buffalo hunt. This clan considered themselves to be the first Omahas. As headman of his clan, Jordan had been signatory to the 1854 treaty signed in Washington DC, which had ceded Omaha land west of the Missouri to accommodate demand created by passage of the Homestead Act.[20]

As a youth, Hollis's father, George Stabler, attended the Carlisle Indian School in Pennsylvania. There, he had shared a dormitory room with Jim Thorpe for two years. Thorpe would later come to be widely regarded as the greatest athlete of the twentieth century. "My dad played baseball. He played with Jim Thorpe. Dad played centerfielder, then second baseman. Yeah, he made semi-pros," Hollis remembered proudly. "The semi-pros worked, they got paid, too. They do it all the time nowadays, but that was a big thing then.[21]

"When they came back from the East, we moved to Walthill, on the Omaha reservation. Dad couldn't get a job." George and Eunice moved to Rosalie and built a small house on Spafford Woodhull's land near the railroad tracks. Hollis continued,

★ They didn't have to pay rent, because it was my grandfather's land. They had a lot of garden stuff. But my mother didn't want to live on the reservation. When I was young, you could take the train to Sioux City for fifty cents, and fifty cents back. My dad went up there and he got a job at the Hanford Creamery. Where the post office now is, that creamery was located just about right there. And he played baseball in the summertime. In those days, baseball was a big thing. He played ball in the summertime, and worked in the wintertime. My mother said one time he went up there and didn't get back for about a week, and we only had one chicken left, and she said we finally had to kill it. So, he moved our family to Sioux City. That was in 1920.[22]

In Sioux City, 7th Street was kind of a main thoroughfare. It had a streetcar running down it. People sold merchandise on the outside in those days, with tables outside with shades over them. We lived on the west side of Sioux Street, between 5th and 6th Streets. Up there was Webster School, on 4th Street, and that's where I started school. It was a big, tall, brick building, with a tower. And in that tower you walked around, kind of at the top of the library. And we'd go up there and we'd have to listen to people read. The playground was brick. My mother said we were the only American Indian students in the school. She said I played with all the boys around there. She said, "Why don't you say something to them?" I said, "I don't have much to say." She wanted me to talk, and I wouldn't talk very much. Anyway, I was the only Indian in my class. But there was a little black girl in there—I don't remember her name. Us boys used to lay the girls' chairs on their sides and go around and jump over them. It wasn't because she was black, it was because she was a girl.[23]

Across the street, on the east side of the street, was a little store. A lady had that store. We'd buy candy and stuff like that. One thing I remember about buying candy in those days was the little sack. It had little colored stripes up and down it. You never see them no more. In those days, one penny could buy a lot of candy. Anyway, that's all she did was sell a little candy and gum and all like that. Spearmint gum was a big thing.[24]

But she and my mother were good friends and we went over there. She always had liver and onions, and my mother would go in there and eat with her, and I'd go, too. Wherever I went, I was always with my mother. One time the lady was over there cooking, and she was drinking wine and she almost fell into the stove. Then my mother said, "Ida, let me finish that cooking." I remember that just as plain as anything.[25]

In those days not many people had a car or buggy. We walked or rode the trolley on 7th Street. If you stayed on the trolley long enough going west you ran into Riverside Park, and if you rode the trolley east you passed through downtown on 4th Street. My dad liked to walk or hike. I think we walked all over the west-side hills along the river bank. We had no canteen, but used a milk bottle wrapped in a damp gunny sack. He carried a pocket knife with one broken blade and he would cut green willows and make us whistles. He always had a paper sack so we could carry back wild grapes and plums and onions.[26]

We were always looking for red willow for my grandfather, Long Wing, Spafford. He used to shave it, and smoke it in his pipe right along with his tobacco. I still have one of his long-stemmed pipes, his calumet. Sometimes he came to visit us. He usually took us for a ride on the trolley to the sand dunes, where there was a small store and a picnic table. He would buy us cream sodas and oyster crackers.

Sometimes he would sing good old American songs, Omaha songs! The name of the soda pop was called Nee-Hi. When we were ready to go back everyone would help push the trolley around on a turntable. Once or twice during the summer our Sunday school class would have a picnic, usually at Riverside Park, and we would all ride in an open trolley there, no sides, singing and laughing and making all kinds of noise. . . . They were good ol' days. [27]

Anyway, down the street at the corner was the Winnebago family, Raymonds, their name was. The well-known Winnebago artist Chuck Raymond was from that family. And on the southeast corner, Italians lived there. Eveningtime, they would sit outside at a big table. You know, they were real noisy people. They had a son that sang. My mother knew those songs, and so she went over there and she'd be out on the porch in the backyard—we had chairs out there—and she'd sing with that son. He'd be singing Italian and my mother would sing with him! I often wonder who that Italian family was. [28]

Everybody said her clan was the singers, and she was a good singer. My mother knew all those old songs and my dad did, too. He played the flute. He made them and he played them. He made drums, too. He was a good musician and he sang in the real Indian way. You know, not English, the Indian way, Indian songs. He'd smoke a cigarette and go out and sing. He took his cane or stick and he'd sing. But that's something a lot of people did then. Later, when we lived in Lawton, Oklahoma, this old blind Comanche, Chief Atakne, he'd sing church songs, and he'd tap a cane on the floor, like a drum, keeping time. [29]

Back in Sioux City, next door to us was a family. Now I don't know if they were Germans or Norwegians or what, but I couldn't understand what that lady said for nothing. I don't know; she spoke English, but I couldn't understand. I think they were German. In those days World War I was just over, and they used to tease boys and girls about being German blood. [30]

My mother and I had, what do you call it? Good rapport. Because I was the oldest one, a lot of times when she wanted to do something, the two little ones, Bob and Marcella, stayed with my dad, and she and I would go. She was pretty religious. Did you ever hear of Billy Sunday, the famous preacher? I saw him a couple of times. In fact, I was there when my mother talked to him in Sioux City. They put a big tent out there and he used to preach—we'd always go. [31]

We went to the first movie in Sioux City together. It was *The Covered Wagon*. Then we went to see Janet McDonald. She sang an Indian song, I can't think of the name—Minnetonka and all, you know. Of course, we couldn't hear, there was no noise. But later we went to see the first "talkie." It was *The Trial of Mary Dugan*, and it talked. When we came out, we were shaking all over with excitement. My mother would talk about that. She must have been young. She would get a sack lunch and we'd walk and talk. Well, she'd sing and talk, like that. [32]

But I do remember one thing. We went to a church called The Helping Hand Mission. Boy, I tell you, we caught, not the measles, but smallpox. All of us did, and they quarantined us. I remember that they had a red sign on the front door. I can't remember exactly what it said on it, but it said [something like] "Smallpox. Keep Out." And Indians are pretty susceptible to it, you know. My dad was out when they did that, and he couldn't get back in. But he still had to go to work. [33]

I didn't have smallpox bad, but my sister and brother had it between their hands and feet. Oh, they had it bad! But I didn't have it bad. My mother didn't get it either. But there was that lady that used to come to visit us, Sister Hanson, they called her. They didn't call her nurse. She was a . . . well, she looked like a big woman and she had either a blue or white uniform on and a cape. The cape was lined red. She didn't wear an overcoat, only a cape. And she had a big hat, a round hat and kind of flat on top; Some kind of health authority. They don't have that anymore, I don't think. But we sweated it out the whole winter. We were really tired. We couldn't go outside or nothing, and the kids were so sick all the time, Bob and Marcella.

Hollis fell silent. [34]

★ That Christmas, my dad came there and knocked on the window. He had a box, about so big. We opened the window and he came in with a box of Eskimo Pies. Do you know what Eskimo Pies are? With ice cream in them? We ate that whole box, we ate all that ice cream! We couldn't keep it because we didn't have an ice box in those days. We'd put stuff outside in the snow. My dad paid for the ice cream by unloading a boxcar of coal by himself. We were about the same size, about five foot eleven or six feet. He was six foot, I was about a quarter inch from making six foot and I never did get that big. He weighed about 160 pounds, so he wasn't a big man, just regular size. It's like we were a little taller than most guys. The rest of the guys were all about three or four inches shorter than we were.[35]

Anyway, on Halloween night, 1925—I was about seven years old and my brother Bob was five. At the corner of 6th and Sioux, there was a big hole in the ground. We called it "The Big Hole." [laughter] It had a billboard running across it and a kind of walkway on it and all of the kids would get on there and lay around and talk, and sit on it. Wintertime, we'd slide down that hole. On one side was a Jewish synagogue, but all these boys I played with were Catholics. I was Protestant, but all these other boys were good Catholics, always trying to take me and my brother to church carnivals and whatever else they had at the Catholic Church.

That night, one Halloween night, one of the guys—I still remember his name, Frank, and his brother Hubert—they were bigger than we were, they said, "Alright, everybody meet down in The Big Hole." That night we all sneaked out. Me and Bob went down there, and they had a horse buggy that they had swiped from an old man who kept it in his barn, and all the boys had taken the wheels off. So they climbed up that synagogue and let ropes down. Everybody pushed that wagon up, and they reassembled it up there on top. It was a big deal. We were just little guys, and we were with the big boys. I often wonder what happened to them. That lady, Ann Landers, she just died, she came from Sioux City. She came from Jackson Street. That's where all the wealthy people lived. She must have been well off. But she was the same age I am. I have often wanted to visit with her. Anyway, there were a lot of Jewish people there in Sioux City, because the war was over. But they're alright.[36]

There was a Jewish family in Macy, on the reservation, and they had a store there. They had a girl about my age, a little short thing, and I used to like to dance with her. Every time I would come up to the reservation to go to Sioux City on the train, well she'd come up, drive me over from Macy. That was her dad that got killed by a railroad car. He must have been drinking; a train hit his car. But their family is gone. I don't know what happened to them. I remember they had those black hats that you see them wear. They were good friends of my mother and me.[37]

There was a lady that was a postmistress in Macy for years. When I was young she was there. When I got older she was still there. Her name was Miss Queen, a very pretty woman. She spoke our language and knew all the Omahas. "What is she doing there all by herself?" I often wondered, "all by herself there on the reservation?" The job must not have paid very much. Maybe she didn't have money to get out, I don't know. But she lived there. My mother used to go visit her. We'd go over to her house, but it's all gone now. One of those things that happens.[38]

Well, anyway, getting back to Sioux City, I don't know what happened the next day after the wagon affair, because I took a train to Walthill, but later I went back and I went up there and the synagogue was gone, the hole was filled up and all the houses were gone. I wanted to write about this a long time ago and send it to Ann Landers.[39]

But the best part was when my mother used to sing with that boy. I often wonder who he was. That boy was a good singer, a tenor. And the old man would be playing that accordion. Then they'd get some Winnebagos start singing up there with their drum. It was not like it is nowadays, you know.[40]

We lived there until about the fourth grade. Then, in 1925, the doctor told my dad, "If you stay here another year, you're going to die of tuberculosis. You have to be out in the sunshine and open air." My mother and dad talked about it. My dad said "Well, I know a man who's going to have a job down there in Lawrence, Kansas." So he applied for a job there and he got a job at Green Construction Company. We had to move to Lawrence. I remember that when we moved, we got on a train, but we ran into a flood. I can't remember where, or what river, the Platte, I think, but we had to get out of the train and walk back through water. Everybody got out of the train and it was a big mess for a while. But we finally got to Lawrence and my dad went to work.[41]

They were building Haskell Stadium. He worked there building a scaffold and stuff like that. It was kind of a horseshoe shape. And then he got a job as gatekeeper when they played games, so every time there was a big football game the whole family got in free. One time they kicked the football out of bounds. He got it and threw it over the fence. Later that night he brought that football home. That was when all those football players—let's see if I can remember, Pete Jeffers, John Levi—were playing there. John Levi Jr., the son, he still writes to me all the time. He lives in Arizona. I played baseball with those guys in the summertime. I remember it was my turn to come up to bat and John Levi's father came over and he said, "Let that ball hit you." We had a runner on third base. I stood there, but that guy didn't hit me. Levi wanted me to let that guy hit me, a sacrifice play.[42]

That was the last football game I saw at the Haskell Stadium, when they played Bucknell. And it was a big deal. Everybody from around here came. Even John Levi, the Arapaho, came. My mother cooked a big dinner for them, a real Indian feast for Jim Thorpe and Levi and two or three other guys. Thorpe and my dad, you know, they were roommates at Carlisle. . . . I can still remember everybody sitting on the porch eating.

Hollis was recalling the first Haskell Indian Powwow, held in October 1926. Probably the first intertribal powwow held on a national level, the event has since become a fixture on the powwow circuit.[43]

★ I got to know Lawrence pretty good, because I was just at that age where I could run around every place. Mrs. Opal J. Kennedy was the principal of my school. I really liked her. I really liked her as much as I liked anybody else, I guess. She was real pretty, small, with black hair, kind of gray, and she wore a smock. But she always had flowers on it and she wore high heels. But when she went anywhere she took her high heels off and carried them in a little bag, and wore her lower heels. I really liked that woman. Yeah, I did a lot of little extra things for her. I was the teacher's pet, so one time I was an usher for her at a dance at the country club. I escorted people to the table for her, dressed like an Indian. Two little white girls dressed like Indians helped, too.[44]

I remember my sixth-grade teacher, my last teacher in grade school, a little, fat, gray-haired woman. She had a whole room to herself, with nice soft lights. I took care of that room. Back then I found out I was a pretty good runner. I would challenge anybody to a race. Anybody, anywhere, we'd go and race. I had some good friends there: Jack, whose father owned the barbershop downtown, and a girl named Lindsey, whose father had a dry cleaning shop, and another guy we called Stephen because his name was spelled like that, but I was the only Indian again. I think it was good for me.[45]

Once when it was a warm April day some guys said, "Let's go swimming." We were sixth grade boys, about ten of us. Well, we couldn't wait until school was out. Kaw River was about five blocks from our school. Right after school got out we took off running over there, all of us. The river flowed by, but it had a kind of a little lake over there, and a high bank. Everybody stripped off and dove in. It was cold. There was a little island out there. I made it to the island, but some of the guys couldn't make it. We had to go back and pull them. After we got dried off, some of the guys didn't want to get back into the water because they were scared of it, and it *was* really cold. Finally, a man came by with a boat and picked these guys up. I'll never forget that.[46]

Then they had a football game on a Halloween night. The KU students built a big bonfire. They had what we called a "shirt tail" parade. Did you ever see one? They took their shirt tails out, like undershirts hanging down, you know. They'd grab onto each other's shirt tails, boys and girls, everybody in it. When they got to the bonfire, they'd sing. It was real exciting for us.[47]

I'll tell you about another Halloween night, okay? Right in the center of town we had a drug store and I knew the guy that worked there; he was in my class. His name was Doody Green—we called him Doody, I don't know why. His dad had the little drug store and my mother traded there quite a bit. We lived about two blocks away. They also had a big Coca-Cola plant there, with a big, high fence. One Halloween night in 1926, the rough element of the kid population decided to raid the plant. We waited until about 12 o'clock. Everybody was hiding in the alley. Bob had a cold and my mother had just bought him a sheepskin coat. They don't wear them no more. It was corduroy, with a sheepskin collar and sheepskin inside. Bob was just small, two years younger than I was. I got in the plant and took three or four bottles, stuck them in Bob's jacket, and crawled out. Bob was still in there. I said "Get out of here." Then the police came. They caught us and took us to jail. They were black policemen. They kept us there until way late. Finally, my dad came after us. We got a police record there. Bob was so loaded down, he couldn't even move, let alone climb a big fence and jump. We laughed about that for a long time, me and Coca-Cola Bob.[48]

After a moment he continued.

★ On Sundays they used to walk around the university, on Mount Oread, where there is a museum and lots of things. People would be singing and selling ice cream out on the lawn. It was different than they do nowadays.[49]

But then my dad's job ran out. They finished Haskell Stadium. The Kansas State University's Memorial Stadium was being expanded, so he started to work over there and he helped build that stadium. So, again, we would see ball games because he got a gate-keeping job. *Everybody* went to the ball games, too. Even if you had to walk twenty miles, you walked to the ball game. That's the way they did then, you know.[50]

At about this time, when I was ten or eleven, I became interested in the stories and songs of the Omaha people. I told my mother I would like to dance at the next powwow. She immediately contacted her family and they started gathering items and pledges of support for the give-away that would take place at the time of my entrance into the arena. This is a part of the tradition of my people.

Anyway, my mother wanted me to dance before I became twelve years old, so that I could put away my baby name and pick up the Black Shoulder clan name that I carry today, Noⁿzhíⁿthia, Slow to Rise, referring to a buffalo. The changing of my name symbolized my growing up and becoming an active member of the tribe. It is considered one of the ceremonies of the four hills of life. When the time came, my mother prepared a real Indian feast for my ceremony. Everyone enjoyed that day as much as my mother did.[51]

With both football stadiums completed, George Stabler found himself unemployed again. Eunice Stabler acquired a position with the Speaker's Bureau of the Republican National Committee addressing Indian issues in 1927. After receiving high praise for her presentations and commitment to the Party, Eunice again put herself in service to the Republicans in 1932. Once, on assignment, Eunice and George had to pack the family up for a visit to Washington DC. Hollis recalled the adventure well.

★ Then my mother got a job in Washington DC. She worked for Vice President Charles Curtis. He was part Kaw Indian, and they spoke the same language. We drove to Washington and camped along the way. When we got to Washington, there was a parade going on, and my father accidentally ended up at the end of the parade. There we were, our first time in DC, in a parade, and the police wouldn't let us out. Finally my mother told my dad to ask a policeman where G Street was, so my dad asked one of them, "Where is g-string?" My mother and I yelled out, "No not g-string! *G Street!*"

Despite her efforts, Eunice's Hoover-Curtis ticket failed to win in 1932, however, and she found herself seeking employment once again. The BIA offered Eunice a position as caretaker to an elderly Osage man, opening up the doors on yet another childhood adventure for Hollis and his siblings.[52]

★ In 1932, my mom got a job at Pawhuska, Oklahoma, taking care of this Osage man, this *Wazházhe* that the white people called John Stink. His Indian name was [John] Ho-tah-moie, Rolling Thunder. We kids called him uncle. He was an old Indian that was rich from oil. That's how we got acquainted with the Osage. That's how we came to know so many people down there in Pawhuska. That, and I had three or four cousins that married down there. Through my friend from the Roe Institute, Morris Sunrise, we became good friends with Mrs. Birdsong, the daughter of Quanah Parker, the Comanche chief and peyote man. The Osage and the Omaha speak the same language. Did you know that? So do the Poncas, Kaws, and Quapaws. We all speak the same language, so we must have been, a long time ago, one group.[53]

Anyway, after we moved to Pawhuska, that was kind of a different deal. We were living in Ho-tah-moie's wooden cabin on top of a big hill right across from a golf course. Once I went walking and he was standing out there watching those guys play golf, and he said, "What those boys chasing that little ball for?" He had ten or twelve dogs. Wherever we went, old-time Indians used to like dogs. Bob and I and my sister had names for them all. One of them was Whiskey. He had Indian names for them all. . . . Then things got messed up. My father got sick and they put him in the hospital. My parents both lost their jobs then.[54]

Ho-tah-moie, Rolling Thunder, was well known to the citizens of Pawhuska. A man of legend, some said he had died in a snowdrift and come back to life in his youth. Another story had it that he passed away in a smallpox epidemic. His body had been rolled in a blanket and placed on the edge of town. Later, he was found alive, starving and filthy, with running sores, hence the name John Stink. After the city passed a license ordinance, under which Ho-tah-moie's dogs didn't pass muster, some of them were confiscated or shot, neither of which endeared the people of Pawhuska to Rolling Thunder. He left the city and never returned. For fifty years, the oil-rich Indian lived with his pack of dogs on the outskirts of Pawhuska, ignored, or worse, ridiculed. Finally, visiting Sioux reported his condition to the Indian agent; his head-right executor was dismissed, and Eunice Stabler was hired to nurse and rehabilitate the old man, then in his eighties. She remained in that position more than two years, until George's health broke down.[55]

★ After we lived there a while, my mother thought it was time to start cutting my ties to her. She said, "I am going to send you to the Presbyterian Mission School, the Roe Institute, in Wichita." I went there and I met a Cherokee boy, Jess Ketcher, and another man, Black Bear Bosin, who made a lot of famous paintings. Morris Sunrise was my good friend, too. These guys were all Presbyterians; we weren't fooling around with those Catholics and Baptists anymore. That was in 1935 or '36.

Morris Sunrise was destined to surface again as one of William Meadows' *Comanche Code Talkers*, published in 2002, but the future was far too distant for young men to fathom in 1936.[56]

★ At the Roe Institute in Wichita I had a good friend, Levi Murdoch. He was a Kickapoo Indian. One time he invited me to his girlfriend's house. There was another girl standing there watching me. Her name was LaVeeda, a white girl, but she was friends with Lillian, the daughter of Henry Roe Cloud [Chief Cloud, a Winnebago, had been adopted as a child by Mrs. Roe]. LaVeeda had her hands crossed in front of her chest. I walked over to her and she said, "I'm going to marry a *Catholic*." I didn't know what to say. I had just met her and I wasn't thinking of getting married. She never was my girlfriend. But after the war, in 1947, we got married. She became the woman of my dreams. I was married to her for fifty-two years. I'll tell you about that later.[57]

After that my parents moved to Lawton, Oklahoma, so my dad could work. He was doing construction at the Fort Sill Indian School. Then, I decided to go to Bacone Indian School in Muskogee to study art under Acee Blue Eagle, a well-known Indian artist at that time. While at Bacone I joined the National Guard, Forty-fifth Division, 180th Infantry Regiment, Company One. It was an all-Indian company. The 1st Sgt. was Bigfoot and the Capt. was Charles Doele.[58]

Acee Blue Eagle (b. 1907–1959), a Pawnee-Creek artist from Anadarko, Oklahoma, garnered a respectable reputation as a student of highly talented Winold Reiss at the University of Oklahoma. His research in archives and museums lent a note of authenticity to his artistic work. Between 1946 and 1965, Blue Eagle's paintings hung in over fifty galleries worldwide, including some in Los Angeles, Chicago, New York, and Washington DC. In 1943, Acee Blue Eagle enlisted in the army air corps. In 1958 he was voted America's outstanding Indian, "a long overdue honor." Today, connoisseurs of fine art especially treasure Blue Eagle's painted glassware. [59]

Had Hollis only known that war lurked just around the corner, he would have realized that his childhood ended at Bacone. Over two thousand Indian soldiers, trained in National Guard units in Oklahoma and New Mexico—one-fifth of all Indians who served in World War II— were destined to serve in the Forty-fifth U.S. Army Infantry Division. With much foresight in 1938, the Forty-fifth changed its traditional emblem, the Navajo swastika—a symbol of good luck—to the more suitable thunderbird. Hollis would soon leave Bacone and the National Guard, but in 1943 he would cross their paths again in Sicily. [60]

★ My roommate at Bacone was a Creek Indian by the name of Chief Saul Terry. We became very good friends. My buddy was Joe Morris, a Cherokee. Years later, after the war, we met again in Wichita, where we both lived. Our Infantry Company wore old World War I uniforms, with flat metal dishpan helmets and wrapped leggings. We had meetings every Monday night. After that, we'd stop at the local bootlegger, so we called him "Monday." The drink was home brew—very strong. [61]

I had a girlfriend then, in Muskogee. Her name was Louella Townsend, and she was a Creek Indian. She used to make me syrup sandwiches. We called them "sprung" sandwiches. She worked in the kitchen, and it was a big deal, because we never got sweet things to eat. That corn syrup used to "spring" us, I guess. [62]

The second semester I returned to Lawton, where my parents were. My father was still working at the Fort Sill Indian School, but I couldn't find a job. Many tribes lived close by, but most of them sent their children to the government schools such as Chilocco, Fort Sill, and the Sherman Institute in Riverside, California. (Later, in 1975, my daughter Wehnona graduated from Riverside Indian School.) I was too late to enroll in public school, so I fooled around. Anyway, I told my mother I wanted to go to a Civilian Conservation Corps camp in Oregon. She had worked there before she was married. I hitchhiked up there, and lots of things happened to me. First I took a bus ride across the desert. I didn't have much money, but I figured four or five dollars, it couldn't cost much. In those days the bus used to stop anywhere, you could just flag it down. I remember it was raining and I got to a railroad track and saw some guys and talked to them and they said, "Well, we're going over to the mountains to catch a train, and you'd better just go, too." I got to thinking about it. I didn't have any clothes at all. I didn't have any except the clothes I had on. I decided to hitch the train with them. We got way up in the mountains where the train goes real slow, almost stopping. All along there I saw railroad guys looking at us. There must have been about fifty of us hobos. A policeman came by there. They called them "bulls." "Everybody get out," he said. "Line up." All of us lined up. I was the first one and I gave him my CCC letter. He said, "I wish you Indians would stay on your reservation. You're from way down in Oklahoma and now you're clear up here." He let me go.[63]

After that I went out on a highway and an old man in a truck came by with a load of sheep. He said, "I'll give you a ride if you help me unload my sheep." We drove all that day and I think partly that night. When we were done he told me how to go to the Indian school at Warm Springs, Oregon. Then I hitchhiked along the big Columbia River and I saw an Indian man. I said "Where's the Indian village, Chmiwa, located?" He said, "All along the river, but they are fishing now." They had kind of a ladder going out by the river and they walked on out there. I think they had nets and they caught big salmon. I watched them walk the ladder. Finally, one of the boys came and talked to me. He asked me where I was from. He knew I was an Indian. I told him I was from Oklahoma. He said, "Come home and eat dinner with me," so we went to his house and camp. His mother was cooking and I don't think she spoke English. He told me to sleep there that night. I told him I was headed for Warm Springs, and he gave me good directions.[64]

The next morning I started hitchhiking up a long, steep road that led to the top of a plateau. A white lady picked me up. She had about five kids. We rode up the big hill to where there was a cemetery, and she had a big lunch basket full of food. We got up to the top about noon and she fed me. From up on the hill I could see a giant team of horses, about fifty of them, pulling two or three combines. There was a big cloud of dust, and all those horses, they made a great, giant turn, right there. They were really something! You don't see things like that any more. Now they use tractors to pull combines like that.[65]

Along this way, a Jewish man picked me up. He was a kind of person you don't see no more. He had a little wagon and little tin cups and he sharpened knives and all that stuff. He didn't talk very good English, though. But he knew a lot of Indians, and he talked to me all the way up there. He told me where to go, so I went down to the Deschutes River. It's a regular highway now, but then it was just a road. The Deschutes was a fast, cold stream.[66]

When I was working for the CCC the foreman put me down there on a river bank. He said, "We'll pick you up in the evening." I said to myself, "That's not right. They always say that they will pick us up, but they never do." I said to him, "Leave me a blanket and something to eat," so he did. All night long I was there, but I had a fire built and I had an axe. I was sitting there and I looked down and there was a big fish right below. The place I was standing, there was a pool, and the water was kind of quiet. "I'll get that fish," I thought, "I'll get it." I walked out there and got the axe like that, and that fish came up there, right there, and I caught him! I chopped his head off and gutted him and I laid him on the fire. I never did eat him though, because they came after me just then. I often wonder what became of that meal, sitting out there like that. I had taken my clothes off so I could swim. Oh, that water was cold, but it had a nice sandy bottom and was clear.[67]

At the CCC we were chasing wild horses. Anyway, there was this stallion, a black stallion, real mean. I mean, he was just like a man, or a dog. He didn't want men around there. Boy, he whistled, and those ears would go up! And they were trying to catch him. It looked awful funny. I don't think they ever did catch him. They just finally had to shoot him because he was dangerous. You don't think a horse can be dangerous, but that horse was dangerous. I wish I had a picture of him. In fact, I often think about drawing him.

Hollis's mind trailed off, looking for his sketchbook, which was where he always kept it, in the box by the side of his easy chair.[68] "After that, I decided to go back to high school," he continued.

★ My mother wanted me to finish high school. It was nice up there in Oregon, but they were telling me that when it gets cold weather up there and snows I wouldn't be able to go anywhere. I thought, "I'd better leave."[69]

Instead of coming back around Salt Lake City, like when I went up there, I decided to go down the coast. Those roads weren't like they are now. I just started hitchhiking and walking, hitchhiking and walking. Once, a man picked me up. We got to talking, and it turned out that the little old Jewish man who had given me a ride on the way to the CCC camp was his father! And, like I said, the hobos helped me. I'd stop at a hobo camp and I'd share what I had and they'd share what they had—soup, coffee, whatever, tea. Finally I got to a certain point, the train was going east and they told me how to catch it. I remember I got off the train at Lone Wolf, Oklahoma. That's in the western part. I don't know how many days it took me, but I got off, and it was just a little town.[70]

I walked up to the store there and got me some sardines and crackers—a big dinner, you know. I was sitting out there and a sailor came out of the store. He had his sleeves rolled up. Do you know any sailors? They used to put their cigarettes in their shirt sleeve, and roll the sleeve up like that. I remember he came out, and in those days I didn't smoke because I ran all the time. He sat down and said, "Why don't you join the navy?" He was talking at me and trying to get me to join the navy. I said, "Well, I've decided to go into the service, but I don't think I want to go into the navy." He was telling me that he was just off the aircraft carrier Lexington. Later on, that ship was bombed and it sank and maybe he was on it, I don't know. But he talked to me quite a while.[71]

He told me how to catch that train. "When it comes up that grade it slows down—that's when you want to get on it." I asked him, "How far is Lawton from here?" He said, "About 200 miles, but I don't know how many towns are between here and there." Then he said, "Go sleep in the icehouse, there's nothing but sawdust in there. Go in there and sleep." So I went in there. It was nice and warm. I was just falling asleep when here comes the train. All I had was a little bag, and a little jacket on, a Levi's jacket. I got out and here came that train and I ran alongside it and was going to try to get an open boxcar, but they were all closed. Finally it started getting its speed up, so I thought I'd better jump on. So I jumped on and it was a flat car and I couldn't get off that danged thing! I couldn't, with that wheel like that, and it was cold, my gosh was it cold, and there was no place for me to go but to stay on there.[72]

Finally, about daybreak, here comes a town, a big town with lots of lights. "I believe it must be Lawton," I said to myself. The train kind of slowed up going through there, and there was a street light there, so I rolled off. It turned out I was only two blocks from my mother's home![73]

It was just like I had a ticket home! I walked up there to my mother's house. In those days, my parents were in good health, but they couldn't find work. They lived off their leased-land money, but it was never enough. I surprised my mother and she said, "My golly, where did you come from?" She was so surprised! She gave me breakfast and then she said "We don't have an extra bed, but we have a bed down in the basement."[74]

I went back to school there in Lawton, but it was too late to play football. I wanted to play basketball. I enrolled, and got to play one whole semester, and to pass my grade. In those days you had to take a slip around, which the teachers had to sign, if you were going to play athletics, an eligibility card, or something.[75]

I was the only Indian there. That didn't bother me, but it must have bothered those other guys, because when I went out for basketball, some article was written about me, for some reason. I was pretty small, about 5'10"and 147 pounds. In those small towns like that, those kids' fathers had played basketball. The fathers wanted their sons to play basketball. They did all kinds of things to get the coach to like their sons. But in Lawton, they didn't know me or anything, and I was Indian. And all the basketball boys and me, we never did like one another. We never did get together. I wouldn't say I disliked them, because I didn't know them that well. But, I had others that were real good friends of mine. That was always my relationship to a group, no matter where I went, because I was never with a lot of Indians, except at Roe Institute. I was always on my own. And that's why I never did meet any Indian girls, because I was always with the white people all the time. It wasn't that I didn't like Indian girls, but I never did *see* any. I didn't hardly even *meet* any![76]

Back in Wichita, at the Roe Institute, there were fifty Indian boys and only four Indian girls. Of course, those girls were pretty well taken up, you know. They were a girl called Evelyn, Mabel Perry, and a girl from Alaska adopted by a white family and she was maybe Eskimo. They lived in a big hotel there in Wichita. Her folks were pretty well off. She was nice but I didn't like being around her parents. And there was another girl, I can't think of her name now. So, those were those four girls. But a lot of boys knew them, so I had other, non-Indian girlfriends.[77]

I knew a lot of Apache people there, too. Mildred Cleghorn and her family used to support me because I was the only Indian on the team. I also knew the grandson of Loco. He was always smiling, but he was mean.[78]

But I'll get back to Lawton. I went out for basketball and I made it. Being a senior, they ask you to help out. My job was to referee junior high basketball games and take tickets. There were two of us doing this together. And every time I went out there, this girl would come and bring a chair for me. I didn't really pay much attention to her, but if I needed a pencil or anything, she'd hand me two or three. Whatever I did, well, there she was. Her name was Ruby. I'd be going here and there, and Ruby would always be there. And I liked to dance, so I danced with her. But I danced with all the other girls I knew, too. My sister Marcella went to the Catholic school, and she knew a lot of people. There were Comanches and Kiowas and Apaches in that area. We even had a Winnebago girl there as a nurse in the hospital.[79]

The Comanche church was there, and it had a big graveyard, a Comanche graveyard. And the village was here, too, the Comanche village. Then, over there, was the hospital. It is just like what it looked like then. Over there was Fort Sill Indian School, a pretty good-sized school. Then, you went on out to the highway to Fort Sill, the big fort. It was pretty active. But, it was strange—there were no Indians at Lawton High School but me. Don't you think that's strange? But like I said, I was used to being with the other people, so it didn't make much difference to me.[80]

One day I thought well, I'd like to get a girlfriend. There were two pretty Mexican girls there at the school, but I never had enough nerve to talk to them. One of them had a boyfriend and he was always with them. And the Mexican boys, you know, they really are possessive, arms around them and hanging on them. Those two sisters were always together, and that guy was always with them. So I never talked to them. I wanted to, but I never did. That one girl, she would smile at me, but she never did talk to me either. Anyway, we were the only ones at Lawton High School that were different; everybody else was white.[81]

To get back to Lawton, they were going to initiate me into the Letterman's Club. I can't tell you the whole truth about what happened with that, but anyway, one night they called me up there to the stadium and they said, "We're going to initiate you." There were about four of us. We had to carry a paddle around. (I had it for years, but I see it's gone now.) They said, "If you don't do what we ask you, or if you don't do it right, we're going to paddle you. You got to run through the lines, too." They never did ask me to do too much. But one of the things they did, they made us put our hands in a big bowl of worms and they made us bite one like it was spaghetti. Things like that, you know. And another thing they did was, they made us go get what women use, you know. A girl cousin of mine lived with our family for a while, and that's how me and Bob knew what women used. One night, one of those fellows I was with said, "I'll get two of them," and he brought me one. It was kind of embarrassing to me.

Finally they told me, "You be at the school at twelve o'clock." We had a nice big building, with big white pillars and big steps. I lived about three or four blocks down. My mother always cooked a lunch for me. I never did eat much. I can't remember what we ate, egg sandwiches mostly, and bread. I came back from lunch and I saw all the kids going to the steps at the front. "Uh-oh," I said. I came walking in and all those lettermen were standing there. They said, "Alright, get up there in the middle," pointing to the patio. Then Ruby walked out there. They said, "We want you to ask her to marry you. Be her boyfriend and marry her."[82]

Now, Ruby was *too* willing, you know. (Keep in mind, none of us knew she was a "beginner.") She said, "Get on your knees." They made me get on my knees and take her hand, so I did that. But the worst part of it, I thought, was Ruby said "yes" instead of being against it! Then everyone left. From then on she was with me everywhere I went. I didn't treat her right. That's one thing I always felt bad about. I just left. I didn't tell her anything, I just left Lawton after I graduated. I often wonder what happened to Ruby. Blonde hair, blue eyes, she was a white girl.[83]

At the senior prom I danced with Velma. She was kind of the queen bee. You ever seen the girls that are kind of the boss? That's what she was. But she was always friendly with me, like, "Hello, are you working?" Like that. So I danced with her, and, by gosh, some guy *jumped* on me! He was saying to her, "I don't want you to be dancing with him." She told him to get out, get away, "I'll dance with him as long as I want." So I danced with her. That guy was a valedictorian or something, always wore a bow tie. I never did trust a guy in a bow tie. I guess that was his girlfriend and I didn't know it. Like I said, I liked to dance, and Velma was a good dancer.[84]

Another time, I got caught in a problem again. That's when they took the picture of the football team (I finally made the team) and I didn't know nothing about it, I wasn't in it. One day I was getting dressed, or undressed, in the gym and the coach came to me. "I want to apologize," he said to me. I didn't know what that apology was for, I really didn't. But they had taken that picture and I wasn't included in it, and he was coming and apologizing. It didn't make any difference to me.[85]

I graduated from Lawton High School in 1938. Then I went to Macy and worked for the Interior Department as a rod-and-chain man. I carried rods and lines for surveyors, and cleared away brush for them. I did that for about four months, then the job ended. Then I decided to join the service. I wanted to take care of myself. I say this because I think women have to do that, too. You have to try to make good decisions. And that's the way I was. Like I said, if a guy didn't like me over here, I always had two that liked me over there.[86]

Hollis tried the navy first, but they told him the quota was filled—he would have to wait to enlist. "But I was too hungry to wait," Hollis explained. So, in September 1939, Hollis Dorion Stabler, great-great-great grandson of Pierre Dorion, stood before the marine in Sioux City who dared advise him to gain weight. Summoning all the dignity and good breeding at his disposal, Hollis took a deep breath and turned on his heel. He left the U.S. Marine recruiting center and joined the army.[87]

TWO

Operation Torch

November 8–11, 1942

★ I remember in 1939 I told my mother I was going into the service, army or navy. She became very concerned about me being treated badly because I was an Indian. I did not find this to be true. I had many friends, many of the white race. Some individuals I did not get along with, and we came to blows and it got to the cussing stage. But it was few and far between, and nobody got hurt.[1]

Thus remembered Hollis in March 2002. When he enlisted in the army in September 1939, the passage of the Selective Training and Service Act—better known as the draft—still lay a year ahead, almost to the day, in the United States' future. Even so, 4,000 Indians were already enlisted in the various branches of the military. When the draft did commence, on September 16, 1940, most able-bodied American Indians didn't need to be compelled to defend American soil. Of the over fifteen million people who would eventually serve the U.S. Armed Forces between 1940 and 1945, 25,000 of them—men and women—were American Indians. For every Indian pressed into service, one and a half, according to government estimates, volunteered.[2]

This is even more compelling when one understands that in 1940 the Indian population of the United States totaled less than 350,000, up from the historic low of 238,000 in 1900. Of this number, 60,000 were Indian males between the ages of twenty-one and forty-four. Despite their small proportion of the total U.S. population, American Indian participation in World War II outranked, per capita, that of any other specialized population in the United States, including whites. Their

1. North Africa

reasons for volunteering were simple. Like other Americans, perhaps moreso, Indians understood the fundamental concept of defense of one's land for the principles of life, liberty, property, and happiness. One Sioux enlisted man said, "As a rule nowadays, most of the fellows don't go in for heroics." Modesty notwithstanding, the Bureau of Indian Affairs would laud Indian participation in the war in 1945.[3] "Reflecting the heroic spirit of Indians at war in every theatre of action, the list of those specially selected to receive military honors grows steadily. We shall never know of all the courageous acts performed 'with utter disregard for personal safety,' but the proved devotion of all Indian peoples on the home front and the conspicuous courage of their sons and daughters in the various services entitle them to share in common the honors bestowed upon the few."[4]

Among the Plains tribes, twice as many Indians enlisted as were drafted. In 1940, almost 1.4 million people lived on the rolling plains of Nebraska. Of these, 3,400 were Native Americans, mostly Omahas. In the years ahead, Nebraska would send almost 140,000 citizens into the war, and one of them was Hollis Stabler.[5]

★ When I graduated from Lawton [Oklahoma] High School in 1938, I had no place to go, no job, so I went to the reservation. I worked for the Interior Department for a while. Then I went to Macy to see my Aunt Jenny. I liked my Aunt Jenny. She was just like my mother. They lived by the river, where the old mission is located. In the morning I told her I was going to go into the service. So, I got one of their horses, old Joe, and rode into Macy. Mrs. Van Cleeve, the missionary, told me, "I'll take you to Sioux City." I tied the bridle on my horse and sent him home.[6]

After enlisting in the army at Sioux City, he reported for duty at Fort Crook, south of Omaha. "I went there and they divided us up into three groups, education-wise: no schooling, elementary and high school, and college. After that, in September 1939, they put us on a luxury train called The Challenger. On that train I made friends with some of the fellows, Wendell C. Peterson from Red Oak, Iowa, and Lowell Walstrom from Spirit Lake, Iowa, who shared a cookie from his mother. Later I met his mother when she was one hundred years old. We got to Hamilton Field and they said I was going to the air force. I said, "I don't want to go to the air force; I want to go to the cavalry." They said to put in for a transfer, so I did that. It took about thirty days. They gave me a bus ticket and some checks to buy food with, no money. After I got my transfer I went to San Francisco."[7]

Hollis arrived in San Francisco just in time to celebrate the Golden Gate Exhibition, commemorating construction of not only the Golden Gate Bridge, but also of the San-Francisco-Oakland Bay Bridge—completed in 1936 and 1937, respectively—two of the largest suspension bridges in the world. A second theme, the unity of all Pacific nations, provided a subtext for the occasion. The city built a venue for the celebration on an artificially constructed island in the bay, christened Treasure Island, an obvious reference to Robert Louis Stevenson, who had lived in Monterey, and used the setting for his novel, published in 1883. A man with an appetite for life and all things sweet, Stevenson, it has been said, "underlined the nameless longings of the reader, the desire for experience. But we are so fond of life that we have no leisure to entertain the terror of death. It is a honeymoon with us all through, and none of the longest. Small blame to us if we give our whole hearts to this glowing bride of ours, to the appetites, to honor, to the hungry curiosity of the mind, to the pleasure of the eyes in nature, and the pride of our own nimble bodies," Stevenson had written, as if especially for Hollis Stabler.[8]

In a letter to the mayor of San Francisco, President Franklin D. Roosevelt wrote, "Unity of the Pacific nations is America's concern and responsibility. San Francisco stands at the doorway to the sea that roars upon the shores of all these nations; and so to the Golden Gate International Exposition I gladly entrust a solemn duty. May this, America's world's fair on the Pacific in 1939, truly serve all nations."[9]

Treasure Island failed to deter Japan from bombing Pearl Harbor, but it would furnish a strategic staging area for the navy in World War II. To Hollis Stabler, in September 1939, it was a sight to behold.[10]

★ I got to Oakland and saw that big bridge, then we got on a ferry and went across the bay to San Francisco. I got on the city bus and told the driver I wanted to go to Monterey. I didn't know it was ninety miles away. He couldn't take me there so I went to the World's Fair. It was like a treasure island. I saw zootsuiters and Mae West and Wrongway Corrigan. Once I looked for the restaurant that Victor McLaglen had. He was an old-time actor and he always acted like a tough marine sergeant. He said, "If any serviceman stops by, I'll give him something to eat and drink." And sure enough, he did. Or at least his restaurant did. They gave me a hamburger and a beer, but Victor never showed up, so I left. Next I went to March Airfield and looked at a dirigible.[11]

After that my transfer came through. I went on to the Presidio at Monterey. When I reached there it was eveningtime. I found the gate and told the MPs I was a transfer from the air force to F Troop, Eleventh Cavalry. (I know all about F Troop on TV. Don't mention it.) The MP told me I was in the right place but the whole regiment was out at Camp Ord. That was a different part of the fort, out on the peninsula. The Presidio was built on the side of a big hill, and right below was the famous Fisherman's Wharf and Cannery Row.[12]

Hollis's description was brief, but the history of the Monterey Presidio was long. Spanish explorer Juan Baptiste de Anza had established the Presidio there in 1776 for some two-hundred mestizo colonists and soldiers, a thousand head of cattle, and a Franciscan priest. Although the colonists found the dunes and scrubland around the fine bay useless for agriculture, the cattle flourished, unlike the native population—the Ohlone—who found themselves at the mercy of the Spaniards. Always poorly supplied, the little colony nevertheless endured. Although Mexican soldiers later manned the Presidio for a brief time, it fell to the Americans in 1846. After the discovery of gold in the region, the Presidio was dedicated for military use in 1850. Successive decades found the Presidio used as a strategic post in the Modoc Indian wars. By 1890, it functioned as a base for military extension into the Pacific Ocean.[13]

In 1939, the old Presidio found itself situated near a crowded tourist town that featured golf courses, tennis courts, polo fields, riding stables and swimming pools, in addition to the pleasures afforded by the beaches. In fact, one historian has written that the only disagreeable feature of life in the Presidio stemmed from the proximity of the sardine factories on the bay, which "wafted rather overpowering aromas over the post whenever the wind was blowing inland, as it often did!"[14]

The Eleventh Cavalry had been organized in Fort Meyer, Virginia, in 1901 as a mounted cavalry unit. Almost immediately, the men of the Eleventh served four years in the Philippines, followed by patrol duty in Cuba, and service with General John J. Pershing on the Mexican border in 1916–17. The Blackhorse Regiment, as they were known, had executed the "last mounted cavalry charge in U.S. history" against

Pancho Villa's army. Having been stationed at Fort Oglethorpe, Georgia, throughout World War I, the Eleventh transferred to the Presidio at Monterey in 1919. By 1921, when the Eleventh Cavalry absorbed the 17th from Hawaii, most of the Presidio's adobe buildings had long been unoccupied and were in need of repair. Even as late as 1939, Hollis had, indeed, stepped back in time.[15]

★ I started walking, carrying my duffle bag; it was dark and raining. A large touring car with two girls in it came by and stopped. They asked me where I was going. I said "F Troop barracks." "Oh," they said, "We know where that is, hop in!" When we got there, they each handed me a business card. Nice girls! They worked at the Lone Star Hotel. They told me, "No credit! Hahaha!" In those days we called that kind of situation a 2/15; that meant $2.00 for 15 minutes.[16]

For that matter, we routinely received our eggs from San Diego. If you looked carefully on the shell you could find a name and address or phone number of a girl on the shell of the eggs. Also, many a romance started because of the laundry, a name or address tucked in a shirt pocket. Every other week a bus ran from San Diego, full of girls ready to go.[17]

When I entered the barracks, nobody was there but a couple of noncommissioneds and a cook. Next day they took me out to Fort Ord. I had nothing but slippers from the air force, but they put me on water call, and I had four horses to water. (The F Troop horses were sorrels, and a few were off-colored.) They took me back to Monterey and fitted me with leather and rubber boots. I also got fatigues. We went back to Fort Ord for a couple more weeks of training, then we moved back to the barracks. There were twelve of us rookies. Our platoon sergeant, Thompson, was a tough ex-policeman, but fair in dealing with us. Everybody had to do something extra if you wanted to make the drill team. I decided to ride a jumper, but I had no experience. I was assigned to an old mare, Lady, who was a good jumper, but she was a charger. When you lined her out and nudged her, away she went! Nothing could stop her, and you better be ready for a good ride. I was scared white![18]

At that time they were filming a movie there called *Primrose Path*. An actress, Ginger Rogers, was standing in the bay, which was very shallow. When we rode by she would pull up her skirt and everybody would whoop and holler. I saw Jane Wyman a couple of times. Ronald

Reagan was a second lieutenant in the Eleventh Cavalry. One time Jane looked especially pretty in a white Cadillac roadster, in a white flowered skirt. We all waved and cheered for her, and Ronald Reagan started waving at us. Then we all booed at him—"Not you! Not you! Jane!"[19]

Reagan, formerly a lieutenant in the Officer's Reserve Corps of the cavalry, worked for the army air force creating training films for the military at Port Embarkation in San Francisco. Poor eyesight had denied him the chance to serve overseas. Reagan transferred to the First Motion Picture Unit, AAF, in June 1942.[20]

★ I had a friend named Allen. One day he asked me if I would like to double-date with his girl and her sister. I said OK. The girls were Japanese, very pretty and nice. We would sit in the father's boat; he was a fisherman. Allen was blonde and blue-eyed, but he sure did like the Japanese girls. Later on, after my daughter Wehnona grew up, she used to tell me, "If you hadn't fraternized with the enemy so much, we could have won the war sooner!"[21]

Our platoon was chosen to be honor guard for an old soldier, a Portuguese or something, in Salinas, about fourteen miles east of Monterey. We arrived early in the morning and marched down Salinas's main street to the cemetery, where we fired a salute to the old vet. After that we were taken to a church and fed a good meal consisting of everything good and drink of any kind. We all ended up drunk and had to be poured into the truck and driven to the barracks.[22]

I'll tell you another story, about the Salinas rodeo. F Troop was invited to take part in this famous rodeo. We demonstrated setting up our machine guns, combat style. Movie actor Roy Rogers was there. He picketed his horse, Trigger, with our horses and ate chow with us. He was about my age. I also saw "Chico the Kid," Leo Carillo, and Homer Holcom, a famous rodeo clown.[23]

Let me tell you about Eleanor's parade. The Eleventh Cavalry was sent to Fort Lewis, Washington, to train and maneuver with the 3rd Infantry Division, who were driving medium M4A3 Sherman tanks, the kind that went 26 miles per hour and had a 75 mm gun. The Eleventh was still on horseback. By that time, my brother, Bob, was stationed at Fort Lewis, but I didn't know that, or I would surely have visited him. Eleanor Roosevelt visited us there, so we put on a dress parade on horseback. We first walked our horses by her stand, very military. The second time we passed her at a trot. So far, so good. The third time, we galloped. Things were looking good, but actually we were having a bit of trouble. It had started to rain. Before the parade, we had cleaned all our riggings with saddle soap. When it started to rain, our reins became so slick we could not control our mounts. After we passed Eleanor's box, we tried to stop. At the end of the parade ground was a grove of trees. We headed for the grove. We had two packhorses. One pack had the machine gun and ammo, the other had our tent and sleeping bags. There were five to six men to a squad. Right in front of me was a large tree, cut down, and we were headed right for it. I was on the left of one of the packhorses, and Allen was on the right. We hit the log about the same time. I and the packhorse cleared it, but Allen's horse tripped, and both he and the horse went head over heels on the other side of the log. The first sergeant was yelling, "See if that horse is okay!" Poor Allen was stretched out cold, but both he and the horse came out okay.[24]

We had lots of new experiences. On one particular day we were crossing a large field when all of a sudden one of the packhorses started to buck and go in circles. The horses had stepped on a wasp's nest and the wasps were stinging them. Most army horses are herd-bound; the horses got loose and headed straight for me. The packhorses had a large pack on their backs, loaded with ammo boxes. I tried to avoid the horses, but a box hit my right knee and broke my kneecap.[25]

Such is the life of a good soldier. Let me tell you about the long ride. The whole regiment took part in this horse-and-man exercise. We started from Monterey, right by the famous Carmel, to Big Sur—two hundred miles apart—over rough country with no roads. I was a corporal. I rode my regular mount, a blue roan gelding named Trammel, and had two packhorses and two extra horses. We were a ten-man machine-gun squad. We made it, but rode back to Monterey in large stock trucks. Many things happened to our squad, but all the men and horses made it back. My old buddy Ellis Whitney made this long ride with me. We were in the same platoon. It was a long ride over land, no roads or rides, only your mount. We did have one bad time. A packhorse started going over a big rock, with bushes on both sides. It got stuck. We had to unpack him, pull him out, and pack him up again. The trip took about two weeks. Ellis has gone to Fiddler's Green to fetch his mount now, as we used to say. That is where all the old horse troopers will go when we leave this world. The bugle will sound and we will mount up and move out together. Cancer took him in January of 1999.[26]

FIDDLER'S GREEN

Half way down the trail to Hell
In a shady meadow green,
Are the souls of all dead troopers camped
Near a good old-time canteen . . .

. . . And so when horse and man go down
Beneath a saber keen,
Or in a roaring charge or fierce melee
You stop a bullet clean,
And the hostiles come to get your scalp,
Just empty your canteen,
And put your pistol to your head
And go to Fiddler's Green.[27]

★ After that long ride I told you about, the government started drafting people, "draftees," they called them. We got into all kinds of fights with those guys, mostly from Chicago, New York, and those kinds of places. They resented us because we were the regular army, and when they came, we all got promoted a rank or two. They didn't like that.[28]

After that, the Eleventh was sent to the Mexican and U.S. border, halfway between San Diego and El Centro. It was a place called Campo, on an Indian reservation with a large lake named Moreno. The dam was very big, and on the other side was the lake, about fifteen feet from the top of the dam. A road about two horses wide was on top of the dam. One morning our officer decided that the regiment would ride across the dam, no railing, except for one about two inches high. We started across, two riders abreast. We had to keep cool, but one horse and rider panicked, and the horse fell into the lake with his rider. We kept going, we did not stop. Horses will get excited if the rider becomes excited. EASY was the word. We made it across and the rider who fell in the lake was pulled out, none the worse for wear.[29]

At this time they made a training film, and I was in it. I sure would like to see it. We made another ride from Campo in the mountains to El Centro in the desert. We used to swim in the great American Canal, the horses, too. We'd swim for about four hours, take a siesta, then go swimming for another four hours in the evening. We were in a place called The Palm of God's Hand, in Spanish. I used to know a girl there, Mary Greenfield, from La Mesa, California. She and her family used to picnic at Moreno Lake. Mary and her folks took lots of pictures. In those days not many people carried a camera. If I could locate her, we'd have a lot of good pictures from that time.[30]

Campo was just across the border from a small Mexican village called Tecate. Nothing there but a cross-street and a bar on each corner. We stayed for the dance in one of those bars. I danced with a pretty Mexican girl, but her mother watched her and me at all times. She told her daughter, "Those Indians are no good." [laughter] What gave her that idea? I never did see her after that. Those were the good old days![31]

We had a basketball team. We practiced in the local gym. Many Indian boys and girls used to come and watch us practice. A cute little Indian girl and I became friends, but one night she ran away. Next morning her brother and relatives came to our camp, and the first sergeant called me out there and asked me what I did with the girl. But I didn't know anything about it. I was innocent. They found her later; she was with someone else. I told you I was innocent.[32]

By late 1940, the economic peace dividend since World War I that had supported the mounted cavalry—last vestige of the old army—had to be redefined. In Europe, fascism threatened the free world, and partial mobilization of the armed forces had already begun, along with the draft. The army now had to wrestle with how to reorganize and modernize the cavalry.[33]

Debate centered on the value of the horse in modern warfare. In 1939, the army had 12 million horses and 4.5 million mules. Many cavalrymen favored complete mechanization. Some supported the use of both horses and machines, while others rejected any idea of mechanization at all. The Fourth and Sixth Cavalry regiments were already partially mechanized by 1939. By late 1940, only the Third and Eleventh regiments were fully mounted. In July 1942, the army inactivated the Eleventh Cavalry, clad it in armor, and rechristened it the Eleventh

Armored Cavalry. Hollis would find himself caught in this juncture between old and new armies. [34]

★ At Campo, my commanding officer was 2nd Lt. Jim Snee, a West Point man, who is still living in San Antonio, Texas. He was a polo player and had a polo pony, a mare named Bermuda. One day (1941) 2nd Lt. Snee told me he was being transferred to Fort Benning. He asked me if I would like to take his pony on a slow-moving freight train from Tijuana to Fort Benning. I had just made corporal then. We loaded up in a boxcar and a corral was built at one end and my bunk at the other. There was hay and a fifty-five-gallon barrel of water in the center of the boxcar. I had water enough for the horse, and I was drinking it, too. I don't remember how long that trip lasted, at least a week.

We were riding across the desert one morning and I heard people talking and I could see their heads bobbing up and down. One of them had my campaign hat on, and I took out my pistol. I soon found out it was a young white couple who were stealing a ride. I scared the piss out of them, but we were soon visiting. They said they were running away to get married and I asked them, "Where?" because we were way out in the middle of the desert, somewhere between Tijuana and San Antonio. At some big city they got off the train, and the boy went to a store and bought cheese, sardines, crackers, and oranges. Whew! I was able to make it alive to Ft. Benning! The army had given me money, canned food, and meal tickets, but no place where I could use them, and NO CAN OPENER! I was hungry enough to gnaw into those cans! We had only stopped for water for the engine, where there were no stores or towns to buy anything to eat. That was before K rations came out. We stopped at a town once, at San Antonio. I took Bermuda to a corral and she just ran around and around in circles, working up a sweat.

The train wasn't leaving 'til midnight, so I walked into town. I got some food and a beer. I had bought a pair of cowboy boots in San Diego, light brown leather with a butterfly on the front. I walked over to the police station and visited with the cops, who were all Mexican. The chief of police liked my boots; they fit him perfectly, so I sold them to him for $20.00. That was a lot of money in those days. I blew it on a friend. When I came out, the train was leaving and I barely caught the caboose. I rode the rest of the way in the caboose. [35]

We finally got to Fort Benning. They took away Bermuda—she was a good show mare—in fact, I never did see her again. I spoke with Snee, who was now a captain. He said, "Do you want to go back, or do you want to stay here?" I said, "I'll stay." He was now a captain in the Second Armored Division. So that's how I got into the Second Armored Division, Sixty-seventh Armored Regiment, E Company—"Hell on Wheels," as they would become known. Later, Snee went on to command the Eleventh Cavalry in Central Europe on horseback, patrolling steep mountain passes.[36]

The first thing we did was go over to maneuvers in Louisiana. That's where we learned to ride motorcycles—Harley-Davidsons. One time I was practicing maneuvers on my bike and I got stuck in mud. Boy, did I get stuck! Anyway, right about that time, Gen. Patton came by. He saw me stuck there, and commanded his men to help me get unstuck! "Get that #@#@ thing out of the way!" is what he said. After they helped me, Patton and his tanks and crew drove away, splashing mud all over me. I just stood there and saluted.[37]

But before that, they put me on K.P. I told them, "I'm a corporal!" but I had to pick up ice, anyway. The iceman came. I took the ice and set it on the table. The cook came and knocked it off. I said, "I'm not going to pick that up." We had a standoff right there. Funny thing was, when it was all over, that guy and I came back from the war—the only guy beside me in that unit that came back. Me and him, and we never even talked to one another. Most all those guys were from the South. Most of us got along real good.

Later, we were crossing a burnt-out area that had had a forest fire. Everything looked like it was cool, but not so. The stumps of the trees were still burning beneath the ground. I was dismounting and I stepped on one of these stumps. My horse jumped one way and I landed with one foot in the fire. I got a big blister on my foot. I had more trouble with my feet during the war than anything else.[38]

On Sunday, December 7th, 1941, I was in Opelika [Alabama], the guest of my platoon sergeant, Sgt. Poland, Red Dog Poland, that's what we called him. He was a real "redneck": redheaded, with a loud mouth, and into white supremacy. He never knew just how to take me. During maneuvers in Louisiana, we had come nose to nose, confronting each other, but nothing ever came of it. By now, we knew each other pretty well and we were still friends.[39]

His mother cooked a big breakfast. Then we decided to go visit his brother-in-law, who had a barbershop in town, before reporting back to Fort Benning. The radio was on, and a special news bulletin came on. We were at war! The Japanese had bombed Pearl Harbor. All military personnel were to report immediately! We didn't know we were preparing for a long, four-year trip.[40]

That year, I spent my Christmas furlough at home in Pawhuska, Oklahoma, where my parents lived. I am glad I was able to be there. My sister, Marcella, then aged nineteen, was very sick with diabetes. We did not know much about it, especially about how to treat it.[41]

After my furlough was over, I started back on a Greyhound bus. When I passed through Tulsa an Indian soldier came on board. We talked and found out we knew a lot of the same people. His name was Cpl. Joe Brunner, from Tulsa. He was in the Second Armored, Forty-first Mechanized Infantry. In fact, his barracks was opposite from mine, the Sixty-seventh Armored Regiment, E Company.

We had to change buses at Fort Smith, Arkansas. It was morning, so we decided to go eat breakfast. We entered a restaurant and sat at the counter to order. I still remember our menu—two fried eggs with chili on them—good southern style! There were not many customers, but in a booth not far from us were two young, pretty girls with loud voices, eating breakfast. They kept throwing beer labels at us, two young and innocent Indian soldiers. We finally gave up and sat down at their table.

We ended up spending the whole day with them. The girl I was with— we corresponded for almost a year. She wanted me to come to visit her and her family in Paris, Arkansas. Her name was on the back of her picture, but I accidentally cut it off when I was trimming it. Now I can't remember her name. She was, perhaps, my paradise lost.[42]

About two weeks after I got back from furlough, a man, but someone not of this earth, came to my bunk one night and woke me up. He told me my sister Marcella was dead. We didn't know she was that sick. I always felt like I never knew her, she was so young, you know. Anyway, she's buried at Pawhuska, with my parents.[43]

Eunice Stabler would never get past the grief of losing her young daughter. She vented her pain in a poem.

> Nineteen years of beautiful comradeship
> Together we sailed life's sea in perfect love and harmony . . .
> Your absence left me desolate—

In its vastness I groped blindly for light;
I prayed, I searched for renewed hope from fate . . .[44]

The bombing of Pearl Harbor had assured the passing of the
mounted cavalry. Hollis traded in packhorses and mules for new,
more potent horsepower. Among them was the U.S. light tank M3
Stuart. Replacing the older M2A4 light tank, which fired a 37 mm tank
gun M5—the British armored troops had used them in the Battle of
Flanders, and found it lacking in armor, and in need of a stronger
suspension—the M3 Stuart was clad in armor measuring from 38–51
mm. The removal of peepholes from the turret had strengthened the
entire turret structure. Grounded idler wheels added stability to the
suspension. Now more effectively able to withstand enemy aircraft
fire, they were affectionately called by servicemen General Stuarts, or
"Honeys," after Confederate General J.E.B. Stuart, and came in two
models—those that consumed gasoline, and those that used diesel.
Hollis had traveled light years since riding old Joe to Mrs. VanCleeve's
house at the mission at Macy, but the journey was far from over.[45]

★ One day we got orders to deploy. Before we left, we had a big party,
with beer and whiskey. The next morning was a Saturday morning and
we were supposed to have an inspection. Everyone was supposed to
have a haircut. I was one of the company barbers. One of the men, 1st
Sgt. Willie Powers, came over to me at the party and said, "Chief, I want
you to give me a haircut like this, I'm gonna tell you how. . . . Leave me
a three-inch patch of hair up on the top, that's all. Then put some hair
oil in it and part it." So I did that. Then everybody came up. They wanted
their hair like that, all bald. It was a big mess. My hair wasn't cut like
that. I had it roached, like a Mohawk. Anyway, the next morning, Capt.
Snee came in for inspection. He looked at all those men and asked me,
"Are you scalping everybody?" There was about three hundred guys or
so. Eventually, I got to know every one—either by their stories or their
heads.[46]

Late one night our convoy went to Norfolk, Virginia. We stayed in a
large warehouse and were instructed not to appear in daytime. All work
and moving was to be done at night. We loaded our M3 Stuart tanks
with four-man crews. They had twin Cadillac motors, a 20 mm cannon,
and two .30 caliber machine guns. Since we were in E Company, all the
tanks had names, starting with our tank, the Empress I. We loaded our

tanks on a light transport carrier, an LTC called the *Seatrain*, and we were put on a ship, the USS *Calvert*. Since we were in the light Stuarts, we were in front, on point. Only the maintenance crew, in their half-track, was ahead of us. It was a large ship, with rope ladders on its sides. When we took our showers, it came out saltwater! Have you ever taken a bath in saltwater before? They issued us warm-weather clothing. We thought we were headed for Guadalcanal where the marines were fighting.[47]

The Second Armored did not go to Guadalcanal. They invaded Safi, Morocco, on North Africa's Atlantic coast, in the first major Western operation of World War II. General George Patton chose to come ashore at three distinct locations, rather than assault Casablanca directly, where 50,000 French stood at arms. He ordered Maj. Gen. Ernest Harmon to land at Safi, secure a position, and be ready to assault the land defenses at Casablanca. The Second was expected to capture the telephone exchange and radio station, undamaged if possible. The safe unloading of the *Seatrain* was of vital concern, as it carried all of the medium tanks headed into battle.[48]

Safi's high cliffs and sparse beach created heavy swells that could dash a light craft onto the rocks, making it a notoriously difficult place to land. However, its harbor was one of three deep-water ports on the Atlantic side of French North Africa. Inside was a wharf with cranes that could help with the unloading of the tanks. If the harbor could be taken, OPERATION TORCH, as the mission was known, would be greatly simplified.[49]

The General expected opposition from one thousand Vichy French forces, but found only half that number training their artillery and machine guns in Safi's defense. With their large guns, the French could have proved a formidable resistance, had they wished. Additionally, at Marrakech, some one hundred miles to the south, well over 3,500 French troops stood ready to reinforce those at Safi.[50]

The U.S. convoy pulled into position on November 7, 1942, at 10:45 p.m. After eating sandwiches and potato salad washed down with coffee, the men started over the side of the *Calvert*. They were surprised that the harbor lights remained on until 2:00 a.m., leading them to realize they had arrived undetected. Finally, at 3:20 a.m., Safi sounded the alert. American gunfire quickly sank the first French ship to fire on them. When the warship entered the harbor, the French commander gave the order to fire, which was answered with a volley of return fire from the Americans that lit up the horizon. Within an hour and ten minutes, Col. E. H. Randal's Forty-seventh Infantry Regiment, Ninth Infantry Division, landed. They held the beachhead while the tanks unloaded.

★ We were on the ship twenty-three days. I made a new friend, a rookie named Delaney. He was an Irish orphan from New York; he only had one sister. We ran into a big storm, and everyone got seasick. We even had to serve as the ship's gun crew because all the sailors were seasick. On the morning of November 8, 1942, we were called on deck. It was sunrise, and we saw Africa. Everything looked gold except the buildings. They were snow white. We were given a lecture on what to do and not do in Africa. We turned in our suntans and were issued olive drabs. We were told to line up as our names were called. We climbed down the rope ladder into small Higgins boats, which then transferred us to the ship where our tanks were. We had practiced this rope climbing at Fort Bragg, so now we knew what to do.[51]

We had a bad accident. Delaney was assigned to the maintenance half-track crew. They were just ahead of us. I was one of the company barbers, so I knew a lot of the guys. Delaney told me he was afraid of water and could not swim. I asked him, "What, they don't swim in Ireland?" and we laughed. The *Calvert* was drifting to and fro and the Higgins boat was dancing all around. When my turn came and I was safe in the Higgins boat, I said, "Where's Delaney?" Someone said he had missed the boat when he slid down the rope. With all the equipment he had on, he had no chance. No noise, no outcry, just gone—the first casualty of the invasion of North Africa. The Sixty-seventh had a short memorial service for him later, when we bivouacked in the cork forest east of Rabat. When I returned from overseas I tried to find his sister, but no luck; too many Delaneys in New York City.[52]

Word came over the loudspeaker that the beach was secured. We were told to go off the right side of the pier. On the left side the current was too swift and the sand banks too crumbly. In fact, we could see some vehicles half in the water. The bank was too high and soft. We did not have to disembark from the LTC by the big door, but by a crane operating on the pier. They unloaded both LTCs and were working on ours when the crane broke. Our platoon was supposed to be on point, but now we were going to be last. Nine tanks besides our three tanks were still in the hold of the ship. We had to stay nearby in case they fixed the crane. [53]

Hollis never knew that a Vichy French nightwatchman, who was shortly identified and ordered to fix it, had damaged the crane. [54]

★ I remember the soldiers telling us to go to the mess anytime and eat. "The cooks will feed you whatever you want: steaks, eggs, ice cream, cakes, a good mess." We had hardly had any sleep because so much was going on and the noise was everywhere. We finally got some sleep and when we woke up we found out that most of the Sixty-seventh had gone on ahead. We had a 2nd Lt., three Stuart tanks, and twelve men, which was one platoon. We ate a good breakfast and were standing by our LTC when French fighter planes came from the right. Everybody was taken by surprise. They were firing on us and the soldiers on the beach. There was no cover on the beach except "scorpions," which was what we called the metal covers for our tanks that we used when we had to come through water. The officer reached ours first, but by the time the other twelve fellows squeezed in, the officer got squeezed out. The scorpion was only big enough for two men. We laughed until it hurt. Pretty soon the navy started firing at those planes, and the last I saw of them, they were on fire. [55]

Then a sniper started shooting at us. We had to be careful. I noticed a small building at the end of the pier, so I walked over to it. It had been turned into a first-aid station and casualties were being brought in. One tank crew was badly burned when their tank caught fire. It made us think about what might happen to our tank. There were also some tankers who would never fight again. They were going home early—dead. [56]

A reconnaissance platoon from the Forty-seventh captured the telegraph and telephone centers, cutting Safi off from the rest of North Africa. By 3:30 p.m., Gen. Harmon had set up headquarters there. He wanted Casablanca next, more than one hundred miles further east up the coast, but the port of Mazagon, which lay between Safi and Casablanca, would have to fall first, and before that, the stronghold at Marrakech. Harmon needed Mazagon for a resupply base. Safi had shown only anemic resistance to the American troops. Eager to press his advantage, Harmon wasted no time. He started his command rolling south, to Marrakech, without Hollis Stabler.

★ By evening they finally had our three tanks on the dock. It was dark as we started up the rocky road to the plateau. I was driving the lead tank, and Sgt. Brooks was the tank commander. It was getting dark and the lieutenant was walking in front with a blue flashlight. Just before we reached the top, Sgt. Brooks told me to stop. He jumped down and was talking to the lieutenant.[57]

It seemed like a long time and I wanted to get started. The officer motioned for me and I dismounted and asked what the matter was. The officer said that Sgt. Brooks refused to go on. He said for me to take charge and get a driver. Just that fast, I became T-4 Stabler! Our radio worked pretty well in the night, so he called a ship and told them what was happening. They sent two marines who came in a half-track and took Brooks back to the ship. We never saw him again.[58]

We finally caught up with the tail end of our column, on the march to Mazagon, on November 9th. From there we were allowed to pass everyone. There was an old French soldier seated in a chair, holding an old rifle, and he would not let anyone go by. We finally just bypassed him. Now we were getting to the desert. All at once we heard shouting and yelling. I will never forget. A young girl came by, riding a fast black pony with a very long mane and tail. She had long dark hair, and wore a white blouse and dark skirt. She carried a flag, streaming in the wind. I think it was a French flag. She was glad to see us, or so we hoped. Just as quickly, she flew past us and disappeared. I have spent many hours since then wondering who she was, and where she came from, as we were in the Moroccan desert—vast, open country—where there was nothing.[59]

That evening, we heard that our goal was Casablanca. We were still in the desert, and at about noon we came upon a small fort with French Legionnaire officers in command of native soldiers, just like in the movies. I was in the tank, and stopped near the soldiers. We had traveled all night and day. Most of the men in the Sixty-seventh now had Mohawks, since I was the barber. Our faces were sunburned and dirty. Except for our goggles, we looked like an Indian war party. I took my helmet off and showed the native soldiers my Mohawk haircut. They pointed at me, and waved, and smiled.[60]

That night, we were pretty much together—trucks, half-tracks, tanks, but no jeeps. When night came, we bivouacked in a circle. We started something to eat, and began to change our clothes, because we were hungry grease balls. I had only my long-handled underwear on when we had an air raid. I jumped on the tank and released a spring-loaded .30 caliber machine gun located on the rim of the turret. I pulled the handle back and started to fire. I could see the path of the bullet as a long, gentle curve—my first shot at the enemy. We were *all* doing something. Everybody had a shot. One fellow was "potting." He was firing his pistol from a squatting position. He said it was a good position to shoot from. That plane was shot down. By now it was sunset, and beginning to cool off. [61]

Early the next morning we started off for Casablanca again. Some of the units headed for Marrakech. By this time we were nearing the coast. The scout cars and half-tracks were ahead of us and the column. When we arrived near the coast we could see a huge ship. Its bow was on the beach, but tilted portside about thirty degrees. Later we heard that it was a war ship that French sailors had sabotaged. [62]

Harmon's first objective was to secure the Mazagon port, where the ships *Cole* and *Bernadau* were being sent from Fedala to refuel and resupply the tanks. The tanks of the Second reached Mazagon at 4:30 a.m. Harmon decided to wait until dawn to attack; by 7:30, the French had surrendered with full military honors. Just as Harmon prepared to move on, he received word that all French forces in North Africa, more than 50,000, had surrendered. [63]

Hollis continued:

★ We soon came to the port of Mazagon, and we could see French artillery lined up on the outskirts of the city. It was about nine or ten in the morning. An American officer walked out to the front of our line with a megaphone and said, "Follow me!" Everyone thought it was Gen. Patton, but I believed it was Gen. Harmon. We later heard that Patton had been in Casablanca, fighting with the rest of the Second Armored Division. [64]

We took the covers off of our 20 mm cannon, gassed up, and followed Gen. Harmon. We were lined up with a road that took us right through a line of six or eight of the enemy's 75 mm cannons. We plowed through, everybody shooting, and the smoke and dust, we finally made it to the edge of Mazagon. We raced to the square at the center of the city and we found two navy fliers. They still had their "Mae West" yellow life vests on—that's what we called them. They waved, but my tank was ordered to block the road that came around the bay.[65]

While we were waiting, we ran out of water. A French boy on a bicycle stopped. He took our canteens, but we almost missed him, as we were told to move out. He saw us leaving and pedaled as fast as he could, finally catching up to us. That canteen had cool, sweet *wine* in it! I never can forget that boy. We threw him a carton of Wing cigarettes. Then we took off for Casablanca. The Americans were having a tough time there, but by the time we got there, it was over for the French. We rested and gassed up and took off for Rabat, the capitol of Morocco, about fifty miles away.[66]

While all this was going on, my brother, Bob, was in the Third Infantry Division, in a reconnaissance outfit. They were invading, too. His ship was sunk and he was injured. Then they all had to swim to shore. They went into battle with only what they carried on them. That happened at Fedala. I went to the hospital at Casablanca to see him during Christmas of 1942, but he had already been discharged. At about five o'clock that afternoon, I got caught in an air raid at the railroad station in Casablanca. I ran into a tunnel. This was my first German air raid. Two Arab girls were in there. My buddy and I followed them up a hill, and they took us to an Arab restaurant. There was a merchant marine in there that spoke Arab and French. Those girls danced for us. We spent the night there and then went back to the railroad station. We found a boxcar selling sandwiches, and we got bread and meat and wine for breakfast.[67]

Hollis had been late to learn that following the surrender at Casablanca, the French torpedoed and sank four U.S. ships at Fedala, fifteen miles north, a disaster that only magnified the loss of manpower the Third had experienced during the initial landing operation there three days earlier.[68]

French Morocco had fallen in four days, and so had 860 Americans. Fifty thousand French troops surrendered. They would be rearmed in the coming months, and trained to serve the Allies. But even as Africa fell, the Germans invaded Tunisia, determined to stymie an anticipated Allied advance on Sicily. They punished the French for their failure to defend North Africa by invading Vichy France. Within a short time, Hollis would face them on both fronts.

★ Anyway, we arrived at Rabat just before dark. It was a large and important city because the Sultan of Morocco had his palace there. They told me and the other tank driver to block a main road coming from the West. We put our tanks on either side of a large, handsome gate. It was a quiet evening. While we were there some horsemen approached from the West. A woman who seemed to be in charge asked in English who was in charge. I told her I was. She said to come with her. I asked her "Why?" I went and told the lieutenant what was happening. He said to go and see what it was all about. I asked her where she wanted me to go, or what she wanted me to see.[69]

She took me into a building not far from where we were on guard. It was a big hall. The only light came from a couple of lanterns. The hall was full of French men. Nobody said anything. We were all quiet, except for the woman who had guided us there. I don't know what she said to those men, but when she was through she gave us each a bottle of beer. I've always wondered who she was and what she said. Everybody seemed to know her, but nobody said a word, they just looked at us. Eventually, some man began to talk, but since we did not understand, we left.

One can't help but wonder if this influential French woman and her comrades simply wanted a closer look at an American Indian.[70]

★ Next day we went to the cork-tree forest at Rabat, which was a bivouac area about fourteen miles from the city. Our platoon and our three tanks had just arrived and were setting up camp when an officer came up to us and said, "Follow me." He was in a jeep, the first one we had seen in quite a while. It wasn't 'til later that we finally got a jeep for everyone. Our three tanks followed him into the woods, which to our surprise was very big. We soon came to a large, dry lakebed. Way out on the sand, we could see a convoy of German soldiers trying to retreat.[71]

The Germans had been caught by surprise when the Allies landed on North Africa. They had expected them to head for the eastern end of the Mediterranean. After OPERATION TORCH, the Germans could either fight or surrender, but evacuation was impossible. They continued to fight.[72]

★ To get into a good spot to shoot we had to decide whether to go down and up some ravines, or go around the lake. We decided to cross the ravines. The first tanker started across them. He went straight down and buried the nose of his tank in dirt and sand and was stuck tight. The second tank started down the slope, tipping from side to side, finally sliding off its tracks. Then our turn came. Slowly, turning side to side, we made it to the bottom of the ravine in one piece. We started up the other side and got into a good position to fire our 20 mm cannon. Each of the crew fired one shot, then the navy planes came over and the German convoy was no more.[73]

Every morning at Rabat a camel caravan would come nearby, or through, our tents in the cork-tree forest. I eventually learned that the caravan carried cork that they burned to make charcoal to use in their vehicles for gasoline. We dug foxholes and had our tents set up over them. Some guys made their set-ups pretty fancy. We were not bad off, except for snakes and insects. The scorpions alone were six inches tall, and not afraid of anything! Centipedes were at least twelve inches long and bright orange. I used to sleep in the tank, and listen to Lord Hah Hah, an English turncoat, on the radio.[74]

Since the bombing of Pearl Harbor, Allied forces in World War II had fought an almost exclusively defensive war against the Axis powers, though a moderately successful one. Defense had centered on patrolling for German submarines, the protection of the Suez Canal, and the support of the Soviet Union. Such offensive measures that had been accomplished were limited to attacks on the German army from the air, for lack of access by land. But between July 1942 and January 1943, a series of Allied defensive victories—the Russian breakthrough at Stalingrad; the British victory at El'Alamein; and most recently the British and American victory in North Africa—allowed the Allies to prosecute an offensive strategy of war. Planners agreed that the European continent would have to be breached, but differed on theories of how it should be accomplished.[75]

The series of meetings between President Franklin Roosevelt and Prime Minister Winston Churchill, together with their Combined Chiefs of Staff, held at Casablanca, Morocco, in mid-January 1943 inaugurated the new offensive strategy. There, Roosevelt, Churchill, and Gen. Eisenhower agreed to push on to Sicily and a possible invasion of Italy, contingent on the execution of the Sicilian campaign. But even as they spoke, German troops poured into Tunisia, hoping to stem just such a plan of attack. Hollis Stabler was destined to play a role in the liberation of Tunisia and the invasion of Sicily.[76]

"At the Casablanca conference, they asked us to be the honor guard for President Roosevelt," Hollis remembered wryly. "They made us wear wool suits and berets and ties, in a closed tank! It was a hundred degrees out, but that was Gen. Patton, you know, that's the way he was."

★ Then we heard that Gen. Patton was going to meet with the Sultan of Morocco, so a friend and I, whose last name was French, got a pass and caught one of those cork-burning buses going to Rabat. The parade was in a large field like a football stadium. It was surrounded by a wall about twelve feet thick and twenty feet high. They gave a large demonstration and parade for our Gen. Patton and his troops, and the Sultan of Morocco and his sheiks. I and French became thirsty, so we persuaded a native to go get us a drink using sign language. We gave him some money, more than enough. I was hoping he would bring us back a drink at least the size of a soda pop. He came back with a bottle the size of a *bath tub*! We drank some, and left the rest for him. I bet he stayed drunk for a month [laughter].[77]

After the parade was over we talked to some of the native cavalrymen. I had a pencil and paper and by drawing, I was able to convince them that I, too, was a cavalryman. We did not speak the same language, but we understood one another. I took my boots off and bought a pair of native sandals. We went into the lobby of a large hotel and sat down, each talking in our own language. Nobody was listening anyway. We traded caps. The native soldier gave me his little red cap, and I gave him mine. While we were sitting there, two American MPs came in and stared at us. The native sergeant kept right on talking, and I pretended that I understood him. Those MPs finally left, and we laughed so hard. We didn't speak the same language, but we shared the same humor.[78]

The native sergeant wanted us to go to their barracks to look at their horses and stables. We stayed, and finally ate some chow with them. They said it was too dangerous to go back after dark. They gave us a bunk and we stayed the night. Before we went to sleep they had a dance. We found out that only men danced, but it was good. To my surprise, a couple of old women loo-looed like our Indian women do. The next day we went back to the cork-tree forest.[79]

I'll tell you another story about Rabat. Chancy was a tall, good-natured drunk from Tennessee. If you wanted a drink, all you had to do was find Chancy. His buddy was Zabol, a Polish boy from Chicago. He, too, liked to drink. And me, I liked to drink, too. When it got dark in Rabat, it signaled curfew for American soldiers. The road leading out of the city going east was a very fancy boulevard. On the north side of the boulevard was the native city called Medina. The south side of the boulevard was a sunken cemetery, about ten feet deep. One time we were out after curfew when we spotted the MP coming down the street, and we rushed to find somewhere to hide. I jumped over the wall and landed in the graveyard. Soon I could hear Chancy calling for me, "Hey Chief, where are you?" All Indians were called "Chief" in the service. "Here I am, way down in the graveyard," I called back. I could hear Chancy and Zabol laughing. We had to figure a way for me to get out. We tied our belts together, and they pulled me up to where I could reach their hands.[80]

We started down the boulevard and we could see the MP coming back. This time we rushed to a doorway in the wall. It was deeply recessed into the building. It was also very high, perhaps three or four stories. We were huddled there, waiting for the MP to pass, when suddenly the door opened behind us! We saw a large room full of natives and lit by candlelight. We looked at them and they looked at us. I put my finger to my lips and said, "Police." A man answered in French, "Enter," so we did. The people were eating bread, cheese, and wine. We were served a fine le dejeuner."[81]

Zabol said he wanted to use the restroom. While he took care of his business, I drew sketches of cowboys and Indians and horses and other animals. Zabol still hadn't returned, so we went to check on him. We found him flushing the stool, trying to get a big, six-inch-by-two-inch turd down a one and a half inch drain hole. Everybody roared with laughter. Later we found out that most French homes had two stools, a small one for women, and a larger one for men.[82]

In the morning we could not get out of the main gate because the French and American soldiers guarded it, so we had to sneak out the back gate. Finally we got back to the bivouac. Later on, a group of Moroccan families camped about a mile from us. I caught a ride with a water truck, and when we got near the camp, there was a lot of activity. They were having a feast, so I dropped off the truck. As soon as they saw me they came over to welcome me. They gave me a pillow to sit on, and a dish with rice, meat, and fruit. They sang songs, and the women loo-looed. One man demonstrated the manual of arms. He must have been an old soldier.[83]

Historians have pondered the propensity of American soldiers to address Indians by the title "Chief." One of the best assessments holds that the war experience represented the first time that most whites had ever met an Indian. In the minds of the uninitiated, American Indian men were stereotyped as warriors. Indeed, few whites questioned the Indians' capabilities as fighters at a time when their own lives were in peril. "Chief," one author has written, signified something other than condescension; it signified respect. Furthermore, some Indians did not resent being addressed as "Chief" on one level—that which reminded them of their heritage. But on the other hand, the stereotype it implied led to expectations about their performance in battle—their "inherited" warrior skills—held by both themselves and their white fellow soldiers that couldn't necessarily be achieved by virtue of race. Thus, it has been said, Indians fought with a fury to live up to their own historic image.[84]

In an ironic twist, Cherokee scholar Tom Holm, writing in 1985, used the example of Bob Stabler, Hollis's brother, to demonstrate American Indian soldiers' propensity to conform to performance expectations. American Indians, he wrote, for the most part accepted these attitudes toward them and often did their best to conform to such views. Robert Stabler, an Omaha Indian, landed "alone under heavy fire to mark the beaches for the infantry in advance of the assault" on Sicily. When asked, Hollis replied, "Bob was just doing his job."[85]

The Second Armored Division regrouped under the cork trees of Rabat, and then transferred by train to Oran, Algeria. Meanwhile, British troops had advanced to within twelve miles of the port of Tunis, determined to push the Germans out. In December, the Germans forced the British back, but mud and intemperate weather would delay Gen. Harmon from attacking Tunisia for months.[86]

OPERATION TORCH had demonstrated that an amphibious force

could be transported across the ocean, land in the face of opposition, and execute its mission. But it also revealed that the American forces were in need of better landing methods. The operation had proven to be a testing ground for both the Second Armored Division and the entire army. It would serve the Allies well in the years ahead. The Second would soon roll across Europe, sans Hollis, earning the nickname "Roosevelt's Butchers" among the Germans. To Americans, they were "Hell on Wheels," and Hollis Stabler had been one of them.[87]

THREE

Operation Husky

July 10–23, 1943

Following the slaughter of the U.S. Army's First Infantry Division at the Kasserine Pass in Tunisia in February 1943, Gen. Harmon rallied the troops. Replacements had to be put into position immediately, and logistics demanded the use of the Second Armored Division. One tank platoon, one officer and twenty-four men of the Second were attached to the First Infantry Division. Due to shipping problems, the Second had to be stripped of its trucks before deploying to Tunisia. An historian has written that some units used this opportunity to get rid of their "most undesirable soldiers, even some from the kitchens." Hollis would live to prove him wrong. It was upon the grit of such tank men as Hollis Stabler that Harmon would earn his reputation as a brilliant "artist in mobile warfare." [1]

Hollis would recall that

★ We received orders to leave Rabat, Morocco. We were told not to take anything except our personal belongings. We mounted trucks and waited. Soon a bunch of Free French soldiers marched in, the French First Armored Division. They took over everything—kitchen, tanks, trucks and half-tracks. We started to the railroad depot and boarded an old train, the beginning of a long trip to Oran, then on to Algiers, and Cape Bone, and Tunis, all by truck. Being seasick was bad enough, but the back of a closed truck on a mountain road, in the cold and rain, and hungry, was worse. Anyway, they put us on a train to Oran, Algeria, the wildest train ride I ever took. [2]

There were four of us sitting together. We had a blanket covering the seat, and we were playing cards, me, a guy named Kushman, Zabel, the

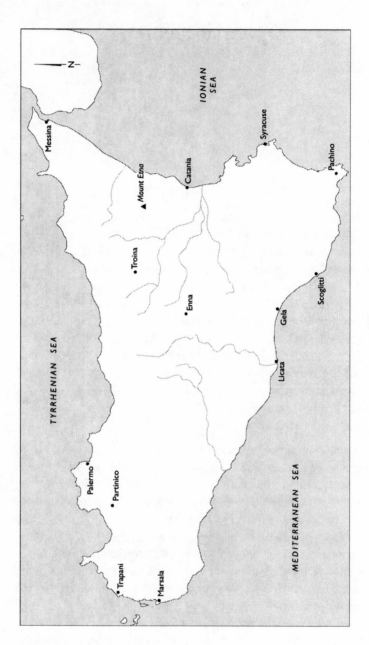

2. Sicily

Polish guy from Chicago, and Charles St. Germaine, the Germ. Every once in a while the Germ would take out his gun and shoot out the windows at Arabs. It made me think about white men shooting Indians from trains in the West. Anyway, we drank a bottle of wine and then Germaine took out his pistol. I told him, "Put that dang thing away!" Then a boy, a blonde-haired boy from Alabama, tried to take it out of his hands. The gun went off and hit Zabel in the knee. The bullet went in here and came out here [Hollis points to the back of his knee], except it didn't come clean through the skin. When they came and got him, why, you could see the bullet hanging down in his skin.

Anyway, the gun went off, everybody stopped, except the train. That conductor wouldn't stop that train for nothing. He was scared I guess. I don't blame him. So that blonde boy, Carter, that was his name, he had the gun in his hand. I told him, "Give me that gun." And he did! Then he ran to the back of the car and tried to jump onto the next train car, but he missed. Of course, the train didn't stop, it just kept on going. Later we heard that some people picked him up and he lost both legs.[3]

Finally we got to Oran, Algeria. Just outside of Oran was a place called St. Cloud. That's where I first heard of the Rangers. I never heard of them before that. I thought to myself, "I'm getting out of this unit, and that's where I'm going." But first we had to get to Tunisia. Oran is where we joined up with the First Infantry Division, Sixteenth Regiment. Then a truck took us to Algiers.

It was a long way, maybe three or four days, and it was cold. We were in the back of the truck, covered up, and we'd stop to rest, you know, and everyone would get out. Then everyone got sick. I said to myself, "I'm not going to get sick," but I did. Oh, I got sick. So there I was, hanging out of the truck for a couple days. We were going to Tunisia, where they had lost that battle.

Then we bivouacked on a high plateau above Algiers. We celebrated the Fourth of July there; some Spanish dancers entertained us. In fact, I was on KP. The captain, a tall red-head with a loud, foghorn voice, almost got killed before we ever got into combat.[4]

We had a large pit dug to dispose of our trash. Some men wanted to burn it, but everyone was afraid to light the match because there was so much gasoline poured on the trash. All of a sudden the captain said, "Give me that match." He walked up to the edge of the pit and threw that match in. There was a terrific explosion! The captain lit up like a

Christmas tree—no hair, no eyebrows, red eyes. His body wasn't hurt too badly, but his pride certainly was!

Then we learned we were going to relieve the First Armored Division, who had taken a beating at Kasserine Pass. We negotiated the pass, and saw what had happened to our men and machines and equipment. We ended up at Mateur, Tunisia, where we were given new M4A3 tanks, Sherman tanks. The first assignment was to set a defense line to be ready to fire at some targets on the other side of the valley, so we started out after the Germans. That was really the first time I ever fought Germans. Before that we mostly fought the Arabs and French. Anyway, it started to rain and rain. Soon, our tank was in deep water. We found we were sitting in the middle of a lake! We couldn't move, and neither could the Germans, but they were shooting at us with a cannon. We didn't feel too bad. They were in the same boat we were. We were all in the middle of that big lake, with a little island in it.[5]

It took about two days for that water to go down. Then, the British came in and the Germans gave up. About this time, my heels became infected *again*. I was sent to a field hospital about fifteen miles from Bizerte, Tunisia. So, I was in a field hospital, hobbling around on crutches. One Sunday afternoon, after we ate, we were sitting up on the bank, with a curving road below us, like a horseshoe. Two trucks started coming along there. We could see German prisoners standing in the back of the truck, and Americans in front.

They stopped almost right below where we were sitting on the bank. The American officer got out. He had a map in his hands. He told the Germans, "You get out and dig here." They got out and dug. Then they uncovered an American soldier. There was nothing left of him, just a skull and a uniform. You could see his belt, boots, leggings, you know, but his body was gone, except his skull. The Americans chased the Germans out of the back of the truck. Then they shook his bones clean and put him in a sack with his dog tags tied around the top and put him in there. After that, hell, we walked around that big hole for two or three days. We didn't know that had been the sight of the battle. We thought that it was pretty interesting that we were right on the battlefield and we didn't know it.[6]

After that we returned to Oran. We were in a park at the head of a beautiful boulevard named after Marshall Petain, the French hero of World War I. To us, it was a pretty good set-up. We made friends with people, like a family where the husband was Spanish and the wife French. The man, Diego, played the accordion. He was very good, and soon picked up some American songs like "Beer Barrel Polka." We had it made because one of our men, Charles St. Germaine, the Germ, spoke French, and another crewman spoke Spanish. The lady washed our clothes, and we furnished soap and money. All the French kids knew us, and we knew them. Everybody called me "Chief" but they pronounced it "Skief." We soldiers picked up some French phrases, too.[7]

We stayed there November and December of 1942 through January, February, March, April . . . May 1943—seven months in Oran, including our time in Tunisia. We got well acquainted with that city. Down below was a dock where they unloaded ships, our jeeps, trucks, and tanks and all that. We got acquainted with people around there. Our job was to go down to the docks, pick up a tank or a jeep or a truck, service it, and the same with our tanks.[8]

At the Casablanca Conference in January 1943, the Allies had agreed to invade Sicily for the purposes of diverting German attention from the Soviet front, securing supply lines in the Mediterranean, and to put pressure on Italians who witnessed the steady fall of Africa and the Allied advance on their own south. Following the German defeat in Tunisia, Hitler ordered his army to invade Sardinia and Sicily, partially to bolster defenses in Italy and protect supply lines in the Mediterranean, but also as an advanced force on Italy, should Mussolini prove unable, or unwilling, to defend it against the Allies, whom it was presumed would invade if they were successful in Sicily.[9]

The Italian military command had acceded to Hitler's wishes and accepted the reconnaissance unit of Hitler's Hermann Goering Division to occupy Sicily in June of 1943. German advisors, already anticipating an Allied invasion of the Italian outer islands, had been in Sicily since the spring of 1943. The Italians, however, lacked the resources to construct much fortification in Sicily, and Hitler had to be content with bolstering the few fortifications already in place. Even as Hitler pondered the stability of Italy, Hollis and his division prepared to invade Sicily.[10]

★ Oran was where we were trained to invade Sicily. Lots of things happened there. We had a good time and plenty of food. We stood formation every Sunday. Right across the street was our tank park. It was our job to train and help tankers from different Allied countries—Scottish tankers, British tankers, French tankers. As they became proficient, they drove their tanks away and a new set would roll in. Once we met some British sailors who invited us to their ship, the HMS Murdock.[11]

We had a nice time on the road between Oran and St. Cloud. We had foot races and boxing matches. We practiced shooting from Higgins boats at targets on shore. We practiced swimming a lot. Don't ever try swimming around an LTC. It looked easy to do, but it was hard to do because on one side the current was so strong we could barely swim against it. Besides, there was nothing to hold onto and rest, so we had to finish once we started. You should try on a navy diving helmet sometime. I did not like diving, it scared me. I found an octopus at least thirty feet long. It was dead, but long.[12]

Not far from our camping area, about a block away, was a whorehouse—Villa de la Rosa—well known by all army personnel. It was only open on weekends. Charles St. Germaine, the Germ, and I were good friends. Since we were almost in the center of Oran, we always had a bunch of people around. We were surrounded by a coiled barbed wire fence, and we stood guard night and day. The Germ and I got acquainted with a couple of Moroccan girls. They all wore long white dresses and veils with only their eyes showing. One of the girls invited me to her home. It was different. We went into a large room, a sitting room with many pillows. She gave me a cup of coffee, but her brother glared at me; he didn't like me. She was very pretty, but we could not visit because we didn't speak the same language. Another thing, all the girls there were called "Fatima," and all the men were named "Mohammed."[13]

That parking lot across the street from us was a big parking lot, I mean, as big as a football field. British soldiers camped near us, tankers. Same with the French. And we got acquainted with Scottish and English platoons, too. There was a British soldier we called Tommy, of course, and the Scottish man, we called him Scotty. He was much older than we were. I was only in my early twenties, and he must have been thirty-five or forty. I couldn't understand him for nothing. But he always came to me and Germ and Kushman. In the evenings, after we had our duty done, well, we'd meet with these guys and go to town. Nothing but bars on either side of the street. We'd go down one way, and then come back up the other way. Of course, there was a cathouse over about two blocks, but it was patrolled by MPs. Certain people could get in, officers, but we couldn't get in.

Diego and his wife gave us a big feast and dance. They lived in a square complex there, built around a common courtyard, and we supplied his wife with everything we could. She was just a little lady, and she had a sister about the same size, just little. And the same with Diego—he wasn't very big. I was a head taller than everybody. We had lots of wine, and Germ got drunk. All of us were eating when suddenly Germ said, "I'm going outside." And he had that damn pistol with him, you see. Some black soldiers were near his jeep. He took a shot at them and shot off an ear or something. He came running in yelling, "Those niggers are after me." I said, "What did you do?" But I knew what he did, so we ran in and locked the door. Those places are built like a fort, with big doors. Pretty soon a couple trucks of black soldiers came up. They yelled, "Peace or war?" I said, "Damn it, Germ, what the . . . Give me that gun!" I took the gun away from him. I didn't know if I should have. We all had guns, but we never carried them, except for Germ. He always had his. He wasn't a big man, either.

So, we waited and waited around that courtyard and fooled around. Finally it got dark and the black soldiers were still there. Finally, about one or two o'clock in the morning we all went to sleep on the floors. Then Diego woke us up and said, "Crawl up this house to the roof and go down there," so that's what we did. We crawled up to the roof and sneaked up there. Those black soldiers were still out there, but they didn't see us. Finally we got back to camp.[14]

Another time, Diego rented out his big barn for a dance. All of us got in there and danced. The French men were in there dancing. And a lady played an accordion. Diego, like I said, would sing Spanish songs and French Songs. I learned some French songs, too. One old lady had a grandson named Joseph. We gave him salt and stuff like that. He was teaching me French. I think Joseph was about fifteen or sixteen years old, kind of underfed, you know, a little guy.[15]

There was a race war in Oran while we were there, between black and white soldiers. Everything was segregated. I never did get involved with that race stuff, so I didn't have many problems. In fact, I never did know any black people until I became a public school teacher in an all-black school in Wichita in 1965. My best years of teaching were there, but that's a different book. Anyway, one time it was a Sunday, which was a big deal for those guys. We were sitting around and suddenly I yelled, "Here come those black soldiers!" They had a band and they were marching down the street. That's when the Swing first came out, you know. Those black soldiers—a British company—they came marching. They gave *everybody* a lesson on marching. They sure could drill! They were good, you know, with music and all that. I looked out for the Germ, but they didn't bother him. We watched them while they passed us on the way to downtown.[16]

But the race problem, the biggest problem was at the Villa, the Villa de la Rosa, between white soldiers and black soldiers. But we stayed away from them. The problem wasn't with our company, it was with another company, but they were all from the Sixty-seventh Regiment.[17]

While we were at Oran, hundreds of German soldiers surrendered nearby, at a place called Cape Bone. No more war! *Le fin de la guerre* for North Africa! German prisoners were all over the place, more than the Army could take care of. I don't know how they fed them. We didn't even have enough to eat. And those Germans were fighting amongst themselves. It was a big fight, so they called us out. We didn't have a tank, we just walked to help out the MPs. That's another thing. No one ever mentions the MPs. At first I didn't care for them, but after a while I had a lot of respect for them. They had the big job.[18]

With Morocco and Tunisia defeated, Gen. Patton aimed his troops at Sicily, where victory hinged on the capture of Gela, a quaint fishing town of some 32,000 Sicilians that sat upon a 150-foot-high hill extending three miles along the shoreline. With the advantage afforded by the city's altitude, army intelligence presumed the Gelans would defend themselves in the streets. Additionally, defensive concrete pillboxes and barbed wire, installed by the Italian Coastal Battalion, surrounded the community some twelve to fifteen miles inland, intended to halt a successful Allied invasion of the Gela beachhead.[19]

German Field Marshal Albert Kesselring, the most powerful German officer in Italy, doubted Sicily's preparedness to withstand an Allied invasion, as did Gen. Alfredo Gozzoni, of the Italian High Command. He complained that the Italian Coastal Battalions were composed primarily of poorly commanded older men who lay thinly stretched on Sicily's southern coast. Gozzoni lacked antinaval guns and artillery, and could station only one tank for every five miles of Sicilian coast. Minefields, antitank ditch works, and concrete fortifications were only sporadically placed. Furthermore, Allied air bombardments had demoralized the Sicilian populace, and rations were low. Sicilian resolve was growing thin. Gozzoni guessed that he could withstand an initial assault, but doubted his defenses could withstand anything more. He urged the transfer of the remainder of the Hermann Goering Division to Sicily.[20]

Gozzoni, anticipating that the Allies would try to capture Sicily's airfields first, created a line of artillery defenses around each, and mined the airstrips against the chance of an Allied victory. The infantry and artillery groups assigned to defend the airfields were augmented with light tanks, armored cars, guns, and some engineering units. A shortage of ammunition and the generally poor constitution of their equipment degraded their potential effectiveness, however. Gozzoni's total resources by the end of June 1943 included six coastal divisions, two coastal brigades, one coastal regiment, four mobile divisions (a total of 200,000 men), and two mobile German divisions. It had earlier been decided that the weak Italian navy, stationed twenty-four hours away in La Spezia, would be called upon only if an especially prodigious opportunity arose, and only if enough fuel were on hand. The antiquated Italian Air Force, meanwhile, had been further decimated by Allied air attacks since May and withdrawn to the Italian mainland, and the German Air force had sustained heavy losses in a series of battles fought between May and July.[21]

The two German divisions appeared highly prepared by comparison. In June 1943, the Hermann Goering Division deployed from southern Italy for Sicily, well-trained and equipped, but with a slightly deficient infantry. Militia navies were directed to remain in defense of their homeports rather than join forces in the event of invasion. German submarines in the Mediterranean, however could not be reinforced, due to the difficulty in crossing the Strait of Gibraltar. Additionally, at Messina, a flotilla of German landing craft sat in the harbor. Altogether, Kesselring found himself in command of some 30,000 men.[22]

Pitifully equipped, yet resolute, the combined Italian and German commands took up their coastal positions in Gela and other strategic Sicilian ports. Behind them, ready to strike at the first sign of Allied incursion beyond the beachhead, lay the German Panzer tank divisions, the only divisions fast and mobile enough to provide an effective reserve for the coastal defenses. German intelligence, anticipating a simultaneous series of invasions at various locations on the Sicilian coast, planned to wipe out each invading force before it could merge with adjacent attackers. Gozzoni hoped to demolish the opposition while they were on the beach, but not yet at sufficient strength to repel an Axis counterattack.[23]

The Allies, meanwhile, planned an invasion presaged by air attack to wipe out strategic Axis aircraft and terrify the Sicilians. The invasion itself was to be carried out by seven divisions along a one hundred—mile stretch of Sicilian shoreline, with a combined force larger than had invaded Normandy the previous year. Planners agreed on July 10–14, when a three-quarter moon allowed enough light for paratroopers to jump onto the island, but enough darkness to conceal the Allied naval advance from Axis patrols some two hours later. Despite the presence of the Italian Navy, Allied planners primarily feared an air attack.[24]

Gen. Patton's Seventh Army Division would come ashore along the seventy miles of the Gulf of Gela. It was hoped that the ports along this stretch of shore would soon facilitate Allied supply lines. Central Command had no firm plan of action once the beachheads were secured, but it was expected that the British command of Field Marshal Sir Bernard Montgomery would take Catania and not stop until they reached Messina, across whose two– twelve mile stretch of waters lay Italy.[25]

The capture of four airfields, including Ponte Olivo at Gela, fell to Gen. Patton to accomplish. Planners also expected him to put the ports at Gela and Licata to work for the Allies. Once accomplished, Patton's Seventh Army Division was to stand by, awaiting further orders. Patton surveyed the field of potential operation, noting the shoreline and the rising swell of Pizza Armerina beyond, and the highway running upon its ridgeline. Capture of these coastal hills would deprive the enemy of its advantage overlooking the invading Allies. Its occupation was imperative to the Allies' securing the beachhead.[26]

Col. William O. Darby and his elite First Ranger Battalion were expected to spearhead the invasion of Gela. A platoon of tanks from the Second Armored Division, among them Hollis Stabler's Empress II, was attached to the First Infantry Division's Sixteenth Regiment, to assist in the operation. Hollis recalled the attack clearly in December 2002.

★ After the surrender of the Germans we knew something was going to happen. It turned out to be the invasion of Sicily! We in the E Company were sent to Algiers, where we trained for landing. Then, we got orders for Sicily. We—meaning one tank and a platoon of the Sixteenth in a Higgins boat—were attached to Gen. Terry Allen's First Infantry Division. But an LTC would be with us, and a company of the Sixteenth would follow. [27]

On the tenth of July at two o'clock in the morning, on the rough seas of a summer storm, the first wave of troops assaulted the beach at Gela, Sicily. Lt. Col. William Darby's Rangers landed at 2:30, and quickly wiped out two Italian coastal batteries before marching on Gela. American infantry units, Hollis among them, whose detachment was assigned to the First Infantry Division, raced ashore along the main stretch of beach as the Rangers diverted the Italians' attention. [28]

The invading fleet represented a substantial improvement over that which had initially invaded North Africa. Much of the new equipment would be tested for the first time in OPERATION HUSKY. Among these were a new series of landing craft and transport ships, including Landing Ship/Tanks, or LSTs; Landing Craft/Tanks, or LTCs; Landing Craft/Infantry vehicles, or LCIs; and Landing Crafts/Vehicle or Personal, known as LCVPs. This equipment was so new it was uncertain if the LCIs would beach in shallow water, or exactly how many men could be contained in an LST or LTC. Hollis remembered the passage well. [29]

"Our tank, the Empress II, an M4A1, one half-track, and a platoon of the Sixteenth Regiment, all in a Higgins boat! The rest of the company was in an LTC. It took about three hours to get to Sicily, and during that time I learned to play Canasta. Our landing zone was to be at the south end of a sandy beach. At the north end of the beach was the city of Gela. It was the Rangers' job to attack and capture this city." [30]

A nine hundred-foot concrete pier split the thousand yard-long port at Gela. To the left of the pier lay Red Beach, or so it was designated by army intelligence. Hollis's unit aimed for Green Beach, a wash of sand eighty yards deep to the right of the pier. Fishing boats bobbing along the shore suggested the beach had not been mined. Of more concern was the steep rise of the cliffs towering over the shoreline. [31]

At midnight, Gen. Gozzoni received word of Allied airborne landings. He immediately ordered the destruction of the Gela pier, just as the spearhead of Ranger Battalions entered the harbor. Within an hour, the Ranger invasion began, under cover of air support. Surprised, the Sicilians were quickly subdued by naval gunfire and the rapid advance of the ground troops. Meanwhile after taking heavy losses, British assault forces finally took Ponte Grande, though a gale delayed and disorganized the American landing at Gela. At midnight, the seas died down enough for the Americans to disembark. [32]

Hunkered down between rough waves and Italian defensive fire from the shore, the combat units assaulted the beach, although all didn't go quite as planned. Several landing craft ran aground on a sandbar some one hundred yards from the beach. The men waded ashore in life vests. Hollis's unit had an easier landing, although the beach proved to be mined after all. [33]

★ We had no trouble landing—the Higgins boat went right up on the beach. After we advanced in our tank we hit a mine that knocked off one of the tracks on the right side of the tank, completely blew it off. When we got out of the tank to check the damage, someone started shooting at us, machine-gun fire. Roby Dee Arnce, our radioman, didn't realize we were fighting a war—everything was new to him. He ran down the beach yelling, "Don't shoot!" and we had to run him down. By then the LTC had backed out, as well as our Higgins boat. We were alone on the beach. [34]

Sgt. Stan Novak said to me, "Go see if you can find our maintenance half-track, so we can repair our blown track." We were about one hundred yards from the cliff. We could see a house beside a small stream about a quarter mile from us. One of the fellows said he wanted to go with me. Three of us started toward the stream. We saw a small building and a truck laying on its side burning, and paper strewn all about. Someone was inside the building. We kicked the door open and surprised a Sicilian. He was obviously stealing money because he offered to give us some. We sent him to Sgt. Novak, and I suppose the sergeant put him to work. [35]

The invading forces had orders to make their way up the cliff, fight their way through town if necessary, and regroup on a farm plain north of the city, a position heavily fortified by the Italians and Germans. [36]

"We looked east and saw a railroad track, a bridge, and a highway, but we decided to go up the path behind the building. It led us to the edge of the bluff, which had trees growing along it. A woman came out from one of the houses to take a pee and never saw us. There was also about ten bodies lined up there on the ground. We later learned that these were the bodies of American paratroopers, victims of friendly fire."[37]

On the night of July 10, the men of the Eighty-second Airborne Division had not been informed until moments before departing from Tunisia that their next landing would be in Sicily, in high winds no less. Headquarters commanded Col. James Gavin's paratroopers to proceed as planned, despite the wind. "If a pilot or jumpmaster could not locate the exact drop zone, the troops would jump and fight the best way they could," Gavin would later recall.[38]

Assigned to stop Italian advances on the Gela beach, the assault for which the Eighty-second had trained for a year dissolved into chaos when inexperienced airmen, some flying their first mission, lost their way to Gela, which is about ninety miles from Tunisia. A strong crosswind added to their disorientation. Gavin found himself in charge of a fleet scattered over a thousand miles of airspace, and paratroopers jumping toward unplanned targets, in a hail of ground fire. Fortunately, American losses were not heavy.[39]

The paratroopers to whom Hollis here refers, however, were more likely those ordered into the sky by Gen. Patton on July 11 to reinforce the center of his advancing front. The troops in the Gela region had withstood fire for twenty-four hours; the rough landing in the harbor had thinned Patton's center front and the mishap of the Eighty-second Airborne had aggravated the plan for reinforcements. Gen. Patton called in two thousand paratroopers from North Africa to relieve the center front.[40]

The transport planes appeared in the skies over Gela, simultaneous with a German air raid. The area had withstood sporadic but intense aerial bombing since the invasion. Headquarters had tried to insure that all commanders had been informed of the impending arrival of the paratroopers from North Africa. Despite precautions, however, antiaircraft gunners on both land and sea mistook the American air fleet for the enemy. Twenty-three American transport planes fell from the sky, while another 37 planes of the 144 total aircraft sustained damage. The force itself suffered a 10 percent casualty rate.[41]

Meanwhile, German and Italian infantry and tank divisions advanced on the Gela airport just as Hollis's First Infantry Division closed in on the vital target. The Americans managed to halt the Italian advance, but the Germans rolled forward, even as the Italians withdrew northeast of the city. Rough terrain, however, would slow the German advance on Gela, allowing American forces to dig in before the appearance of the Germans. When the Germans did arrive, they were met by the First Armored Division, Darby's Rangers, and, most importantly in this instance, heavy shelling from navy gunboats.[42]

"We crossed the stream and started up a large sand dune," Hollis continued.

★ From there, we could see the airfield about three or four miles east of us. Down below was a railroad station or depot. The three of us started walking south on the sand dune. I was in the middle, the two crewmen on either side of me. They each had a tommy gun and I had a Springfield bolt-action thirty-ought six rifle. I was the only soldier to qualify on it in my old company in the cavalry, so anytime one showed up, they brought it to me.[43]

We were walking slowly when we suddenly heard a lot of gunfire. Two German Stukas came barreling down on either side of the sand dune. We were in the open, with no hiding places. I could see the plane on my right and I was ready for him. I fired until my gun was empty. I could see the pilot; he looked right at me. I fired until they were gone. That was at the battle of the airport at Gela.[44]

Despite their rough landing, the elite forces of the Eighty-second Airborne had succeeded in capturing a crucial road junction between the beach and Gela, ensuring access to the Ponte Olivo airfield. They also netted twenty enemy machine guns and almost 500,000 rounds of ammunition, as well as the first German prisoners of war in Sicily.[45]

At Gela, ground troops endured heavy air attacks. At two o'clock in the afternoon, four planes strafed the beaches while a high-flying bomber dropped five bombs of its own. Later that night came a massive attack on the Gela harbor, and, as one historian put it, "The sky over Gela became a confused jumble of friendly and enemy aircraft flying among the puffs of smoke of ground and naval antiaircraft fire."[46]

★ We finally found the maintenance half-track. We also found the kitchen truck, so we grabbed something to eat. Then another air raid!

Four planes came over, one of them right over our heads. Pendarvis jumped on the half-track and started to shoot. Nobody wanted him in their tank, but I saw he was doing OK. He ran out of bullets and didn't know how to reload. I jumped on the half-track and loaded the gun for him. He was ready. He must have been a rich man's son. He used to talk about a country home and sailboats, and said he was an admiral.[47]

While we were taking a break, someone said to look up in the sky. To the north of us a German bomber let go a large bomb. We could see it drop out of the plane, long and silver. It glided down slowly and hit the sand dune, but it did not explode. Instead, it kept gliding along the sand dune and headed straight for us. We had only olive trees for protection. The bomb kept going almost to where we were standing. It stopped. We could see it, but it did not explode. If it had, I would not be here telling about it.[48]

While we stood there talking about the bomb, four GI trucks drove up, hauling 105 mm guns. They stopped right below us. They unloaded the big guns and started to fire at the thirty or forty German tanks coming toward us. The artillery guns each fired about ten or twelve rounds like they were automatic. They packed up in about ten minutes and were gone, a sight I will never forget.[49]

German tanks were burning all around us. About this time a platoon of GIs came by, the same group that had come over in the Higgins boat. I decided to go with them because I heard shots and realized I would be hit if I didn't move, so when this platoon came by I joined them.[50]

We were on the west side of a highway in a ditch. The sergeant said to follow him and ran across the road to the brick depot and went into the building. Inside was a large room, with seats next to the wall. In the center was a large table or platform. There were five or six girls sitting on the table. They were our enemy. They cursed us and spit on us, but we didn't have time to fool with them. There was a GI already in the building. He said there was a German tank outside the door. The sergeant opened the door and tossed a hand grenade into the tank. We ducked, then saw another tank on the other side of the house. The sergeant ran to the tank and I followed. I don't know what happened to his platoon; I guess I was the only one with him.[51]

When we looked into the tank the motor was still running and the radio going full-blast, but no crew. I never did see them. I reached into the tank and picked up a nice pair of binoculars, a very nice pistol, and a wallet with lots of pictures. But we still didn't know what happened to the crew.[52]

All this time the U.S. Navy was sending big shells over us, a dozen German tanks were burning. The airport was on fire, too—hot time! This was at the Gela airport battle. All of a sudden it seemed like GIs were all over the place, heading for the airport hangar. I saw our recon half-track driven by Sgt. Poland, the redneck with red hair, green eyes, big belly, and a voice to remember. I had been eating breakfast at his mother's house the morning the Japanese bombed Pearl Harbor. I jumped onto his vehicle and rode to the burning hangar. There was an airplane outside, but what was strange was the gun mounted on the back of the cockpit. It must have been thirteen-feet long, about fifty caliber size! I didn't notice if it was clip-fed, single-shot, or automatic.[53]

With the beach and the airfield secured within hours of landing, Hollis and his fellow soldiers ascended the narrow winding road to the city above. Most of the heavy fighting had already ceased, as the Italian defense collapsed under the American assault. Rangers had successfully fought hand to tank in the city streets. The Germans, however, launched a counterattack from the plains north of the city. After a day of heavy fighting, during which the First took the brunt against more than one hundred German tanks, the enemy retreated.[54]

★ Poland and I decided to go to Gela to see if we could locate our tank. When we arrived at Gela the Rangers had already captured it. We were told some of the American medium tanks had started inland, so we took off.[55]

We started up the mountain road and finally reached the top, a large prairie. It was eveningtime, but we hurried on after we ate and gassed up. Someone in the front of the column reported over the radio, "Get ready! Gas attack!" I was riding on the turret and we could see a large, ominous white cloud drifting toward us. It was moonlight and we could see our tanks stopping, but it was too late. Nobody had gas masks! They were the first thing we soldiers jettisoned when necessary. Someone yelled, "Get your handkerchiefs and piss on them. Hold it to your face!" I don't know if anyone actually *did* it. Then the white cloud hit us. We were coughing, heaving, eyes smarting! But it passed us without any serious effects. The Germans had blown up a sulfur mine.[56]

I was still with the half-track. We saw a German motorcycle near the road, so I got out and started the cycle and mounted. There we were, me and Poland, just like when we were on maneuvers in Louisiana in 1941— tanks, half-tracks, and motorcycles. We started inland by going over a mountain range. We passed through a small village with a fountain in the center of the square. We had gone two miles when we found out we were out of water, so I volunteered to get some. I gathered up all the bottles and canteens and started back to fill them.[57]

Hollis may, in fact, have happened upon the motorcycle left behind when two Germans were arrested on the highway by Col. James Gavin:

> "Wanting to see the German forces for himself . . . Gavin took the paratroop engineers and began walking along the highway. . . . A German officer and a soldier on a motorcycle suddenly came around a bend in the road and were captured. Though the two made no effort to resist, they refused to give information."[58]

★ My old buddy, Germaine, the Germ, wanted to go with me. He mounted behind me on the motorcycle and we started back to the village. A large convoy was passing and I found out it was the Oklahoma Forty-fifth Division. I used to belong to it, the 180th Infantry Regiment, Company One, an all-Indian company from Bacone College, when I studied with Acee Blue Eagle. I yelled words of encouragement, like "New meat!" We were going down a steep road and my brakes went out. We were dragging our feet but could not slow down, let alone stop. I saw a curve and a high bank behind the road. I told Germaine to get ready to bail out. Up the bank we went, and so did our water-canteens, scattered all over the place! Germ hurt his knee and I broke my little finger on my right hand. We gathered the canteens and caught a ride with a truck. It was empty, so we had plenty of room.[59]

We were passing a mountain village and all of a sudden there was Sgt. Novak, waving for us to stop. He said he had no crew and was as glad to see us as we were to see him. Roby Dee, our radioman, was the only crew he had. There are supposed to be five men in an M4A1.[60]

Although the celebrated Darby's Rangers, with the support of the armored divisions, captured both Gela and the admiration of the free world in Sicily, they did not do it alone. One-third of the men who thronged the beach at Gela were combat engineers, on their first mission of the war. The casualties at Safi and Fedala had not been counted lightly, and Headquarters was determined not to have a repeat performance at Gela. Once on land, the combat engineers continued to support the troops. Hollis remembered them well.

★ Our column was unable to move because the Germans had blown up the only bridge across a small and swift mountain stream. While we were waiting the German Luftwaffe bombed it again. The Seventeenth Combat Engineers kept right on working—brave soldiers! They finished the job and our column started across. It was tricky to cross a sixty-ton tank on a pontoon bridge. While waiting for our turn we were parked next to a garden. I dismounted to get out and take a look at some big, red, juicy tomatoes: a bacon-and-tomato sandwich was what I was thinking about. We had no bread, only big English biscuits or crackers. We made some sandwiches—good, but a little hard. They satisfied us for the moment, however.[61]

Our turn to cross was coming up when diarrhea hit us. Then, an air raid started. We were so sick we were hoping a bomb *would* hit us! Sgt. Novak, the only one who wasn't sick, said he knew better than to eat tomatoes fertilized with human excrement! He put out a call for a medic, who finally showed up with some medicine that plugged us up for a week, but that's another story! [laughter] We finally crossed the stream, after some shaky moments.[62]

The seaport towns of Sicily's southern shoreline—Scoglitti, Gela, and Licata—had fallen to the Forty-fifth Infantry Division, the Eighty-second Airborne, and the First and Third Infantry divisions in less than three days. Furthermore, the British Eighth Army had taken Pachino, and, more importantly, Syracuse, located even further south and east. Within ten days the Second Armored Division would take Marsala and Trapani in the northwest from the Italian and German armies before turning northeast upon Palermo. The cost had been high. On July 11 alone, the second and most deadly day of the invasion, the Army had lost 2,300 men.[63]

The drive to Messina proved to be the most pivotal portion of the entire campaign. The British Eighth Army unexpectedly encountered increasingly rough terrain on their march north and east from the Sicilian coast. Even as they wrestled with transportation, elite paratroopers from Vichy France swarmed down among them. Field Marshal Montgomery asked the Seventh Army for permission to extend the British west flank into American-held territory. The move left Gen. Patton in the position of protecting the Eighth's flank, rather than leading the way north. [64]

The request was not without forethought, or indeed a bit of malice. The British had formerly implied that it was more fitting for them to lead the way than their "junior partner from across the Atlantic." Furthermore, formal plans for Sicily had never been cemented, beyond the taking of the initial D-Day campaign. Montgomery proceeded onto Messina, avoiding the line of strongest German resistance. The halt of the American Seventh on Highway 124, and its rerouting westward, however, allowed the enemy time to withdraw to a new line of defense between Catania and Enna. [65]

Gen. Patton and the other American generals fumed under the decision, having presumed they would be allowed to assist in the capture of Messina. Not one to take a backseat, Gen. Patton asked for permission to swing west and take Palermo, the capital city. His army then darted through the weak Italian defense, the German Panzers having been previously withdrawn to central Sicily. It took only seventy-two hours to capture the city. The next several days would see them seizing control of the entire western half of the island, at a cost of 272 American lives. [66]

Fortuitously enough for Gen. Patton, Montgomery's drive to Messina bogged down at Catania, along the coast south of Messina. He asked permission to redraw the boundaries once again, thereby reincorporating the Seventh Army in the Messina effort. Messina, though, protected by Mount Etna and the Caronie Mountains, would not fall as easily as had Palermo. The Allied troops would first have to cross the Germans' Etna Line surrounding Messina. Although Gen. Gozzoni had resolved to defend Sicily to the death, the Germans were already making plans to withdraw from the island. They planned to hold the Allies on the Etna Line while they evacuated. Hollis, however, fought at neither Palermo not Messina. [67]

★ The Sicily campaign was over. The British were still fighting at Messina, but it wouldn't last long. The Sixty-seventh was not far from

Palermo, but we didn't enter it. Some of our tanks went into Palermo, but the Sixty-seventh bivouacked near the railroad line between Partinico and Palermo, about two miles south of the city. We were between the railroad tracks, a busy highway, and the coast. The coastline was rugged, but there were lots of good swimming and fishing holes. We also had a gun range where we practiced with our weapons.[68]

About a mile down the railroad tracks was a beautiful palace that belonged to the Prince of Orange. I walked down to take a look around. Everything looked so nice! Someone was in the stables, cooking. He gave me a bowl of soup—it was so-o-o good! I gave him a pack of American cigarettes—a good trade, you know.[69]

Scholars have acknowledged the assimilative role played by military service on the lives of Indian soldiers. Shared battle experiences and hardships on the frontlines tended to reduce friction within military units to a personal basis. As one historian has written, "Because soldiers from different worlds shared essentially the same war-time experiences, they came to accept one another as equals and friends." That is, of course, unless one was found to be a "rat." Hollis explained.[70]

★ We settled down for a long stay in Sicily. I'll tell you a story I call "The Recreation Incident." One day on our company bulletin board someone put a notice that on the coming Saturday a truck would take a group of fun-lovers to Fun City, located on the other side of Partinico.

Fun City was simply a long, two-story white building. The lower floor was divided into two sections. At one end was a bar and dance floor, and there were pool tables at the other end. The top floor had many small rooms with a hallway running from one end to the other.

There were no doors on the rooms. Instead they were covered with a sheet. Inside each room was an "exercise" bed. A pretty girl was in the doorway of each room, waiting for the fun to begin. It began when the music started and couples started dancing downstairs. The soldiers and the girls began to mingle and talk . . . business deals. No Italian lira changed hands; only the Allied invasion money was accepted.

Soon it was time to leave. We told our newfound friends that we would be back. We did not know that this pleasant occasion might not be repeated. It seems that after we returned to our bivouac area, someone wrote a letter home describing in detail what recreation was like in Fun City.

Maybe it was a jealous girlfriend, a wife, or a mother. Anyway, someone wrote to Gen. Harmon and told him to stop it. Gen. Harmon immediately put Fun City off-limits. The news hit us like a bombshell. Some guys even talked about deserting. Everyone was under suspicion for spilling the beans, except the few who could not read or write. We never did find out who the "rat" was.[71]

Before I left, a Sicilian family we knew invited our tank crew for a dinner. We went toward the town of Partinico, crossed a creek, and went up a hill to the family's home—a large, long house with a barn-like door. The living quarters were on a built-up ledge about four feet high above the barn. It had a large fireplace and a long table to eat on. Behind that was a loft containing beds.[72]

The lady told us to sit at the table. She cleaned a board about three feet in diameter and put it on the table. She and her eldest daughter stood chopping cheese around it. Then she made a spaghetti nest and poured tomato sauce in it, and gave us each a bottle of wine.[73]

The women did not eat with the men. It was a meal I will never forget! Somebody got drunk and fell off the ledge. We had one boy with us that spoke Italian. He said the family was so poor they did not have money for shoes. When we left, we all gave them our boots. It was a generous gesture, but I have tender feet and was almost dead when we finally got back to camp. My heels became infected again and I was sent to the hospital.[74]

While Hollis bivouacked south of Palermo, Gen. Patton marched on Messina. The First Infantry Division, exhausted by two weeks of nonstop campaigning, found its greatest obstacle at Troina, where German Panzers and Italian troops fired down on the poorly concealed Americans. For six days ground and air troops fought for control of Troina. At last, the Germans evacuated, later acknowledging the Americans' tenacity in the affair. The Etna Line had been broken. On the morning of August 17, Americans marched into Messina, just hours after the hasty departure of the last Germans. Gen. Patton now worried that he would have to defend the city from the British, who had coveted it so dearly.[75]

★ When I was released from the hospital I found out that the Second Armored Division had been sent back to England. None of us knew anything about this here D-Day thing; we never heard anything about it, but that's what they had gone to train for. While I was waiting at the replacement depot to rejoin the Second Armored Division, I noticed a crowd, with some Rangers there. Those Rangers asked for volunteers to form a little cannon company. A cannon company had half-tracks and armored cars and light tanks. I was tired of waiting to catch up to the Second, so I volunteered to join them. Like I told you, I always liked to keep moving. So they took me, me and another guy. I never did see him afterwards. They put us in the Rangers and sent us to Agropoli and that's how I ended up in Darby's Rangers.[76]

Sicily had toppled in thirty-nine days. Twenty-nine thousand enemy soldiers had fallen, at the cost of 2,237 American and 12,843 British lives, respectively. Next to the invasion of Normandy the following year, the invasion of Sicily would prove to be the largest Allied amphibious assault of the war. Watching the Allied assault on July 10, one journalist had written, "[It] was as if all the army, navy, and air ministers of the world had combined to produce it, the whole terrible, logical culminating menace of modern industry, the whole theater of war—a very World's Fair of War—land, sea, air lay here before me in all its gigantic, splendid, overwhelming meaninglessness."[77]

The Italians had panicked and terminated Mussolini's leadership on July 5, 1943. Hitler moved Rommel's army into position in Italy during July and August, ready to face an Allied invasion. On the German's eastern front they fought heatedly with the Russians over Orel. At Messina, Sicily, only between three and twelve miles across the Strait from Italy, Allied forces prepared to invade. The demolition of the Third Reich had begun, but the price would be Anzio.

Back in the United States, the moral, political, ethical, and cultural implications of World War II did not slip past Eunice Stabler unnoticed. One of the most progressive Indian women of her time, Eunice nevertheless seems to have spent much time reflecting on the contradiction between the assimilation of the American Indians as citizens, and the obligation of citizens to serve the country in war. Eunice, who had for so long sought to strike a balance between acculturation and cultural preservation, found herself penning a book whose title, How Beautiful the Land of My Forefathers, betrayed her internal predicament. With two sons on the war's frontlines, and Marcella's recent death, Eunice looked to her heritage for reassurance. Early in 1943 she wrote,

The most beautiful and inspiring philosophy of Omaha Indian belief is the future after death. He realized death was an inevitable event in life. No one could escape it. He resolved to face it without fear. . . . His belief was that life did not end with death, for the soul of man is immortal. He viewed death as but a change of condition, or as one would go on a journey into another country to live, to enter upon new and larger life. Wakonda was so perfect in his creative work and his love was so complete for man that he had provided a home for him after he departed from this life, to live on in a higher sphere of continuance of life.[78]

FOUR

Operation Shingle

January–May 1944

Anzio. Who could add more to the memory of that already illustrious, disastrous operation on Italy's western coast that took the lives of 4,400 Allied soldiers—2,800 Americans—in four months? Hollis would live to tell of it, but for him, Anzio would not be about those who survived, but about those who died, just as it had been for Nero, who was said to have played the fiddle there while Rome burned, in the days when Anzio was called Antium.[1]

Following the Allied invasion of Sicily, the Germans braced for the Fifth Army's expected advance on Italy. They established the Gustav Line of defense across the "leg" of the Italian peninsula, midway between Naples and Anzio. Rome, the Eternal City, lay some thirty miles north of Anzio, and Hitler was determined to hold it against the Allies. Throughout the early winter of 1943–44, American forces fought their way through the mountains of southern Italy, advancing on the Gustav Line, past untold numbers of German Tenth Army concrete pillboxes, bunkers, and minefields. By mid-December 1943 American troops opposed the Gustav Line, hunkered down against an unusually severe winter of freezing rain and mud, a position they termed the "Winter Line Campaign," and held until early January 1944. With the forward advance, they could now look down far below on Highway 6—Via Casilina—wending its way past beautiful Monte Casino on its way to Rome. But between them and Rome lay the formidable Gustav Line.[2]

On the western shore of Italy, the Allies prepared to invade the fifteen-mile long beachhead at Anzio, far north of the Gustav Line, intent on

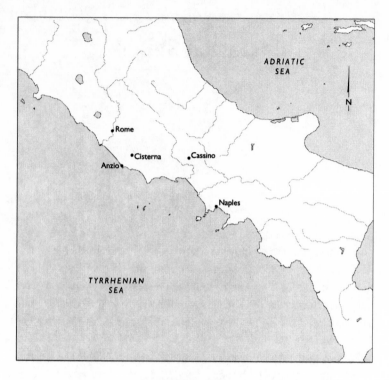

3. Anzio, Italy

diverting German troops from the advancing Winter Line campaigners, who would then press the advantage northward. Hollis recalled his role in December 2002.

★ The campaign in Sicily was over in less than a month, I think. After I joined the Rangers, first they took us to Cisterna, the city of Italian kings, then they took us to Pozzuoli, a coastal city west of Naples. While I was in Cisterna they were executing German spies there, shooting them, but I didn't see it happen. First thing we did when we got there was get our boots. They had a big pile of them, and you sat in a chair and tried some on until you found ones that fit.[3]

Then we got trousers. You'd go over there and look for your size; same thing with the shirts. The Rangers dressed a little bit different from the other units—we had to have a new set of clothes. Nice big coats, and pants real baggy, all kind of light green. Those pants had big pockets, and suspenders on them, too, big wide suspenders, and you could wear pants under those baggy ones if you wanted to, white pants and shirts, with our patch on them. Nice, real nice. That's why I still like pockets. Every time I get a T-shirt I want a pocket in it.[4]

After I got to Pozzuoli they told me they had dropped the idea of a cannon company. Instead, they wanted to put me in Headquarters Company because I had a little radio training in the cavalry. They put me in communications. There were about ten of us, all qualified on radio. The kind of radio we had was called a 536; it was about two feet high and a foot square. It was kind of heavy. But there were two parts to it, and you'd have to crank it if you didn't have batteries. Then, too, we had to lay wire everywhere we went. But I liked it. Riflemen would run past us every morning with big packs on their backs, and shake their fists at us because we didn't have to do that. But our biggest problem was carrying those batteries. They were about the size of a motorcycle, but we had to carry them. They're no good if they get broken, you know.[5]

Here in the Rangers, there were three other Indian men. One was Arthur Leblanc, a Cree Indian, I think, or an Ojibwa, from Michigan. Another was Thomas Bear Paw, a Cherokee from Tahlequah, Oklahoma. Just before we invaded Anzio, someone told me, "Chief, there is another chief in the Headquarters Company—His name is Sam One Skunk." I met him, he was a Lakota from South Dakota, and we went to take in a show. After that we went to the home of some Italian people who were his friends. We sure had a good time, pasta and vino. Then we were sent to Anzio. I don't remember seeing him again until his death was announced in the paper in 1979.[6]

Hollis was not aware that Sampson P. One Skunk, known as One Shot, had become a national celebrity back home. His distinctive name, 6'2", 150-pound frame, and very real skills in the field, had caught the attention of Associated Press reporters. They kept the home front advised of Ranger One Skunk's prowess, which eventually earned this most distinctive of Darby's Rangers the American Defense Service Medal, the EAME Campaign Medal, an American Theater Medal, a Combat Infantrymen's badge, the Good Conduct Medal, two Oak Leaf Clusters to the Presidential Citation Medal, a Silver Star Medal, and a Legion of Merit Medal. It wasn't long before *Life Magazine*, the *Saturday Evening Post*, and *True Comics Magazine* featured the fascinating One Skunk in their publications, often running anecdotes in the following vein:

> Private P. One Skunk was a man of few words. He seldom said anything but "ugh," which meant "yes," "no," or "maybe," or anything he wanted it to mean. Even in Britain, where taciturnity is a national trait, Private One Skunk was a very quiet man. . . . The Rangers went into some heavily wooded country on maneuvers, an exercise particularly in traveling through underbrush without making any noise. A British officer [noticed] Private One Skunk was not paying much attention. "Well you see, sir," an American officer replied, "this is just child's play to him. He's probably known how to sneak right up on a chipmunk since he was six years old."[7]

★ Anyway, The Rangers did some training there at Pozzuoli. We were getting ready to go to Anzio, but we didn't know it. It was wintertime, January 1944. I was assigned to a lieutenant and given a little walkie-talkie. It had batteries, too. That was the worst part, all those batteries. So we trained around there, and one day they said we were going to make a landing. So we practiced on a little island that was around there. Every evening we would go out there in a row boat and crawl up all around the mountains. Finally we were ready. They told us we were going to land about thirty miles from Rome.[8]

Hollis must no doubt have been referring to WEBFOOT, a landing exercise practiced on the beaches south of Salerno, January 17–19, 1943. While drilling, the Third Division lost a ship during bad weather. Though few men were killed, the same could not be said for their equipment; a battalion of the Forty-fifth Army Infantry Division took their place at Anzio.[9]

Even as they practiced, the southern Allied troops—French, British, and American—attacked the Gustav Line. But, faced with the impregnable mountain fastnesses secured by Germans, the advance on the Gustav Line bogged down with heavy losses by January 22, the date set for the invasion at Anzio. The Allies had not been able to break the Line, but they kept the enemy engaged at Cassino long enough to divert German forces posted around Rome. OPERATION SHINGLE proceeded as planned.[10]

Hollis continued:

★ At Pozzouli I went to the movies on the evening of January 21, 1944, the night before the invasion. It was the hometown of Sophia Loren. They had a little theater there. That night they had free theater. They had a bar, where you could buy shrimp and wine and stuff like octopus fried in a circle. I sat next to a guy who had a Third Infantry Division patch on his arm. I said, "Are you in the Third Infantry?" He said, "Yes." I told him my brother was in the Third Reconnaissance Company, and I asked him where they were bivouacked. He said "You have to go around the lake, over near the Roman ruins at Agropoli." We were next to the lake, and it was steamy all the time, with hot, hot water. The lake was under the rim of a volcano. He told me they were bivouacked up on the rim of the volcano, so after the show was over I tried to get someone to go with me, but no one would go. I left the theater and walked over there.[11]

The guards soon challenged me, asking me to identify myself and all that, but the guy in the theater had pretty well told me how to get there. So I went up and found my brother. Oh, he was glad to see me! Bob and I were kind of alike. He said, "We've got a room over here." We went in there, and it must have been filled about this high with GI blankets, all over the floor. There were two girls in there. My gosh, it turned into a big party, all the guys coming in. Bob and me just sat there, talking and drinking. We had a good visit and a good talk, drinking beer or wine or whatever was at hand. Finally I said, "I'd better hurry back to my unit." So I left. I said, "I'll see you, Bob." He said, "Okay." It was the last time I saw my brother alive. [12]

Early in the morning I went back to my unit. They had been getting ready to go to Anzio when I went to find Bob. I got back about daybreak. The guys had already moved; not a thing left behind. Someone had said earlier that if you get lost to go to a camouflaged building, a school building, and my guys would be in there. I went looking for Headquarters Company. It was still dark. I was asking everybody "Where's the Headquarters Company?" The answer was always, "Go that way," or "We don't know." I walked all around looking for those guys. They must have had all my equipment, because I didn't have anything, just my clothes, my uniform. [13]

Finally an officer came over. He asked, "Are you from Headquarters?" I said, "Yes, sir." It was Major Royal Murray, his group. He said, "I think they are already loaded." Then he asked me, "Can you drive a truck?" I said, "Yes." He said, "Well, why don't you drive this truck for me. We can't find our driver." That happened a lot there, you know, guys missing, and going to the wrong places. But you never can stop, see, you just got to keep going in the army. [14]

He told me to come with him. I didn't even tell my sergeant. He said not to worry about it, that he'd take care of it. I was put into a group that was driving trucks. I was in a six-by-six. I got in and slept until we lined up and drove into an LTC. I went down and ate some breakfast. I told that officer, "I don't have any equipment." So he gave me a belt, a canteen, and a medicine pouch. Then I said, "I've got to have a weapon." He said, "Oh, we'll look for one." Then he got me this carbine with a little clip on it, a banana clip, maybe nine or ten rounds. That's all I had to invade Anzio. I said, "Okay, that's better than nothing." [15]

We sat there and the boat took off. I think it was an all-day trip. By nighttime on January 22 some Rangers had already landed at Anzio. Bob's Third Infantry landed, too, but my group was still in the water. There was smoke everywhere, and everybody shooting and all that, you know. We kind of eased up into the port. I got out of my truck and was sitting on the LTC right in front of a gun platform, a kind of tub that had a machine gun in it, but I didn't know it at the time. I was up there, and two or three of the guys were with me. Overhead a loudspeaker said, "We are going to the dock. Everybody get ready to move out." That meant it was time for us to rig the trucks so we could carry wounded men in them. Our ship moved and we got in line with other LTCs ahead of us. I was sitting next to that tub when suddenly here comes a dive-bomber, coming straight at us. Well, those guys with the machine gun opened up, started shooting. That's where I hurt my ears, that first time; it was just like being in a drum. Oh, my golly, it hurt! Finally the bombing stopped. I thought, "I'd better get downstairs." I went down and found my truck and got in. The lieutenant said, "Follow that truck." I was about the third truck in line. We went right onto the dock. The ship door opened and we just drove out, right into town. We drove through that town just as fast as we could go.[16]

The Allies had landed under less enemy fire than they had anticipated, even given the necessary diversion of German troops to the Gustav Line. German intelligence had anticipated an allied invasion further north; the stealth of OPERATION SHINGLE had caught them off-guard. Only a skeleton force of German troops was available to defend Anzio, and it had been caught unprepared. Wasting no time, Bob Stabler's Third Reconnaissance troops ran the line of the Mussolini Canal along the Allies' right flank, blowing up bridges. Hollis and the Rangers landed just to the south of Anzio harbor and took the port. They then scaled the cliffs rising above the beach, and captured the city, much to the surprise of both the Italians and Germans. In exactly twenty-four hours, the Allies would unload 36,000 men at Anzio; two were Stablers.[17]

"Anzio was a pretty little town, a tourist town. We went through the city on the left side, near the shoreline," Hollis continued.

★ We went right through the edge of the city. I was looking at things. There was nobody out, just the buildings to look at. We lined up on the road and started driving. Here came a Stuka right over us. They shot us all up that time. We were driving along the beach when a British soldier directed the first truck to turn into a big field and the second truck followed it. I was the third truck and I pulled in, too. A British soldier jumped on my truck, and I couldn't understand that bloke for nothing. He was yelling something. An air raid was going on, too, see, so we went out in the middle of the field.[18]

I saw a wooden fence, maybe thirty or forty yards away. I got out of that truck, and boy, I took off for that fence for cover. It's a good thing I did, too. I don't know what ever happened to that British soldier, but boy he was hanging on, with my truck bouncing all over. But anyway, I had left my helmet in the truck and had lost the carbine. So there I was, invading Anzio, with no helmet and no gun, just a belt and a canteen. I laid down by the fence there. There were no soldiers, no one around, just burning trucks, including mine. I could see the convoy still going down the road. Everybody was shooting, but I didn't know who they were shooting at.[19]

After a while, everything quieted down. I looked around, but there was no one there. I was out there by myself, just a big old prairie, the fence line, and the road to Anzio. I started walking back to the dock. Finally I came to the outlying buildings, but there was no one around. Back in Pozzuoli they had told us if we ever get lost, go to the casino. Finally I ran into an Italian man and asked him where the casino was. He pointed it out, a big white building on a hill. I started walking up there. Rangers were all around. I said, "I'm looking for Headquarters Company." "Well, you better go up to the casino, you'll find them up there," they told me. By the time I got to the casino, the Headquarters Company had already started out to take the town of Cisterna.[20]

Hollis could not know that the Germans had dispatched troops en masse to Anzio, and were already fighting hard to retain control of the bridge at Cisterna di Latina—some fifteen miles northeast of the beach Hollis had landed on—the city through which St. Paul had traveled on his way to trial in Rome in the first century AD, and which had been ancient even then. A favorite resting place on the Appian Way, it hosted travelers en route to Rome, and ever found itself in the path of war. Now, Bob and the Third Infantry Division fought with Germans for its control.[21]

★ I fooled around there at the casino for a while, trying to find a gun. Finally someone gave me another carbine, fifteen rounds. Nobody liked them because the bullets were too small, thirty caliber, just a little gun. A guy offered to take me out to where the Fourth Battalion was, so we got into a jeep or truck, I can't remember. We drove all night.

Someplace along the way we got on a highway and we caught up with the Fourth Battalion by eveningtime, on the side of a small hill. They asked me if I had eaten. I said no, and they gave me a little can of food, a K-ration. The thing I was most worried about was that I only had a light field jacket on over an undershirt and shirt. I didn't think I had enough clothes on, but there was nothing I could do. Everything had been in the trucks that burned up.[22]

They introduced me to a Lieutenant Dick Porter. He said that I would be his radioman and he handed me one of those little walkie-talkies. They are no good. They work all right if you've got good batteries all the time. But that was the worst part, no batteries. He and I went together. We lined up down there. There was a rifle platoon in front of us and the Headquarters Company right behind them. Maj. Roy Murray was in charge, and Lt. Porter was attached to him. They each had a radioman; I was Lt. Porter's.[23]

Hollis may or may not have known that Roy Murray, a close associate of the fated Col. William Darby, had already led the First Ranger Battalion in its successful raid on Sicily. Following the battles for Anzio and Cisterna, Murray would lead the First Ranger Battalion's Fox Company raid on Dieppe in northern France, but Hollis would not be with him.[24]

★ We waited about one or two hours. There were all sorts of star shells bursting above us—big mortar shells—but we didn't know where they came from. It was cold; everybody was frozen, but we didn't move. We could hear on the radio that the First and Third Battalions were having a hard time. "We need help," they said, "send up the Fourth." Major Murry said, "Okay you guys, let's go."[25]

A flare lit up above our heads. We were not supposed to move when a flare was lit, but that flare took forever to come down, so we started out. Then we would have to stop again because of the flares. We stopped and started for about an hour. It took us a long time to get started. Finally we moved out. The platoon ahead of us was going pretty fast. We were walking right behind them—me and the major and lieutenant and the medical officer, and the major's driver, about six or seven of us all together—maybe one hundred yards.[26]

I could hear by listening to the radio that the First Ranger Battalion was hollering—they needed some help, some reinforcements. We were going up to try to help them, but most of them got killed. We got up there and they said, "There's a tank on the right side of the road, and we think there's some machine guns on the left." Boy that was the biggest mess you've ever seen. I don't know how I got out of it, but I didn't get hit. Those guys in front of us walked right into it. Every one of them got killed. We were right behind them. Maj. Murray and the doctor, all of us, went off to the side, in front of a house there, and laid down on a little knoll. We couldn't see anything, all we could hear was shooting, and people talking and yelling. No more tanks came. A good thing they didn't come—they would sure have had us![27]

At daybreak the next morning I looked out, and it was the biggest mess you ever saw on that road, and on both sides of it. All of those guys were dead. They got caught square between the tanks and the machine guns. We had to pick them up. The medic captain and the major were both crying—they knew those guys. I didn't know them, so it didn't bother me too much, but we had to bring them in. The doctor was taking their dog tags. He was covered with blood, and so were the dog tags. He was crying because he knew them. We had been right behind them. I don't know how we got out. I could see those bullets flying, but here I am. I don't know why. Maybe because a priest at Macy gave me a St. Christopher medal. I'm not Catholic, but I had it with me.[28]

A jeep came down there about that time. It had stretchers and could take about four men, dead men. We laid them up in there. Pretty soon an ambulance came, and they took some more. We sent out about twenty dead guys. We didn't know what happened to the battalion that had been behind us, just that they scattered out when the firing started. Anyway, we never did catch up with the First Ranger Battalion. Good thing we didn't, or I wouldn't be here. Then we went down to a terrace ditch. The ditches followed the contour of the ground to hold water. We followed that—it was about three or four feet high. We could lay down behind it. Right in front of us was a big stone fort or structure. I don't know what it was, but it was big. We were there on top of this hill, where the contour was, and the slope went down to a big deep drainage ditch that ran into the Mussolini Canal, which was about a hundred yards wide, just like a river. Anzio was real flat, on land reclaimed from the ocean. The canals drained it. Highway 7 [the Appian Way] ran through Anzio, and went into Rome, about thirty miles away. But it would take us months get there.[29]

There must have been a thousand yards between the ditch and the fort. The Germans were in the fort, but you could not see anybody. Someone came over and said the Third Infantry had lost some men over there—one was an Indian boy. Later on, I walked over there by the fort. I saw my brother, Bob. I didn't look at his face. I couldn't look at his face. I looked at his hand. It was Bob; he had his ring on. There were four of those guys stretched out there. They had run through the blockade, and then they had tried to run back, but they didn't make it. We had heard the fight on the radio, but I didn't know it was Bob. That was January 31, 1944, at Cisterna, Italy. Another Indian boy, Bob's good friend Estes from South Dakota, he was there when they buried Bob at Nettuno, Italy. Later, in 1948, we brought him back to Pawhuska.[30]

I used to have a whole bunch of things that Bob left—letters and stuff. My son, Hollis Jr., has them now. Back then, everybody knew Bob. He was the welterweight champion of the Third Infantry Division. He used to know this boy from Texas who had won so many medals. It was Audie Murphy. (When I was at Bacone I went to school with Audie Murphy's future wife, Opal Lee Archer.) He was in L Company. He became a movie star and got killed in an accident. Murphy won the Congressional Medal of Honor and everything. Bob earned the Silver Star Medal for action "beyond the call of duty" at the invasion of Sicily. Later, after he died, he got the Purple Heart and the Oak Leaf Cluster.[31]

After I found Bob, I really wasn't scared, but you know, I thought I would be a little more careful. I didn't know what to do. None of the guys in my company knew him, but everyone in the Third Infantry knew him. I walked back over there later on, to a toilet in a big tent. Some guy looked at me like he was really scared. He asked, "Who are you?" I told him. "Are you Bob's brother?" I said yes. "I thought you were Bob," he said. Me and Bob were about the same age.[32]

The *Wichita Beacon* announced Bob's death. "Private Stabler had received on August 29, 1943, commendation from Major General L. K. Truscott for heroism in the landing at Sicily. In that action, Private Stabler volunteered to land in advance of Allied units on the Sicilian coast to mark under heavy enemy fire possible landing beaches for Allied landing barges."[33]

★ After I came back to my unit we tried to take the big stone farm where the Germans were. The battle started in the morning. All of a sudden a half-track came nearby. I went over to get some batteries—always looking for batteries! They were a big deal, you know. [laughter] While I was standing there they brought a wounded Ranger in who had been shot in the arm. It was Sgt. Janko from Wichita, Kansas. I didn't get to meet him then, he was in pain, but we met again later after the war. But we put him in the half-track and the medic gave him a shot. Just then—ping!—somebody shot and hit our half-track. About three or four of us were standing around there. Boy, we ducked down—but I got my batteries first! I didn't want to have to go back again. I crawled back to the ditch.[34]

One of the guys we were laying with was named Brown. He and I were laying there together. One of the guys said, "What color is shit?" We all yelled out, "Brown!" and laughed. We were always teasing him like that. Then I said, "Did you see that?" One of the guys said, "Yeah." I thought I saw something move around the corner of the building. I kept looking, and I saw it again. I couldn't tell what it was, but something was moving. It was a long way away, but I had good eyes. Someone was trying to get to the corner of the building! I said to Brown, "Watch that place over there," but he couldn't see it. So I said, "Let me have your gun." I only had that carbine, remember. Then I went back to the corner of the building and waited. I didn't aim at the corner, but another place, about waist high, where I figured a man would be. Sure enough, that guy jumped up. I pulled the trigger, and I hit him. It was a long way. I bet it was in the thousand-yard range! I didn't have a scope or anything, all I had was the leaf scope. No one else could see him but me, but I knew what he was going to do. I knew where I had to aim. He got up and I hit him. That shot was for Bob, you know.[35]

After my long shot, we were still on the hillside behind a terrace. At daybreak some officer called out, "Fix bayonets!" My partner, Denny, and I looked at each other. We were in charge of a large, two-part radio that had to be cranked to supply power, but we had no officer to tell us what to do. So we waited, saying we could kill the Krauts with batteries.[36]

We stayed all night there on the hill. The next morning the officers came around there and we got our radio going. But, those damn 536s, it took two men to carry them around, you know. Anyway, the whistle blew and the Rangers were ready. They started fast, whooping and yelling, but the Germans were ready, too. They laid down a barrage—

none but a few could have survived. Denny and I had started running, and were about midway to a ditch when we heard the call to fall back. I made it back to our side of the terrace, still dragging my half of the radio, but I never saw the other guy again. One thing I can distinctly remember is someone calling for help, "My eyes! My eyes!" I don't know what happened. Believe it or not, I was so tired, I fell asleep in the ditch, right in the middle of the battle! I don't know how long I slept.[37]

Then I heard a whistle, and somebody saying to go back to the starting place. We had just got back to the terrace when a Ranger fell right beside us. He was one of the Fourth Battalion medics, shot dead through the heart. Later, the Thirtieth Infantry came and got the dead out of there. After it got dark, we decided to relocate. We were trying to get back to Highway 7. We got to a farmhouse and stayed in a concrete stable. There was a dead cow out there and someone had butchered it, took steaks out of it. Headquarters was in there. Inside, there were a couple of dead cows. I don't know how they got killed, but there they were. I saw a concrete manger and I said, "I'm going to sleep in there." I was sitting in there and I looked out the back window. I could see the German tanks going round and round. They couldn't get over to us because we had a drainage ditch between us and them. Still, I could see them. Suddenly, one of the tanks turned towards our stable and pointed his gun right at me. I knew he couldn't see me, but he came right straight for me. Boy, I ducked down to get out of the way of that bullet. Finally they turned off. Later on, years later, I went back and visited that place. A lot of those guys in the First and Third got killed or captured there. My unit just wasn't fast enough to be in the action.[38]

Anyway, we stayed there a couple months. This is in January, February, March 1944. One night an Italian man came to the door looking for his little boy. We didn't know where he was. I never knew what happened to that man. About then I got ingrown toenails, real bad. My feet got infected again. I had to cut the toes out of my boots, and it was freezing. Finally my sergeant said, "You better report in."[39]

I said "okay" and I started walking. I was going toward the highway, across a field. I thought I noticed something white in the rows. I looked, and it was that little boy, dead. I walked to the highway, hobbling, really. Pretty soon another Ranger came along with a bad knee or foot or something. Suddenly we came up to a German tank, with no one in it, just a hand laying there on the ground. Then a photographer came up, a newsman. He had a green armband on that said "PRESS." He said, "Do you guys mind if I take your picture?" So he put that hand on the tank, and me and the other guy got up on the tank on either side and he took our picture. I sure wish I had that one. We told him he was still a long ways from the fighting, about a mile away. "That's where you can get killed," I told him.[40]

Then we hobbled into town. They put us on a barge and rowed us out to a British hospital ship with British nurses. They were real nice, those British nurses. They called them "sisters." They took us to Naples. All those seriously wounded guys and me with my ingrown toenails. Later I told my wife I was really ashamed. Some guy would come in and say, "What's the matter with you?" and I'd have to tell him I had ingrown toenails. I can't get over that, with all those guys laying there shot up, you know.[41]

Anyway, they got me to Naples and put me in a hospital. In there, those Italians were always bootlegging. They sold me a little bottle of red stuff. I thought it was alcohol, it looked like soda pop. It was strong, but I found out you have to mix it with water or something. It was a mixer. After I drank it a guy came in and gave me a urine test. He came back and said, "All I can say is, your horse has kidney problems," but he was just kidding. I guess we'd drink anything.[42]

So I got up there on the exam table and they held a sheet in front of me and gave me a shot to kill the feeling in my toes. Boy, I was fighting them. Then they took my nails off, with pliers I think. I came out of there and my toes were raw, you know. I was in that hospital about two weeks. One time I went to a bar in Naples, in my robe with my crutches. I met a man named McCafferty in there; we would eventually serve together. Then they sent me back to Anzio.[43]

I got there in the evening. Two or three other guys and me started walking across the real flat part. About halfway across, there was an air raid. We ran to find cover, and stopped next to an anti-aircraft gun, the same kind that had hurt my ears. It had four machine guns, I think, swinging around on top. I noticed an airplane out on the field, nose down in the ground. I could see it was an American plane. One of the guys said, "That plane was piloted by black pilots." At the time, I didn't know there was such a thing.[44]

Me and another guy—a sergeant with a long red mustache whom I didn't know—we finally got to the little brick building where we were supposed to report in, but the ground all around it was on fire from a phosphorous shell. The sergeant went in first and I waited outside. Then my turn came and I went inside. Suddenly a shot rang out. That sergeant had shot himself in the foot. Two Ranger officers, already inside the hut, picked him up and threw him against the wall. Eventually a medic came and dressed his wound.

There was also a Lt. Fieldman inside. He started telling us where to report. I started in the direction he led us, walking along the side of a ditch that we called the Bowling Alley. While we were talking, the Krauts took a shot, and that ball came roaring down that alley! We all hugged the ground. Down in the ditch there were yellow flags that said *minas*, mines. He left me, and said to follow the yellow ribbons, and to be careful when I crossed the ditch because there were mines on both sides.[45]

All I had with me was my bag and a rifle. I didn't use a helmet anymore because I couldn't hear if I did. If I got shot in the head, why, *that's all*, you know. I followed a river, across a ditch, and across a field. I came to a little house and there were three guys in there, Americans. One guy was on a machine gun. Another Ranger reported in right about then, just like me. Later I found out he was a famous football player, but we were both privates. Anyway, we got there, and the sergeant had been shot and he was going crazy. And one of the other guys was just as bad. Only the guy on the machine gun was doing okay. The football player said, "I'll take these guys back." We could see that he was the kind of guy you didn't want to fool with. There was a dog in there that was pooping around, and he shot her and threw her out the window. You've got to be careful with people like that, you know.[46]

But he and I needed to string some radio wire. There was an old jeep in there and he knew how to fix it. I wasn't very good at mechanics. Then he said, "Instead of walking down there, we'll take this jeep down the highway." He got in and started it and we positioned the wire so we could lay it out, right down that highway. Just like a bowling alley, with mines on the side. The Germans shot at us as we drove. I often wondered who that guy was. Anyway, we got back safely.[47]

Another time they called me and said, "You have to go down there and fix that telephone line again. Take a wire down there." Well, we took some wire, a little spool, with my toolkit, pliers, screwdriver, knife. We got down to a little building, no roof, just sides. They had a machine gun set up there. Then an airplane came over. We could hear other airplanes coming, too. That first one kept getting lower and lower, but we couldn't see it, only hear it. It was a B-24, crashing. We looked out, and those guys were bailing out. One of them jumped out and landed almost in front of us on the other side of the canal, over where the Germans were.[48]

Everybody motioned for him to come over here, but it was too far away for us to talk. We never found out what happened to him, probably captured. At about the same time, here came a German Stuka. About five or six of us dived into the same hole, about three feet across. I don't know how I squeezed in there.[49]

One night, a few days later, we were camped in the vicinity of the Mussolini Canal on Highway 7. At about one or two in the morning they woke up my partner McCafferty and me and told us we were needed at a certain gun emplacement at an old house. McCafferty was kind of nuts, the kind of guy you had to watch out for, like I told you. We gathered our weapons and tools that we would need and started walking down the highway. A jeep with blue lights came by and we flagged it down. I said I would sit in the center on some barracks bags. McCafferty sat up front with the driver. I don't know why the lights were blue. We had only gone about a hundred yards when all hell broke loose. All I remember was tracers in front of us, followed by a deafening noise, and then silence. Nothing.[50]

When I awoke I was flat on my back, staring into a dark sky with a lot of stars in it, tracers, flares, stars. I couldn't hear a thing because of my ears. I sat up; I was all by myself on Highway 7. Nobody in front of me, nobody behind me, nobody around. There were no people; there was no jeep. Some movement caught my eye and I could see McCafferty laying face up in the ditch, with his body in the water. His face was very white, like a white dish. He said, "Chief, help me." I reached down and pulled him by his suspenders and I laid him on the highway. His voice sounded like he was in a deep hole, far away.[51]

Then I found where the jeep was sitting. The driver was still in there, dead. I straddled McCafferty and dragged him down the highway to a house occupied by the Eighty-second Airborne. They were here to relieve us, the Fourth Battalion. I put a blanket over us and used a flashlight. I could see he was hurt bad. One paratrooper said, "Bring him in here." They had about four or five blankets you had to go through to get inside. I laid him on his stomach on the floor, then I found a flashlight to look at him. I could see the wound in his back. The shrapnel had entered in the front and come out the back, down there. "You know what?" "What?" he asked me. "You've got a new asshole," I told him. Then I ran to tell Captain Hardenbrook, our medic, what had happened.[52]

At first, when I found Hardenbrook, I couldn't talk. Then he gave me a shot to quiet me down, and also a cup of whiskey. Finally I told him where McCafferty was. I slept eighteen hours. When I woke up, I couldn't hear. About a week later my right ear popped. Then, water came out of my left ear. My left eardrum had been broken. I had been wearing a steel helmet. A piece of shrapnel must have hit the helmet but did not penetrate it. It sure made a lot of noise. Because of this incident I have had to wear hearing aids to get along. But I guess they took McCafferty to Naples, to the hospital. Later on, after the war, the government gave me 90 percent disability for my ears. I told Nonie, my daughter, I'm going to sue them for that other 10 percent, so I could claim 100-percent disability, but I never did.[53]

One day someone said, "Dick Porter got wounded, let's go see him. He's down there in that house." Medics were taking care of him there. Three or four of us went to visit him. He said to us, "Man, did I get hit." But he wasn't very proud of his wound. He got hit right in the butt.[54]

Anyway, we stayed there that night. About the middle of the night, here comes a sergeant. He said, "Get your guns and be quiet." We all got our guns and followed him down a slanting road. We laid down and I could see Germans, maybe a whole company of them, walking right below us. We were quiet, didn't say a word. Nothing happened that night, but the next morning, the sergeant said, "I think I hear something." He went out and a bullet hit him right in the chest. We looked outside, and there was a bunch of dead sheep outside, all dead except for one. One was kind of sitting up, and somebody had to shoot it to put it out of its misery. There must have been about a hundred dead sheep out there.[55]

There was a barn out there, too, with an open door. You don't see many of those kind of doors any more. There was a GI laying in the doorway, dead. But, you know, whenever I saw those dead men, they looked to me like they were growing into the ground, just melting in, just flat. That's why I could never look at their faces. Not even my brother. All I had to do was see if they were melting into the earth, and I could tell they were dead. Anyway, we didn't know who he was or where he came from or how he got there.[56]

After that, our line started moving up a little bit, just a little. On March 9 we were located on the west side of the Mussolini Canal, near Conca. We were in a large, two-story house with a large barn. The first night two cows grazing nearby were killed by a shell-burst. During the night a couple of the Rangers went out and butchered them. We had lots of meat, steak and soup, but no bread. Somebody knew how to cook. He had a tub full of that meat, cut in long strips, Indian style. I'd give that guy a medal if I knew who he was. We found a sack of flour, but there was no baking powder, so one smart Ranger suggested trying tooth powder, Pepsodent, and it worked—a little. And we had wine, to help it all go down.[57]

Anyway, I finally fell asleep and then Sgt. Stewart received a call that a communication line had been cut. He sent me and a guy named Smith to go down and repair it. I didn't know Smith too well—all I knew was that he was from Arkansas—but we worked well together. We had to carry a brand new roll of copper wire—heavy. We had the roll suspended on a stick between us so we could share the load. We mounted it on the front of the house and started out with the end of the wire. All of the roads and highways were elevated six to eight feet above the surrounding ground, because the land was so flat that rain would make it impassable otherwise. It had rained the night before, so the ditches were filled with water. Nonetheless, we stayed off the highway because the Germans had it zeroed in with their guns. When a target appeared, they could pull their half-track-mounted gun up onto the road and fire. They would then back down before we could return fire.[58]

We started out. It was rainy and cool in the midday. We were walking on the side of the road because of the flooded ditches. We came to a small bridge leading to a farmhouse. We could either go under the bridge and wade through the water, or go over the top of the bridge. We talked about it and decided to chance it and go across the top. We started across and were adjusting our load when we heard "Thump! Thump!" A shell hit Smith in the chest. The second shell hit me on the left side in five places—shoulder, hip, thigh, foot, and in the middle of my back. I was knocked into the water. Smith walked around the ditch, down to the water's edge, and sat down. He said, "Help me, Chief, help me." I couldn't help him. I looked at him and his face was turning an orangish yellow, then blue. He laid down and died.[59]

When I hit the water I realized I was wounded. It hurt, stinging like when firecrackers burst in your hand. I tried to stand up and found I could not. I crawled to the bank. I wasn't there too long when two Eighty-second Airborne medics came down the bank. One guy came to help me and the other went to check on Smith, but I knew he was dead.[60]

My medic cut my pants leg off. It was the first time I could see the wound. It was my left leg, all laid open. I could see that white bone in there. I thought, "I'm going to have one leg." I was about a half mile from where my brother Bob had been buried. The medic doctored me up, gave me a shot, put a big pack on my leg, and wrapped me up. He said an ambulance would be coming. I told him to be careful because the Germans might shoot again. Sure enough, as soon as the ambulance got there, the gun fired at it, but it didn't hit it. They pushed me into that ambulance, and we took off down that highway, going about sixty or seventy miles an hour. We drove a while and then they stopped. They took me into a lone farmhouse, laid me on a table, and another medic looked me over. They said they would take me onto the beachhead. All these little boys and girls were standing around looking at me there. They doctored me again, put me in the ambulance, and took me to the beach. I arrived about noon or one o'clock.[61]

I was in a field hospital. It had no walls or roof. There were no men around, just nurses in fatigues. They had a tent, and a little generator. We were outdoors, not even a door. Just an operating table and a gas engine running the generator. Three nurses were working with their hair in handkerchiefs. The woman doctor was a major. The other two were nurses. They laid me on my belly on the operating table. Using big scissors, they started cutting my uniform off. When they came to the boot on my left foot I said, "Hey! That hurt! What happened?" "Well," the nurse said, "you got shot through the foot, too." That piece of shrapnel stayed in my foot until 1989, when I finally had it removed.[62]

Then they turned me over. It was cold March weather and they had taken my clothes off. They tied my right arm to a two-inch-by-four-inch piece of lumber sticking out of the table. The nurse said to count backwards from ninety-nine to one. I started counting. The next thing

I knew, I was in a tent hospital! I looked up and there were a lot of little holes all around. [laughter] They were shrapnel holes, you know.[63]

I was still groggy and not able to see very good. An Indian nurse came in. She sat on my bed and asked me my name and my tribe. My leg was tied up in a two-by-four, and I was on my stomach. I told her, "Don't throw away my jacket! I want to save it." She rolled it up and put it under my head. She told me her name and tribe, but I cannot remember it. She asked me what I wanted. I said I'd like to have a drink. A day or two later a medic came to our ward and asked for me. I did not know him, but he left me a black plastic canteen. All the medic said was that a lieutenant had sent it to me. I wish I could remember her name, but anyway, we were both Indians, and a bond was there. The canteen was full of cognac. Very strong, you can't drink a lot. It lasted me a couple days. I never did see her again. I always wanted to thank her for her gift. We lost quite a few girls who were serving as nurses at Anzio—seventeen, I think.[64]

I recall another girl from home that was at Anzio, but she was a white nurse. Her name was Sue Woods. I don't know if she was there when I was or not. She was awarded a Bronze Star. She was about my age. I knew her real well, we used to go to Sioux City, and to football games and everything else. She worked at the Winnebago Indian Hospital. The last I heard, she lives in Iowa someplace.[65]

True to Hollis's memory, 2nd Lt. Sue E. Wood of the Army Nurse Corps received a citation for bravery in Italy for continuing at her post during an enemy raid, "comforting and caring for her patients, although in great danger." She received commendation for "outstanding courage and high devotion to duty, bringing the highest credit upon herself, her profession, and the military services."[66]

Hollis continued:

★ I've got to tell you something kind of strange. There was a guy laying right behind me, a black man. Every time an airplane would come over, boy he went crazy, used to cry for his mother at night. I asked, "What's the matter with him?" They said that he was a psycho. He was an engineer who had been laying metal mats on the beach so the tanks could come up. They had an air raid and he jumped into a foxhole. His friend was already in there, but he didn't have a head. This guy went into shock.[67]

That field hospital was at Cisterna. They took me from Cisterna to Anzio to load me onto a British hospital ship. When I got to Anzio they had an air raid. All of us guys were laying on the open ground in stretchers. Boy, they sure did rush us into shelters—they put me in a catacomb! After the all-clear, they brought us back out. British soldiers came along. One of them started to pick me up and I asked, "Hey, where are you going?" The other litter carrier said, "This bloody bloke's a Yank—ha, ha, ha." They loaded me on a barge and took us out to the ship, a British hospital ship."[68]

We sailed to Naples and were delivered to the hospital that was located on the old fair grounds. They must have had a World's Fair there a long time ago, because the people still talked about it. The Forty-fifth General Hospital was from Mobile, Alabama, and nearly all the nurses talked with a nice, soft, southern drawl. I was placed on a second-floor ward that was large and roomy. It held fifty beds for serious, but treatable, wounds. Most of the wounded came from Anzio, Casino, and Venafore.[69]

In the hospital we were lined up head to toe, head to toe, two rows deep. My partner was a paratrooper named Casebeer with a bad stomach wound. When they cleaned him the smell was not very nice. They kept a fishbowl on his stomach. The soldier at my feet was from the Third Infantry Division. He was shot in the hand and the bullet went through his arm. He was in a lot of pain. He would call for his mother at night, too.[70]

A nurse sat in the corner at nighttime. She was the only one who had a light. Next to me was a lieutenant from the Third Infantry. We used to talk. I told him about my brother and all that. One night that lieutenant suddenly threw his covers off. He didn't have any clothes on. He got up, walked by that nurse, and went out to take a piss. That nurse didn't move a wink. [laughter] She just watched him go out and come back in without saying a word. The next morning, we all told that lieutenant what he had done. "Ah, I didn't do that," he said. He didn't remember. We tried to give him the benefit of the doubt.[71]

We did not need lights at night. Mount Vesuvius was erupting, so the volcano's fires lit up our second-story ward with its big bay window all night. I remained in the hospital from March 9 until June 10, 1944. While I was there the Normandy invasion took place, on June 6. I was still recuperating when they told me about the landing on the beaches.

They mentioned the name Omaha Beach. I said, "Omaha Beach?" I was thinking, "Well, I'm an Omaha Indian!" But of course, no one knew I was an Omaha Indian. The entire time I was in the army, *no one ever asked me what tribe I was from*, except other Indians of course, so I just kept silent. They always called me Chief—*ni'kagahi* in the Omaha language, but they didn't know that. That was my Anzio experience.[72]

Hollis's participation in the Omaha naming ceremony had symbolized his transition from childhood to youth. His experience in the National Guard at Bacone, likewise, had marked his passage to young-adulthood. Now, Anzio—and the death of his brother—would make him a man. Back home in Wichita, Kansas, a frantic Eunice Woodhull Stabler started a war of her own. She had lost her daughter Marcella to diabetes in 1941, and Bob at Cisterna in January 1944. If it were within her power, she would not lose Hollis, too.

Hollis had written to his parents in Wichita on January 16, 1944, wishing them a belated Merry Christmas. He informed his parents of his transfer into the Rangers. "I think I will like this outfit," he wrote optimistically. Hollis asked her if she had heard from Bob. He wrote that Bob was bivouacked in his vicinity, and hoped to find his brother soon. He complained that he hadn't been paid in several months, and reassured his mother that if she didn't hear from him in a while, "remember I am OK."[73]

There is no indication that Hollis wrote to his mother immediately after the death of Bob in late January. A very worried Eunice finally received a letter from Hollis written March 16, 1944, from the hospital in Naples, to inform her of his injuries. "They are only leg wounds, and I hope to be up and about soon. . . . I haven't sent any money because I haven't been paid. . . . So long for now, and don't worry, dear mother," he wrote.[74]

But worry Eunice did. In fact, true to her character, she took action. Writing her congressman, State Senator Hugh Butler, on April 1, she queried him as to why she had not received formal notification of her son Hollis's injuries. She further informed the senator that she wanted her surviving son to be returned stateside. Butler forwarded the communication to Brig. Gen. Robert Dunlop, the army adjutant general. Meanwhile, the Brig. Gen. had sent Eunice her formal notification of Hollis's injuries. "It is most distressing to me that this information relative to your son was not submitted at an earlier date to the War Department for prompt transmission to you."[75]

In the interim, Hollis had written his mother again. "I am getting along just fine. . . . What is dad doing and how is the car? . . . It sure is nice weather here, but I wish I was home." The Brig. Gen. had by now responded to Senator Butler's inquiry regarding Eunice's letter. He wrote the senator, "I appreciate your interest on behalf of Mr. and Mrs. Stabler. . . . The desire of Private Stabler's parents to have him returned to the United States is fully understandable . . . however, his return is not being contemplated." At almost the same moment, Hollis wrote to his mother again. "I sure hope you are well and comfortable. Myself, I am walking with a slight limp and hope that I will leave soon. Where I go from here I do not know, so please don't worry, as I will be OK."[76]

Eunice did not take no for an answer. She took her requests to a higher authority than Butler. Her records hold condolences for Hollis's injuries from Congressman Arthur Caffen and Senator Clyde Reed, but neither held promises of being able to bring him home. At last, Brig. Gen. Dunlop mailed an official response to her request. "Adequate medical facilities exist for the proper treatment of your son at the Forty-fifth General Hospital. He is convalescing satisfactorily and upon completion of the convalescence period he will be returned to duty in the theater of operations in which he is now serving." But Eunice wasn't yet ready to admit defeat.[77]

As early as the end of January, 71,000 German troops outnumbered the 61,300 Allied troops at Anzio. Even so, American troops, including Hollis, would march into Rome on June 4, 1944.

★ After I got better they said, "You're going back to your company." That meant with Sgt. Cisco, as a machine gunner. So they sent us by truck to Rome. After we got there we marched to the Pope's summer palace. We were looking for guns. We found a big brick building, with railroad tracks running into it. In there we found a big gun. Strange thing was, they were Orientals manning it. I don't know what kind. Someone said maybe Tibetans. They were sitting up there on the barrel of the gun.[78]

After the fall of Rome, Hollis would find himself fighting in France. Historians would argue over OPERATION SHINGLE in the decades following, claiming that the Allies had bogged down at Anzio, and failed to take the Appian Way and Via Casalina as soon as possible, thereby allowing the Germans to resupply in the region. Others would claim the fault lay in the Allies' failure to foresee that Hitler would not divert his troops from Cassino to Anzio, or to anticipate the speed with which German troops north of Rome would reach Anzio, allowing them to hold the Gustav Line. But for those who were there, Anzio was not an abstract argument, but a conflagration that only the fortunate survived.[79]

1. George Stabler and Eunice Woodhull Stabler

2. Sampson Stabler

3. Marcella, Bob, and Hollis Stabler

4. Hollis and Eunice Stabler, 1939

5. Stuart M3 Light Tank, sketch by Hollis Stabler

6. Robert Stabler

7. LaVeeda Alexander
Stabler

8. Hollis in *hethúshka* regalia

9. Hollis, 1939

10. Hollis, 1945

FIVE

Operation Anvil/Dragoon

August 15–17, 1944

Following the bloodbath at Anzio and the Normandy invasion, Allied forces turned their attention to the French Riviera. Plans for France had been broached since the Quebec Conference of August 1943, but did not solidify until a year later, due to the urgency of the Normandy invasion in June 1944.[1]

At that point, the European theater of war had only been engaged in Italy and, after June 1944, in northern France. The German Wehrmacht divisions occupying the French Riviera had thus far escaped direct assault by Allied troops. But the Allies—with the exception of Churchill—felt that a supply route to the northern front, where Allied troops would land at Normandy, could be cut north and east out of the Riviera between Toulon and Marseilles, which had been occupied by German troops since shortly after the Allied invasion of North Africa. In order to secure these ports, the outer French coast would first have to be taken.[2]

Winston Churchill, who feared the depletion of Allied troop strength in Italy, was not alone in opposing the Second Invasion of France, as it would be known. The German High Command also hoped the planned invasion would not materialize. The German Nineteenth Army lay thinly spread along the Rhône River where it emptied into the Mediterranean of southeast France. Further dilution of troops to defend Marseilles and Toulon would jeopardize their strategic hold on the Rhône.[3]

Despite Churchill's objections, and contrary to German hopes, plans for OPERATION ANVIL, the invasion of southern France, went forward. In principle, ANVIL would close the distance between the Riviera and

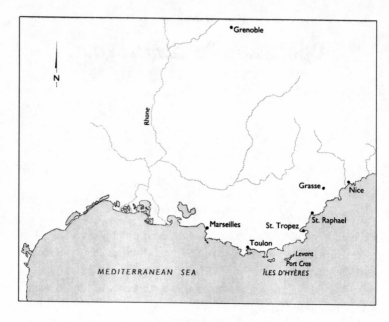

4. Southern France

Normandy, where troops of OPERATION HAMMER, later OVERLORD, had stormed the beaches in June. The Americans volunteered sixty-six landing craft for the operation, which the French hoped could be used for the Italian campaign, as well, but which Allied commanders relegated to the ANVIL operation only, touching off a tempest between the two allies. In the end, the Americans agreed to send nineteen landing craft.[4]

Rome fell to the Allies on June 4, 1944, and the D-Day landing at Normandy occurred two days later. Initially optimistic regarding the American invasion of northern France, Gen. Eisenhower watched with dismay as the advantage turned to the Germans at Normandy. Although the invasion had cost fewer lives than anticipated, American troops soon battled storms and rough terrain just to get a shot at the enemy. At this point, the advantage of a southern supply line became apparent to Eisenhower.[5]

Feeling that he'd been dragged into cooperating, Churchill renamed the operation DRAGOON. Lt. General Alexander M. Patch Jr., fresh from cleaning up Guadalcanal in the Pacific, was assigned to command the Seventh Army in March 1944. French staff officers with detailed knowledge of the coast were consulted. In late April, allied planes began "softening" the field of engagement, taking out roads, bridges, railroad tracks, ammo dumps, and airfields that might impede the invading Allied troops. After Allied forces invaded Normandy in June 1944, a supply route from the south had become imperative in order to support the troops marching east toward the Seine. Most importantly, German morale had never been lower, or their losses higher. Even the Luftwaffe had shrunk to 70 available fighters and 130 bombers.[6]

The American command continued to push forward with plans for ANVIL/DRAGOON even as Churchill sulked. Of utmost consideration was the training of the First Special Services Force. This crack team of seasoned troops, who had fought at both the Aleutians and Anzio under the command of Col. Edwin A. Walker, would be responsible for invading and securing two groups of islands, the Levant and Port Cros, eight miles from the shoreline between St. Tropez and Toulon. The capture of Levant, whose eastern shore overlooked the sea lanes to the west, and the Ile de Port Cros, with its ancient fortress, Fort du Moulin, were thought to be key to the capture of the ports of Marseilles and Toulon, for planners feared these islands might hide German long-range guns. On the night of August 14, 1944, Special Forces moved their boats into position in the sultry waters of the Mediterranean, with Hollis Stabler at the helm.[7]

★ After I was discharged from the hospital in Naples, following Anzio, I was sent to join the First Special Services Force, First Regiment, Sixth Company. This was a commando outfit very much like the Rangers. It was made up of American and Canadian volunteers, and we made a very alert and aggressive force. About half of us in the group were ex-Rangers. They sent us to Caserta, Italy, the main headquarters of the Fifth Army. That's where the royal palace of Italian kings was. But of course, it's a democratic country now. While we were waiting to be issued new clothing, the Americans there executed some German soldiers. I never did know why.[8]

We were given new clothing and a check on payday. Our boots had buckles on the side. I liked them because they were easy to take on and off. And we had baggy pants, with big pockets and suspenders. In those days we wore little jackets, with our red patches. There was no place to spend my money, so I sent it home. After we got our supplies, they sent us to Agropoli, Italy, south of Naples, for special training, which mostly meant crawling around on a lot of little islands with a full pack. We did this everyday, and it really made me strong, that's all I can say.[9]

Our first sergeant was a Mexican named Cisco. The commanding officer was Captain Peterson. We were training with ten-man rubber boats. We would row to some island, land on one side, and carry all our equipment to the other side. My leg was not quite well, but I think the exercise helped me use it more. I was the first man on the right side of the boat, and a left-handed man sat on the opposite side.

Then one night they came up and said, "We're going to France!" So we got together and everybody had a big party. We rented a room up in the hotel, and that was the biggest drunk you ever saw. We ran out of wine toward morning, so we sent a couple guys with money to get some more. They came back with a big old bottle with a rope wrapped around it. One of the guys was passed out, and I poured some wine on him.[10]

On the morning of August 14 we loaded onto a British destroyer, stacking our rubber boats three or four high in the center of the ship. It was a very fast ship. I was put in a machine gun squad as the gunner.

The squad included the gunner, assistant gunner, and three riflemen as ammunition carriers. With two machine guns on our boat, plus the ammo boxes, it was quite a load.[11]

We were told we were going to a group of islands not far from St. Raphael, France. The islands we would land on were called Îles D'Hyères, the Islands of Yesterday, they said. We were going to invade the ones called Levant and Port Cros. When I sat down at the edge of the destroyer I could touch the water. About midday they gave us a good meal, which we ate on the open deck. As soon as the sun went down it became cold.

At 3:00 p.m. we got busy checking our rubber boats because they were going to be towed by a British torpedo boat. When we were within a mile of the coast of France we put our boats in the water, ten men to a boat. My boat had two machine gun squads in it. I was on the right-hand side, and the left-handed guy on the other side, like I said. The British torpedo boat came into our midst and we hooked our rubber boats onto a long cable. There seemed to be ten or eleven rubber boats hooked to that torpedo boat.[12]

We noticed some small bags on the floor of the boat. We looked inside and found wooden pins about 12–15 inches long and an inch in diameter. A note said, "Use these to plug up bullet holes." We laughed because no one volunteered for the job![13]

Final plans for ANVIL had included an elaborate counterintelligence effort code-named FERDINAND, which conducted fake parachute drops, false radio communications, and misleading sailing plans to confuse the Germans. Part of the plans for FERDINAND called for code names for the target beaches, which were to be marked with colored lights. SITKA became the code name for the shores of the target islands. Two thousand Allied troops prepared to invade the Îles D'Hyères.[14]

"We had a marker, a blue light set into a cone that someone had installed, and they planted it on the shore. No one could see it unless they were directly in front of it. I always wondered who put those lights on the shore. Navy swimmers? My brother Bob had received the Silver Star for volunteering to do the same thing during the invasion of Sicily."[15]

On Levant, the Force men, after scaling the forty- to fifty-foot-high cliffs, wasted no time driving the 850 German troops into the island's port and rounding them up. The feared German guns turned out to be wooden dummies. Hollis's detachment, assigned to Port Cros, would find their situation slightly more complicated when the Germans refused to surrender. [16]

★ The torpedo boat towed us to within a thousand yards of the island we were going to, which had a big fort on it that looked like an old, old castle, a medieval castle. There were two other islands there. One was very large, with cows and crops on it. The other one wasn't very big, but it was big enough to hide people on it. Then they cut us loose from the ships. The man opposite of me kept a good rowing pace, always lined up with the blue light in sight. It was nighttime, with a full moon. We finally reached the shore. No sandy beach, nothing but rocks, and a cliff about two or three stories high. When we hit the beach I climbed out to hold the boat steady. [17]

The wind came up and we had a time holding the boat steady until we were unloaded. I stepped off a rock and my carbine slipped off my shoulder into the water! I reached down to catch it and my helmet fell off! So there I was, somewhere on an island in the Mediterranean, just like at Anzio, wet, tired, sleepy and hungry, with no gun and no helmet! I kept thinking about my girlfriend, and wondering who she was with and what they were eating and drinking. [18]

Anyway, the riflemen crawled up the cliffs and dropped ropes down and pulled us up. That's pretty hard to do when you're carrying a machine gun, and we had a load, two machine guns and ammo. We were finally making our way to the top. Just as we reached the top of the cliff, someone fired a single shot at us. We froze, but nothing else happened. We found ourselves facing a thick willow grove. The trees were about an inch in diameter, six or eight feet tall, and very springy, but we had to go through it. According to the map, we knew we must be close to the road that ran along the top edge of the cliff. We took a rest, wringing with sweat. All of a sudden someone came up near us and said, "Hey Chief, they want you and your machine gun up front." It turned out we were just a few steps from the road. If we had pushed on just a little further we would have made it. [19]

Dawn was just breaking. We reassembled on the road and took off our *muzette* bags and started toward the action. Do you know what a *muzette* bag is? It's kind of like a purse, but with a flap on it. We heard yells and shots so the captain motioned for me to take my gun up a small, wooded hill. My gunner was with me. After I set my machine gun up I was looking down the hill onto a winding road. A German machine gun was firing at our forces when they tried to cross the road. But we were doing the same thing to the Germans! It was kind of a duel, you know. Soon they backed up and our men began to advance. We went back to get our bags. [20]

We took a break, and the squad went back to where we had left our packs and bags. Someone had robbed us and taken everything of value! I had a large silver Napoleon coin that the French and Spanish family, Diego's family, with whom I had become friends in Oran, had given me, but it was gone. *C'est la guerre.* And that coin even had a likeness of Julius Caesar on one side. It was probably worth a lot of money. It was a big coin. [21]

We were hungry, but before we could do something about it an 88 mm shell landed about a hundred yards to the right of where we were standing. Then, a second shell landed about fifty yards closer. We realized the next shell would be right where we were standing. Instantly we scattered, looking for shelter! I started digging in the ground, but only got to the depth of two or three inches when I hit solid rock. My hole was only three inches deep; even the buttons on my shirt were in the way! We had to pile up rocks. Whoever stopped that last shot—he or they—we thank them because that next shell would have been on top of us. We believed it was the American paratroopers dropping in there who had saved us. [22]

That island was about as big as four or five football fields. In the middle was the hill, with the castle on it. Down below was a pond that used to be a lake, I imagine. And the island had roads all around it. It also had a nice little inlet where little boats could get in. A big boat couldn't get in there, but a rowboat or a rubber boat could come in pretty easily. We finally reached the bottom of the road. [23]

They called us "Hurry up, hurry up," to help them attack the German gun pad. We hurried down the road, but when we arrived they had already taken it. It was a large, round structure with a ramp on one side and a room underneath. It was thirty or forty feet in diameter on the sea side, and quite high. It had no large gun, but it looked like something had once been mounted on it. [24]

As the Force men on Levant had already discovered, the Germans had no big guns on the islands, only "well-camouflaged dummies."[25]

★ We set our machine gun on the pad, facing the ramp. One man was on the gun all the time. There were five men in the squad. We built a fire at the base of the ramp using our k-ration boxes. I was facing the pad and the other three men were busy cooking something to eat. All of a sudden a German soldier stood up right behind them. "Don't look now, but there is a German soldier behind you," I whispered. All three of those guys turned and looked at the same time. I could see that the German was very young and very scared. He put his hands way up high. He had a broken leg from jumping off the gun pad. Our military police came and carried him away.[26]

They came and told me to get ready to attack the castle that night. They said we were going to get the gate of that old castle, way up at the top. Across from where we were we could see the gate, and the high wall surrounding that fort. All the rocks, trees, and shrubbery were cleared and piled up back to the moat. We were on the side, between the gun pad, the dry moat, and the castle. The piled-up bushes and tree limbs were like a fire break—ready to burn.[27]

We moved closer to the moat and found some huts—caves, really, with beds, rugs, and a cooking stove. We also found some canned food. Unable to read German, we opened on and found meat! We tried a taste and found it wasn't bad. Later, someone who could read German told us it was horse meat.[28]

After resting and eating we checked our guns. The evening was nice, and we weren't worried . . . at least, I wasn't. Just as darkness fell we heard a loud "poof" and the ring of brush at the base of the hill caught fire! The Germans must have set a fuse to go off when it became dark. Our combat team decided to move on the fort anyway. We started out across the pond. It was damp and muddy, but it didn't stop us. I was carrying the gun tripod and a box of ammo. Half way across, the Germans opened up with a couple of machine guns. The bullets went right over our heads and made us nervous; we got down on our knees, in water. But we kept crossing the moat.[29]

The German gunner could not lower his gun to hit us because of the contour of the hill. I was following a rifleman. All he had in his hand was a rifle, so he moved fast. But a machine gun, you know, that's about twenty pounds, plus the tripod. It wasn't really heavy, just awkward. We had to find an opening through the burning brush. He finally found one, like a burning tunnel, and we dashed through the flames so as not to get burned. Safe on the other side, we started up the hill in single file, but we were kind of strung out, and it was dark. Our target was the main gate to that old fort.[30]

We were about a 100 or 150 yards from the spot we were headed for. Near the top of the hill, the march stopped. I was about four or five feet behind the man in front of me. My assistant gunner trailed me by about the same difference. It was dark and quiet. I could barely see the man in front of me. All I could see was the soles of his boots. The only weapon I had on me was a .45 caliber pistol in a holster on my web belt, but I was lying on top of it.[31]

My ear was to the ground. I thought I heard footsteps. Everything was very quiet. My position was about three-quarters of the way up the top of the hill. Again, I thought I heard footsteps. This time I knew they were footsteps, and I wondered if the men in front and back of me could hear them, too. I rolled over very quietly and shifted my pistol so it would be ready to handle. You know that when you cock a .45 you pull the slide back, and it's pretty noisy.[32]

Suddenly an American boot was right in front of my face. We scared each other. A voice asked what company this was. I told him it was the Sixth Company. The voice said we were to pull back because something was going to happen. "Tell your men to move back; go back the same way you came." So we backed down the hill, crossed back over the burning brush and crossed the moat to the other hill to wait until morning, in some little hooches the Germans had made, with canned stuff and lights. They had it all fixed up in there. By then it was getting light in the East, the morning of August 16. A loudspeaker told our regiment to gather on the west side of the island because U.S. Navy planes were going to bomb the old fort.[33]

At about three or four o'clock, two Navy planes appeared and circled our island two or three times. The first plane dive-bombed and hit right in the center of the fort, but the second dive-bomber was way off. He couldn't see because of the dust and debris from the first dive-bomber. We hollered and cheered him on, anyway. After that they said, OK, let's try it. So another company started up the hill. But they had to come back because there were German machine guns firing at them from up on the hill.[34]

Then the loudspeaker said, "Stay in your position. A British battleship is going to try its luck." About an hour later it said, "Here it comes!" A sixteen-inch shell came rumbling like a freight train on flat wheels. It landed this side of the fort and shook the whole island. Then another shell barely skimmed the top of the fort. A third shell hit the fort, gouging a hole large enough for a train to go through it. Just then a German soldier ran a white flag up on top of the fort. Our Sixth Company was glad, because we were scheduled to attack it that night. We got sent up anyway, so we hurried up the hill the same way we had the night before. Troops were jumping into that castle all over the place. We set up our gun, but we didn't need it; we couldn't shoot anyway because of all those guys jumping in. We just didn't know what was happening to them after they jumped in.[35]

We arrived just as a Force man, who had climbed the wall and dropped into the compound, was opening the big gate. We passed through a room—the orderly room—and I picked up a red Nazi armband with a swastika and some other pins on it. I later sent it to my mother. She kept it for me and I got it back, but years later I gave it to another Special Forces guy that I met, a major, or a lieutenant, I forgot, and it got stolen from him. I sure wish I had it now. Anyway, the next room was a kitchen of some sort. A large wooden barrel stood against one wall. We opened the lid. Sauerkraut! Nothing but sauerkraut! I don't know how the Germans stood it. The smell was terrible! We did not taste it; no one was that brave. I looked around outside in the courtyard. There were a lot of dead animals—cows, pigs, chickens—and some dead German soldiers down at the end. Most of the German prisoners were really young guys, maybe eighteen or nineteen. I never did see their officer. Well, everything on the island was very old.[36]

The fighting on Port Cros had continued into August 17. Not until the British battleship *Ramillies* pounded the fort with twelve rounds of fifteen-inch shells did the Germans surrender. Had Hollis had time to inquire, he could have learned that the islands of the Îles D'Hyères, now known as part of France's Côte d'Azur, and accessible only by ferry, housed several substantial forts. These had been commissioned by the likes of Cardinal Richelieu and Francois I in the early sixteenth century, and then manned by convicts—rewarded with the right of asylum—as a defense against pirates. Today the islands constitute a national park, known for scuba diving and nude sunbathing.[37]

Within hours, the outer islands of the French Riviera had fallen to the Allied troops. Meanwhile, as the men of the Special Forces distracted the Germans on the Îles D'Hyères, the Allies were landing 60,000 troops and 6,500 military vehicles on the shores of southern France, the leading edge of a force that would eventually number 250,000 troops. The Allies would capture 2,000 German prisoners, but lose 200 Americans, in addition to almost forty French marines. Churchill, who had been conferring with British commanders in Italy, sailed in to watch the mainland invasion from off-shore. German divisions raced up the roads north of Toulon in hasty retreat. With their heavy camouflage, they looked like "a forest in motion" to those observing them, and "strangely silent."[38]

The central targets, the DELTA beaches, covered a five thousand-foot-long strip of sand at Boughton Bay, northwest of Sainte-Maxim. The beaches west of DELTA were dubbed the ALPHA beaches, and those to the east, the CAMEL beaches.[39]

The ALPHA beaches fell surprisingly easily to the Third and Fifteenth Infantry Divisions. ALPHA YELLOW would later be remembered as the site of one of Sgt. Audie Murphy's heroics, but he was not yet the most highly decorated soldier of World War II. Likewise, the DELTA invaders found less resistance than expected. It was the CAMEL beaches that would prove to be the biggest challenge.[40]

CAMEL RED, lying at the mouth of the Gulf of Fréjus, could have opened a route to the interior, but heavy fortification and a rain of enemy fire prevented an assault. Rear Adm. Spencer S. Lewis, in charge of the CAMEL RED landing, diverted his 142nd Infantry to CAMEL GREEN instead, ten miles east of their intended target. Lewis had been unable to contact Thirty-sixth Infantry Division Commander John E. Dahlquist, who was already on-shore. The unexpected maneuver upset American Sixth Corps Commander Maj. Gen. Lucien K. Truscott because it delayed an advance on the Germans and the airfield at Fréjus, but Dahlquist's career survived. Back in the field, it was agreed that CAMEL BLUE and CAMEL GREEN would have to be taken first.[41]

Despite some enemy artillery fire aimed at the landing craft below,

CAMEL GREEN, a small, heavily fortified beach lined with high cliffs, fell easily to the 141st Infantry because troops in Toulon had delayed German artillery destined for the island. CAMEL BLUE proved to be a bigger challenge. Hollis and the exhausted Force men proved they were up to the job, however.[42]

"Next morning we were told we were going to the main land, to head for the city of Grasse. At that time, Grasse was the perfume center of the world. It was located just above the French Riviera." As Hollis remembered, planners on the eastern front intended to prevent Germans from moving in from Italy. "While we were waiting the black French colonial soldiers came up. They wore big old white pants, and sandals, I think, and red jackets on with little red tassels. Their lieutenant was a white man, a French man. They swarmed in over the hills."[43]

Free French forces—consisting of Frenchmen, North Africans, and Africans—played an important role in the southern French invasion. Following the capture of the islands, French troops secured the left flank of Cavalier Bay, on the mainland. Their objectives would be Toulon and Marseilles.[44]

Grasse, it has been said, is in the balcony of France's Côte d'Azur, perched on the slopes of the Provençal Alps, overlooking the French Riviera since the seventh century. As one writer has observed, long before trendy Cannes, Menton, or Nice, Northern Europeans escaping frozen winters visited Grasse. Historically a city of leather tanners reknowned for their gloves made of supple sheep and goat leathers, Grasse had the good sense to build a perfume factory for its tannery when scented gloves were all the fashion during the rule of the French and Spanish courts of the early eighteenth century. A modern tourist can explore the perfume factories of Grasse, but as one traveler has observed, "Whatever perfumery you will visit, the Holy of Holies will never be revealed to you. The perfumers will receive you in the parlor but not in the kitchen."[45]

Hollis continued:

★ Our island had a little inlet for small craft, so we went down there in the morning, and rowed out to an American minesweeper. I took some canned rations with me, and some horsemeat. I was hungry, I was going to eat it. We climbed aboard by a rope ladder. I was tired from having almost no sleep for two nights, and very little food.[46]

An Indian sailor stopped to visit with me. We talked about home. He was a Sioux from one of the Dakotas. He asked me if I needed anything and I told him I was hungry, and I showed him my can of horsemeat and gave it to him. "Wait," he said. "You can have it if you want. What are you hungry for?" I said, "Anything." He left, but came back with a jacket in his arms. He sat down beside me and pulled out a hot loaf of bread with a large slab of butter in the center, and some jam or peanut butter, I don't remember, and a canteen full of milk. Oh, that was the best thing I ever tasted! He saved me. I, in turn, gave him a fine pistol I had picked up at the bombed fort. Lots of guys picked up souvenirs but I carried only what I had to. I wish I could remember that Indian's name. He was on a minesweeper near St. Raphael, in the First Special Service Force unit. He was an Indian, and so was I. We recognized that "brotherhood." If he's not dead, I sure wish I could find him. [47]

The minesweeper took us to the shore at the city of St. Raphael, which was a big city. The Vichy French were still fighting there, but we supported de Gaulle. The road was brick, and it ended right in the water, waist-deep, so we had a good landing. We had to pass under an ancient aqueduct, huge. Everybody was saying to take a picture right there, so we took one, you know. I had to go so bad I felt like pissing on that aqueduct, so I did. Later we saw a sign, "Kilroy was here." We laughed, and wondered if we could catch up to him, but we never did. [48]

We had to run through the streets because there were snipers. Up ahead we could hear a lot of gunfire, and people hollering. We reached a large square—a big one—where there must have been a firefight. Debris, clothing, and wagons were in a pile, burning. But we were running, we didn't stop. We hurried through that plaza. As we passed a pile of clothing, something exploded, "pop!" and hit me in the ankle. I wasn't sure what it was, but it must have been a shell. It bruised me, but it could have been worse. [49]

We reached a well-traveled road or highway and kept moving as fast as we could, then we set up a bivouac and rested. There were already some guys there, paratroopers I think. They were everywhere, trying to clean up snipers. I noticed a jeep coming from our rear, with two men laying a communication line. I knew this, because it was the same thing I had done as a Ranger at Anzio. I looked at one of those guys and I said "Boy, that's an Indian. That's an Indian." How did I know that? I don't know, I just did. Not only that, he was an Omaha like me. They stopped right in front of us. "Dave, is that you?" I asked. It was Dave Walker! We were friends when we were younger. I knew his family. We shook hands and parted. He had to go. I did not see him again until after the war, back home in Macy. He is gone now, but I wish he was around. He must have been on the same trail as me.[50]

Anyway, then they put us in trucks, American trucks, and they took us along the coast, maybe a couple hours drive. We finally got out and I was thinking, "This is just all too fast, everything is in a hurry." We got off the highway and went up a ditch and then we came to a trail, not a road. On either side of it they had little yellow flags, to warn about mines.[51]

Hollis had not yet learned that Hitler had ordered the retreat of the German army up the Rhône Valley, abandoning all except Toulon and Marseilles. The American troops raced to cut off their retreat. Meanwhile, First French Infantry division commenced the liberation of Toulon, beginning with the nearby town of Hyères. By August 23, they had scaled the cliffs and stormed the city. German troops began surrendering, although pockets of resistance remained until the fall of the harbor, which huddled under a heavy rain of artillery fire from Allied warships.[52]

Even as Toulon fell, Allies attacked Marseilles. Within hours, with the help of French infantry, the city was surrounded and cut off. In the city, French resistance forces fought in the streets, while Allied warships bombarded the harbor. By August 27 the Germans had been pushed out of the city and down to the docks, where they stubbornly destroyed as many of the facilities there as possible before being forced to surrender. With the ports liberated, American troops and allies rushed north toward the retreating Germans. They traveled so quickly that they soon outran their supply lines. By September 12, the First Armored Division would break through to Gen. George Patton's Third Army, marching from Normandy. In the interim, Hollis and the Special Forces men raced through the lush district of Provence, east of Toulon and Marseilles.[53]

★ We took off across the country, following small trails that had the yellow German flags with the word *mina*—mine—on them. We finally reached a nice road through a beautiful valley, a huge vineyard with a big chateau on one side and the rugged coast on the other, big trees and big homes. The road following the coast was lined with nice, well-kept yards. It seemed to be used a lot, but was narrow, lined with trees and flowers on either side. We didn't see anybody. If I were younger I would go there again.[54]

It was getting dark, and nature called, but we did not slow down our pace, a quick step. I finally told my assistant gunner that I had to take a dump, you know. He said, "Hold it." Finally we got to a place with big tall pine trees, with cut grass and bushes, which was bad because of snipers. They watch for people using the bathroom. My gunner told me, "Good luck!" I dropped out of line and went about twenty steps away from the road.[55]

I had to take my web belt and harness off. It had a canteen, a medicine kit, a pistol, and a shovel attached. I also had a raincoat that functioned as my sleeping roll, and a muzette bag for personal items, which I laid around me so I could reach them quickly. I also had my machine gun with me. Then I took out the most important item—toilet paper—which was the liner of a cigarette package. We soldiers saved all paper. That was the scary part. Some guys would almost come to blows over a nice piece of paper. We used to keep it for toilet paper, folded up in our helmets. Nobody ever tells you about that, do they? Oh, and another thing, don't ever eat little green grapes. They looked nice, you know, but . . .[56]

The Force men I was marching with never stopped or even slowed down while I was taking care of my business. That column kept up that quick pace. I could tell it wasn't going to slow down or stop unless commanded. I finally finished and put my gear back on. I started after them, trying to catch up with my company. When I reached them, I dropped back into line. We had nothing to eat except our K-rations. On the left side of the road was the valley. Every inch of ground was covered with grape vines—vineyards. In the center of the field was a chateau, and buildings connected with growing grapes. Usually a squad of men would have stopped to check it out, but that column just kept going. The whole place was beautiful and restful. I didn't know what we were going to do, but we were on our way to an unknown fight.[57]

We walked and ran, mostly in silence, too tired to talk. I was carrying the machine gun. All night long we ran. Sometime during the night the column stopped. It was dark, but a big moon was coming up, and the night was nice. I leaned against a rock wall, the machine gun cradled in my arms. The next thing I knew, I woke up. There was a long line of soldiers gaining on me from behind, and no one in front of me. I hurried down the road, again, to catch up with the column. I don't know how long I had napped. When I found the column, I stepped back into line.[58]

Those guys I was with—paratroopers, Rangers—were a lot different than the other guys I had been with. They were really aggressive. You had to learn to take care of yourself, you know. That's the way it was.[59]

By morning we neared our target, Grasse, across the valley from us, on a big hill. We were on a big, high hill, too. Suddenly dawn broke and we were marching into a valley, with a stream running through it. Across the center of the stream lay a small house, or maybe a mill. The stream was cleared of timber to about a hundred yards on either side of it. Our road crossed the stream near the mill and continued across the valley up a mountain. Suddenly we were taking machine gun fire from a gun placed at the base of the road.[60]

Capt. Peterson was right behind me. He told me to set up the gun and fire to the left of the road going up the mountain. "Bang! Bang!" I fired an entire belt at that target. Soon, a white flag appeared on a stick. We packed up and crossed the stream. Four or five young Germans stood over there, lined up, about fifteen or sixteen years old, it seemed. I could also see a couple of soldiers lying on the ground in the bushes. My shooting had been good. It was still payback for my brother, Bob.[61]

By this time, all these Force men were running up either side, going across that valley. The Germans were up on that other hill, and never did see me. We marched on down that hill. Soon, a bunch of French people joined us. They had been waiting for us, hiding behind the bushes. They had flowers and flags and wine and sandwiches. There was a lot of backslapping, talking, passing the jug; I think it was Chianti. One old guy wanted to carry my *muzette* bag, and he even wanted to carry my gun. I let him carry my bag, and my box of ammunition.[62]

As at Cannes, the joy of the liberated French spilled out into the streets. News footage of their exhilaration not only punctuated the Allied victory, but served as powerful demoralizing propaganda against the enemy.[63]

★ We crossed the valley and started up a winding road covered with foliage, going to Grasse. The civilians were still with us. When we came to the top of the hill we found a railroad track that a German machine gun had zeroed in on. We kept going. Each squad crossed that track by running together. When my turn came, the old civilian carrying my *muzette* bag went right alongside me—real cool! There seemed to be small firefights everywhere and it was getting dark again. Before he left me he gave me a bottle of perfume, which I put in my pants pocket. It was real low, around my knees.[64]

Grasse is real steep, with a lot of steps. We were sitting on the steps and Capt. Peterson walked up to me and said, "Where are you from?" I said, "Nebraska." That's all he ever said to me, Capt. Peterson. Then he told our squad to go to the next terrace. He said it would be about midnight when we got there. He said we could go through the backyard of the people living there. We started out on our right and found a bunch of people sitting there eating something. Lordy I was hungry! You know, those French they don't eat till late. They kept right on eating like we were not there. Finally an old lady asked me, "*très faim?*" "*Oui, très faim,*" I answered her, and she gave me a large bowl of soup and a piece of bread. It was good. She fed about six of us guys. We gave them all our cigarettes and candy.[65]

We finished our march through that family's tier in Grasse. We found an empty building, and everyone conked out until daybreak, except me. It was hot; I just had a shirt on, with big loose pants, no cap or nothing. I took about three canteens to fill at a spring we had noticed nearby. You know, we really hadn't eaten or slept from the time we left Italy until now! No eating, no sleeping! A French man and I began to visit by hand signals. He offered me a drink from a fancy bottle. It wasn't wine, it was stronger. We had not slept for more than forty-eight hours, and had marched all night at quickstep. I was tired and hungry. The next thing I knew, it was morning and I was laying down in a nice, soft, clean bed. I looked around, and I was alone in a bedroom![66]

I had no shirt on, and my boots were standing very neatly by my bed. By the bedside was some wine and a piece of cake in a dish. I had a headache—the biggest headache of my life! Oh, my head was hurting. I looked for someone, but no one was around. I put my shirt and boots on, but I was afraid to drink the wine, I couldn't stand to drink it. I found some water and washed up and combed my hair.[67]

I finally started out, but to where? I had no idea, but I started down the mountain, a nice, curving road. I jumped on a French truck going down. When we finally reached the bottom I found my company, just getting ready to march into Nice. I didn't care where we were going because I still had that big headache.[68]

They said there was going to be a parade. Oh! I still had that headache. A parade was the last thing I wanted to be in. I washed my face a little bit and tried to eat and put on a steel helmet and got my tommy gun. I don't know where it came from, but suddenly we had a band leading us. Soon women of all ages and sizes surrounded us. It was all flowers, wine, color, and music![69]

We marched through town, and the only way you could keep going was if you kept drinking. If you didn't drink enough they wouldn't let you pass. We went through one section of town where all the girls had purple hair, pink hair, orange hair, you know. Guys were dropping out of the parade all over the place.[70] [laughter]

Actually, I have to say that I really can't remember much that happened after that. I was with this other guy and I told him, "Boy I got the biggest headache in the world. I don't know if I can make it anymore." We sat down on chairs that lined the sidewalk. We were so tired and dirty and I had that headache. We noticed a small hotel, Hotel Plasene, nearby. On the spur of the moment we decided to rent a couple of rooms. Then we went to a restaurant. When I sat down, I broke the bottle of perfume the old Frenchman had given me. Man, did I smell! After that I took a shower and laid down and passed out.[71]

We stayed almost a month—thirty days—in that hotel in Nice, going back to the camp outside of town only to eat or change out of our clothes. I had been wearing a steel helmet, and carrying a tommy gun in the parade on that first day. For all I know, they may still be in that Hotel Plasene! Later, the city had a banquet and a dance for us in one of the larger hotels on the Promenade Grande. I liked to dance; one girl even asked me to dance. But they didn't dance like we do. That was when we were learning to do the swing and stuff.[72]

There were all kinds of outfits there, Force men and paratroopers and others. They showed a movie about the First Special Services Force (us), and it's true, you might have heard, the Force men got drunk and mean and fought amongst themselves. I had a date, so I missed all the exciting parts![73]

That hotel I was in was built on a cliff, and it had an elevator that took you up and down. They told me that before the war they had closed up that elevator. But a man was in there. When they opened it up again, he was dead. That guy I was sharing the room with, he kind of disappeared after a while. He got a girlfriend and he disappeared. I'd see him every now and then. It was just like we were living a vacation. We got our hair cut, we'd eat breakfast. I walked down the Promenade. I got acquainted with everyone in that area. There were two or three people who spoke English. The hardest thing was finding food to eat, American food. What they ate was different. Once I went to Monaco, to the casino. There was a lady in there playing music. I was in there with some other guys. She said, "Can anyone dance?" So I danced with her. She must have been a big shot. I did real good. But she was all alone in there.[74]

I did meet a girl there in Nice, too. It happened at that dance. I decided I had to go to the bathroom. The bathroom was full, so a guy told me to go down to the basement. I went down there and there was nothing but potatoes and storage stuff, and a bathroom for men, kind of a trough.[75]

I came out, and a girl was there. She had followed me downstairs, and next thing I knew we were going at it. When we got through, we went back upstairs and I was ready to dance and drink some more. That girl talked to an older woman that was with her. I couldn't understand them, but they left. I had to follow them because the girl had a hold of me. I let her go, and danced with somebody else. Later on, I met that girl again. She must have kept track of me; she knew where I was going. Anyway, my unit finally ended up in the city of Grenoble. So, that was it, the end of the Champaign Campaign.[76]

As historians later realized, the behavior of American troops in France was not above reproach. They were accused of "helping themselves" from French homes at random, including provisions, family heirlooms, and clothing. French officials begged military leaders to order the soldiers to desist from plundering, though they did not begrudge the soldiers "wine and spirits and food." Additionally, American commanders eventually put Cannes, Nice, and Monaco "off-limits" to curb the soldiers' behavior.[77]

On September 12, 1944, some thirteen weeks after the initial invasion of southern France, the southern Allied divisions shook hands with the men of the Normandy invasion on the banks of the Seine. The Allies had failed to capture most of the retreating German troops, but the combined forces of 263,476 personnel, 56,318 vehicles, and 526,039 tons of cargo had ransomed France. Despite their failure to prevent a German retreat, 79,000 Germans had been captured, at a cost of more then 13,000 lives, including 3,000 Americans. Most importantly, the supply line to the north had been opened.[78]

Unbeknownst to Hollis Stabler, his mother Eunice Woodhull continued her battle against the War Department as Hollis rested in Grenoble. Senator Hugh Butler contacted her on October 31, 1944. "Enclosed is a copy of a letter just received from Brigadier General Robert H. Dunlop regarding Hollis. I was happy to hear that Hollis has now recovered and has been released from the hospital. If there is anything further I may do, do not hesitate to call me." But the response from Brig. Gen. Dunlop was not what Eunice wanted to hear.[79]

"I again refer to your letter of November 6, 1944, with enclosures from Mrs. Eunice W. Stabler, Decatur, Nebraska, requesting that her sole surviving son be assigned to non-combat duty. The recently announced War Department policy on this subject applies only where two or more sons in one family have been lost or killed and the only surviving son is in the army. It does not apply to families that have three sons in the service. . . . I understand the grave concern that prompted Mrs. Stabler to write and she may be assured that her son's well-being will be safe-guarded while he is in the military service, and that he will be assigned only those duties commensurate with his physical condition . . ."[80]

The War Department's words not withstanding, who can say with certainty what brought Hollis home in the end: Eunice's prayers, her letters? But in early February 1946, Hollis got the news he had been waiting for—Eunice had won her war.

★ One day a notice came out of the first sergeant's office with my name on it. It was my pass to go back to the states! After thirty-four months, five campaigns, and many battles, I was going home! I had made it, but my brother had not.[81]

These stories are my recollections of an important experience in my life. I was not a hero. I was not the only man fighting the war. I was always part of a team. In this final campaign, I was just one man in a gunnery squad of five. We were a team, working together. I made it home, but many good men, including my brother, Bob, were not so lucky.[82]

SIX

Tígthe: **Home**

Home. To the Omaha Indians, home meant tígthe. In any language, no place is more sacred, no memory so cherished, as home. The word embraces the most universal of ideas, but is predicated upon an idea even more basic: war. War and home, home and war—inextricably, paradoxically linked in the human pantheon of archetypes. And so it was for the Omaha Indians: kikína, war, and tígthe, home. One would not exist without the other. But for Hollis Stabler, as for thousands of other Native American veterans, coming home to a postwar world was a confusing experience at best.

★ They put out a list, with my name on it. I was glad to be going home. I was through. I was ready to go home. That list came out and they got us on a train, a French train with eight horses and twenty men, something like that. I went to Fontainebleau and Paris. We got off at Paris. When we were going over there a man, a sergeant, jumped on the train. He was there talking to us. We told him we were going to Paris. He said, "I'm an ex-soldier. I'm getting ready to go back to Paris. I have a shop there." We said, "A shop?" He was an American soldier, a staff sergeant. He was French, but he joined the U.S. Army. He had a dress shop there in Paris. We didn't meet too many of them.[1]

We got to Paris and we were staying there a couple days, then we got a train and went to Orléans. That's where they trained for the "The Bulge." (I didn't end up going to The Bulge.) While I was there I saw a man get executed, an American GI. They marched him up on the scaffold in a hood and gloves. Then they cut his buttons off. They hanged him. Then everyone did an about-face and marched away. I think they hanged him for murder. The whole thing only took about ten or fifteen minutes. Then I was in Orléans when Roosevelt died. I spent six months there. While we were there they brought in two big trailers. They made us walk through them in raincoats and boots. They sprayed us down because there was typhus there.[2]

Hollis, in fact, spent Christmas of 1944 in Monte Carlo. He sent his mother a postcard postmarked such, and significant for a brevity that would later haunt him. "Hello, Mother, how are you? I am well; your son, Hollis."[3]

★ After Orléans I was sent to Le Havre. I stayed there about a month. That place was full of sunken ships, just the tops showing. They took us out into the bay to a big ship, and that ship took us home. We went to New York City, then to Fort Dix, New Jersey. When I was in New York, that's when I tried to find Delaney's sister. That's also when a B24 crashed into the Empire State Building. We all thought, "An airplane in a building, huh?" So that's the first thing we did, we went and looked for it. And it was in there! Smoke coming out, just the tail end sticking out. They were working on trying to get it out.[4]

But anyway, this Italian boy invited me to a dinner. He lived in Brooklyn; he had some friends with him. *Real* Italians, his mother and dad. They treated us real good. We fooled around there. About two or three o'clock he invited me to a wedding. He was used to New York City. We jumped up and caught a train, then another train. He knew exactly how to do it. We got to this big Italian wedding. That's when I saw girls jitterbugging. Oh, they were good at it! I danced with a couple of those girls. They asked me, "Are you Indian?" "Yes, I'm Indian," I said, and they were interested in me and I was interested in them.[5]

Then my mother and dad showed up in New York, because I was the only child left, I guess. They took me to the Rockettes at Radio City Music Hall, and took me different places. There was a girl here that died at Sioux City a while back; she was in the Rockettes at that time. I never did get to talk to her. I was wanting to visit her, but she died before I could talk with her. Anyway, my parents had driven to New York City. My dad had that old Chevy with yellow wheels on it. While we were in New York City, he drove in to Grand Central Station, with the big limousines and all that. The car broke down and we got stuck. [laughter] He and I had to push that car out of the way! Oh man. And while we were in New York, the Eighty-second Airborne had a big parade.[6]

But my parents came on home, and I went to Hattiesburg, Mississippi, and got discharged. I got there and it was just chaos. Everything all mixed up, people coming in and out. I wanted to get *out*. I was ready to get out. Then they gave us a "short arm." Do you know what a "short arm" is? That's to see if you've got a venereal disease. The doctor was up on a stage, you know, and they called you and you had to walk up there with just boots and a raincoat on. [laughter] Everybody else would be down there clapping! [laughter] They'd be whistling and hollering, you know! [laughter] Oh gosh! I used to think, "Oh, if only LaVeeda could have seen that!" Everybody hollering! [laughter] But anyway, that's when they medically check you for shots and all that.[7]

LaVeeda, of course, and millions of other wives, lovers, mothers, and daughters would never know the true extent, and function, of prostitution in World War II. Understandably, as one contemporary news columnist put it, "Hotel Street," the "new crossroads of the world," would never be part of the "official chronicles or the enshrined memories" of the war. Few returning soldiers were likely to share tales of "Hotel Street" with the women in their lives.[8]

The rate of venereal disease among World War I soldiers had reached staggering proportions. War planners intended to avoid a repeat performance in the current war. Despite enactment of the May Act of July 1941, which commanded military officials to wage war on prostitution aimed at U.S. servicemen, military commanders abroad found themselves simultaneously endorsing and condemning houses of ill repute. The most farsighted understood that prostitution could not be outlawed and was best managed under military oversight, while others fought a hopeless war of extermination on elusive local establishments. Officials found themselves caught between an acknowledged need for regulated brothels and the dictates of the May Act.[9]

Nor were the power politics related to prostitution restricted to military leaders. Local communities played a role in the sanction, or not, of prostitution in wartime communities. In Hawaii, the issue of prostitution during World War II had a direct bearing on early postcolonial restructuring of race and gender relations. Although documentation is lacking, it may be presumed that prostitution in the Arab and Muslim countries of North Africa during the war challenged existing social standards with regard to race, class, gender, and money.[10]

In Honolulu alone, for example, the wartime sex industry serviced 30,000 men a day throughout the duration of the war. Two hundred and fifty "registered" women served their clients under a strict condition of sale, "$3 for 3 minutes." Despite the volume, and due to inflexible controls—such as the use of prophylactics—Hawaii military installations maintained a low incidence of venereal disease. More significant were the profits to be made off the trade. In Hawaii, it was not unusual for a madam to end the war with a six-figure sum in her savings. Even a common prostitute could earn 30,000–40,000 dollars per year. But although Hollis had behaved no better or worse than his contemporaries, like all returning veterans, he now faced the real-world challenge of human relationships.[11]

Hollis continued his story:

★ I went outside with my barracks bag, and a guy comes along selling fifths of whiskey. There were a whole bunch of us out there, but little by little they disappeared. Pretty soon it was just me and two other guys, one from Lincoln. They let me off at Omaha. I got out at Union Station, now the Western Heritage Museum. I started across the walkway there. At the end of it was a bar. I wanted a beer and hamburger, so I went in there. Unknown to me, somebody called the police. Here comes a policeman in there. He said, "Are you drinking?" I said "Yeah," you know. "Indians aren't supposed to drink." That's what he said to me. I just dropped the bottle and walked out. I still had my uniform on. It was a city policeman, not an MP. . . . It made me wonder what I'd been fighting for. I never went back to that place.[12]

Like many returning Indian veterans, Hollis's encounter with American racism was abrupt, as if to emphasize that not much had changed on the home front in his absence, despite the service of 25,000 Indians in the war and at least that many at home. Legislation in 1802 had excluded Native Americans from legal alcohol consumption. As one historian observes, however, drinking had become a symbol of equality in the service. Returning veterans would not be long in overturning the old law, with mixed repercussions for Indian communities.[13]

★ I started out and went to the bus station. That place was full of people. That's where I met that girl, Grace, from Macy. She was a waitress, and she used to go visit a little girl in the hospital who had casts on both her legs up to the hip. I don't know who I was looking for there. I didn't even know anybody. But everything seemed all mixed up, too. In Omaha I got to a hotel, called Ike's Barn. All the Indian soldiers stayed there, and I had some cousins there, too. It was nothing but drinking. Grace was with me. My Aunt Jenny gave me money for clothes. I bought shoes, pants, a shirt, a camel coat, and a yellow scarf. I had a cousin there in Omaha, Nina. She was married to Hank Sheridan, the one from the 101st that jumped at D-Day. He got shot in the arm. My uncle, George Woodhull Jr., warned me to leave. "You better go on home." I told him, "I don't know where. I don't know where my mother and dad are now." They were living in Lincoln, somebody told me that. So I got on a bus and went to Lincoln.[14]

Grace went on home to Macy, but I stayed in Lincoln. My parents lived near the Capital, south of it. We could see the back of the Capital out the window. I stayed there and went to a counselor to go to school. All GIs had a counselor. And he said, "You better go back to Sioux City and check in." So I moved back to Walthill. My mother and Dad moved back, too. They were just following me because they had no place, they had nothing better to do than keep track of me, and I'm glad they did.[15]

I got here [Walthill] and I thought I could get a job. I wasn't ready to work, but I decided I better. They gave me a job to go to Cudahey's Meat. So I went to Sioux City, and they put me in the job called the "beef kill." Have you ever heard of a "beef kill"? You've never been in a slaughterhouse? I had a good friend in there. Me and him were about the same—tall, skinny guys. They had these big old beeves, too. There's a pen they put the cattle in. Then there was a man, a black man, with a big old sledgehammer. He'd get the cow and knock him down. Then they'd turn a thing and the cow would slide down like that. Our job was to hook them up. Then after you finished that, then you'd have to help them slay the cow, and that was hard to do. Lay it down on its back, put those spikes in them to keep the legs up. Then the skinner would come along, but before that they would cut the cow's throat, blood all around. I worked there about two months. I got a couple paydays. I thought, "I don't want this. I don't want to spend my life like this."[16]

So I told my mother. She said, "Well, let's go to that counselor." She went with me everywhere I went. And that man said, "We'll give you an aptitude test. You've been out of school for ten years. Let's see what you can do." So they gave me the aptitude test, and I did pretty good. He said, "What kind of school do you want to go to?" I said, "Any kind of school." I thought about the University of Nebraska. They sent me back to Lincoln, so my mother and dad moved back again. I got a counselor at the university. He said, "If I were you, you've been out so long, I'd go to a smaller school." So he sent me to that little college in Lincoln, that church one [Wesleyan]. While I was there I started thinking, "Well, I know where a little school is." I was thinking about Friends University, in Wichita, a Quaker school. I knew all about it. The counselor said, "Whatever you do, I would go to a smaller school. You'd do good on teaching, drafting," and he named off quite a few things. [17]

I wanted to get away from Cudahey's. I could have stayed there, but I just didn't want to. Grace came down there to Lincoln, she followed me there. One time they gave me a job at Yankee Hill Brick Company, to unload a flatcar. Two or three of us went down there. Talk about a tough job. That was it. I don't know how many bricks—we had to set them in a wheelbarrow, wheel them down, stack them up. We did that for a couple weeks, got paid. I thought, "I don't think I want to do this for long." It was while I was working at the Yankee Hill Brick Company that I heard about the atomic bomb. I was surprised to hear how many people died. "What kind of bomb is that?" I wondered. I think they should have done it earlier. It would have saved a lot of lives. My dad was working at a farm. There used to be a big farm right on South Street, where the park is. My dad was a maintenance man there, so he hired me. We worked there for a while. Drinking was what got me. Grace was living with me. My mother said. "If you're going to live with that girl, marry her." [18]

I didn't even think about it. I said, "Okay." "Let's go get married," I told Grace. She said she really didn't want to do it, Grace didn't. So finally, they had that old courthouse down there, it's gone now. I said to her, "Let's go. If you're going to stay with me, let's go." She said, "Alright." I asked for the papers and asked her to sign and she wouldn't do it. I asked her, "Why?" She said, "I'm married." So that settled it right there, you know. She said, "I can't." I have her picture here someplace. One day I'll show it to you. She was a nice-looking girl, but that was the end of it. I didn't even know she was married. I never knew who he was, but he must have been a white boy. They moved to

Plattsmouth. I guess she's still living there. "Dang, I don't want to do that again," I told myself.[19]

After I had been out of the service about a year, the hethúshka warrior society welcomed me home. Mr. La Flesche's brother was a guest. My cousin's daughter painted my wounded leg. All I had on was a breech-cloth, a long piece of cloth that you had to wrap and twist between your legs and let it hang down, front and back. My cousin Mary Lyn embarrassed me by yelling out, "Watch your shonde, don't accidentally twist it!" Henry Blackbird and George Woodhull Jr., called Horse Chief, gave me a song. All the women loo-looed and the men blew whistles the first time they sang my song.[20]

I went to Wichita. Grace followed me down there to Wichita, even after she told me she was married. We didn't get along. From then on it was no good. Finally she told me she was going to see her sister. She left and I never did see her again. They tell me she has a daughter, but of course I've never met her. So in Wichita I went to school. I called LaVeeda's mother. LaVeeda was the girl who told me she was going to marry a Catholic. Her mother and I were good friends. I always got along with older women. I visited with her for a long time. I didn't ask her about LaVeeda. I told her I was going back to school. One day she called me, left a message for me to call her. So I called her and she said, "You better come down here. I'm going to have a dinner—you can meet someone you ought to know," or something like that.[21]

I asked a friend to take me down there. She had a nice dinner, and LaVeeda was there. We got to talking and got acquainted again. Not long after that, she said, "I'm getting a divorce." I didn't even know she was married! I never saw any of these guys! I don't know who these guys were that my girlfriends had. She left then, I don't know where she went, but I went back to school, trying to get things started. One day LaVeeda called me again and asked, "Can I come out to see you?" So she came out to my mother's house. They lived out there by Boeing, those cheap houses. My mother gave me a room upstairs when I started going to school. One day LaVeeda called out there and said, "Come down and see me." She was working there at Montgomery Ward. We got to talking again. I don't even remember asking her to get married. She said, "I think we ought to get married." I must be pretty weak; I said, "Okay." So we had to take the blood tests and all that stuff. Before we got married I talked to my mother. My mother said,

"You know she's been married before. You're going to have to accept that. My advice—don't ask her about anything, unless she tells you." So that's what I did. So I never did ask her about anything. If she wanted to tell me, she told me. She had her faults, too, but we got along good. We didn't argue, only when I drank.

Eunice, still concerned with maintaining Omaha clan tradition, arranged to have LaVeeda adopted into the Nation by a tribal member, thereby insuring that her apparent daughter-in-law belonged to an appropriate clan before marrying her son. [22]

Like most returning Indian veterans, Hollis would find himself living in a postwar economy that no longer needed an influx of Indian workers to run the war factories. Although many veterans chose to return to their reservation homes, where an even bleaker employment situation presented itself, some, like Hollis, would pursue careers in the larger society. For many Indians, even those as progressive as Hollis, big-city life called for changes. [23]

★ One day LaVeeda said, "Why don't you get a car?" See, I never even *thought* about getting a car. I said, "That's a good idea, let's go." Her father knew a guy who sold Plymouths. Just like that, we had a little Plymouth coup. We bought it. She was good at managing money. For three years I went to school, then I worked for the city as a draftsman. I got acquainted with everyone in the city. I did drafting work for them, wire diagrams and stuff. I worked with a lot of people, the mayor, I knew everybody, because they knew me. Then I graduated from Friends and I said, "I wonder what I should do?" I went out to Boeing and they asked, "You have a degree in Industrial Arts and Art?" They hired me as a quality control, an inspector. [24]

Unlike Lockheed, who refused to hire Indians during the war, other companies such as Boeing refused to consider race in the hiring process and enthusiastically capitalized on the expanded labor pool. [25]

★ They sent me out to Shipping and Receiving, way at the south end, a big long building with a porch on it. They put me in there and they said, "Do you mind working with a woman boss?" I said, "No I don't mind!" They put me in with a woman called Letha Jones, boss in quality control. She and I got along good, but a lot of guys didn't want to work with her. I worked there about a year. I did a lot of things. Then they found out I was an artist, a draftsman. So I did a lot of drafting for them, too. Then one day they said "We have an opening for an inspector in small fabrication parts, checking rivet patterns." So I said, "I might as well learn how to do that." That's one thing I liked about Boeing. Whatever you wanted to do, well, they'd send you to school.[26]

They sent me to that fabrication school. I was checking rivet patterns. On a Saturday I went to the first class. They had what they call "expeditors"; they bring around drawings for whatever you're working on, and you have to check it to see if you are doing the right thing. Here comes this expeditor, he came in. I can picture him, a big fat guy with a flat top, white T-shirt, overalls, shoes with white socks. He says, "Hey Indian."

Boy, that made me just so mad. I just grabbed him. He was on a bicycle. Just his toes were touching. I flopped him right on the floor. He got up, all dirty and greasy in the back, and all clean in front. I said, "I'm your inspector. What have you got for me?" He never said a word, just got up. Everybody in the shop saw that happen. From then on, I had no problems.[27]

I got acquainted with all those guys; they found out I was in the service, and there were a lot of service guys. I just got along good. I kept working my way up. Finally they put me in Final Assembly, that's the fuselage, in the 41 section, with B52s. Before that, I had a lot of parts for the B47. That's the airplane that Jimmy Stewart flew. I was checking wiring, all kinds of wiring. One time I was checking cables on the fuselage on the B52 and the door opened up and I jumped off and it caught my pants, ripped them right off. Everybody laughed about that. But I got along pretty good. When you're an inspector . . . well, I didn't have much trouble. Once in a while some guys didn't like it, wanted to argue with me. But they'd do the work over again.[28]

I worked myself up to Flight Line. Flight Line was three big metal fences, with a plane in each one, with a runway over here. There was a bus that went through there, no sides on it, you just catch it. I was waiting for it. I started jumping on, and a guy took a swing at me. I just grabbed his arm—off he went. The bus driver was watching, he didn't say anything, just laughed. That guy was on the road out there. I don't know why he didn't like me. I never did know who he was. You know how they are. Then one night I was in a hangar. I crawled under a fuselage, and a guy took a swing at me. They do that, you know—you have to watch yourself. Just like the service, that's the same way the service was. Then we got into it. The manager, one of the big shots, came out on the balcony and called, "Hey!" We stopped. That guy went his way. I went mine. I still don't know why he did it. But he knew I was an inspector. Inspectors weren't really liked. Those workers had to do what was right, that's all I can say.[29]

Anyway, I worked out on the Flight Line. One time Jimmy Stewart showed up in his airplane, a B47, a big bomber. It has two men in it. He had hit a big eagle, that's why he stopped at Boeing. I was an inspector so they sent me up there to check it, the leading edge of the wing. It didn't hurt the aircraft: kind of dented it a little bit. Feathers and blood around it, that's about all. But I saw Jimmy Stewart walking around talking. You know who Jimmy Stewart is? It was a pretty good job, I liked it.[30]

At that time we bought a new house, LaVeeda and I, on Richland [Street]. That's where my son Hollis D. was born. Hollis D. was eight years older than my daughter, Nonie. He and LaVeeda were there. We had a dog, Freckles, the same age as Hollis D. They grew up together. We had a nice little house. I put a pump in there, had a lot of trees. We didn't have enough money to fix the water main. I had to dig a hole. The hardest job I ever did. LaVeeda couldn't work; she had Hollis D.[31]

One time I came home and LaVeeda was in the backyard. She said, "I'm back here." So I went back there. She had this big old black eye! I said, "My gosh, what happened?" She turned the other way, and she had another black eye! I said "Well, what happened?" She said she and Hollis D were laying in bed together to take a nap and he hit her with his bottle. He was two years old. Then he picked up my golf club and she was trying to get it. She had to step down. My golf club was out there, she stepped onto the step and the golf club came up and hit her in the other eye! Two black eyes! Everybody thought I had hit her, but I didn't even touch her.[32]

That girl! It's a good thing she married me. I always believed I was here to protect her. I don't know what those other guys would have done with her. Another time I came back and she was all bandaged up, her breasts and stuff. I said, "Now what happened?" She had a sun lamp. She and Hollis D. were taking sun. Hollis D. tripped and the sunlamp burned her. "LaVeeda," I said, "Good God." Being married to her changed me, because I had to take care of her. We didn't have any more children for a long time. Then she said to me, "I'd like to have a girl." I told her, "I don't know what I can do except keep plugging away." I was working all the time. Then I got interested in archery, and so did LaVeeda. It was about eight years between babies. We were just getting ready to adopt a little Pottawatomie girl, then here LaVeeda got pregnant again with Spafford, and right about a year later with Nonie.[33]

I felt like I should be with LaVeeda all the time. That's the way it was, we didn't have any problems at all, until I got started drinking. I'd get to drinking, and I knew I couldn't drive, so I'd throw my keys on the roof.

Hollis does not directly say so, but his consumption of alcohol during the early years of his marriage may have been related to federal legislation in 1953 that legalized consumption by Native Americans.[34] Like many returned Indian veterans, Hollis used his VA benefits to acquire a home. It should be acknowledged that in buying an off-reservation home, Hollis did not sever his relations with the Omaha Reservation. Unlike many Omaha Indians, Eunice and her children still held allotments on the reservation. Leasing fees would afford Eunice and George Stabler a meager income in their older years.[35]

★ We bought a nice big home in Wichita. One day, a man came up to me. He was kind of famous because he wouldn't pay taxes. So he and I got acquainted. He lived in a nice big three-story house, big basement. He said, "Do you think LaVeeda could do some paperwork for me?" So she'd go over there and do paperwork. But he didn't finish off the garage, the cement floor. After we got the house, Hollis D.'s grandfather gave him an armadillo. And you know, those little things stink like anything. So we built a little cage for him out there in the garage and he'd dig way down in that dirt and down he'd go. We'd have to pull him out. That happened a lot.[36]

Mr. Walter "Tex" Alexander, LaVeeda's father and Hollis D.'s grandfather, was a man to be remembered. A Texan and employee of General Mills for thirty years, the man had only missed three days of work in his career. He was also a well-known square-dance caller, a pastime Hollis and LaVeeda also enjoyed together. Her father's only child, LaVeeda had expectations of her husband. "I had a tough record to follow. But, I didn't care. I always worked anyway." Hollis recalled wryly.[37]

★ LaVeeda had a lot of relatives in Texas. We went there a couple of times when we first got married. I met her aunts and uncles. Most of them were rednecks. When we got back LaVeeda said, "If I'm going to live with you, I want to learn to dance Indian." My mother gave her a buckskin dress. I said, "Go ahead. Dance." She had light brown hair and big blue eyes. She said, "I'm going to the dance tonight." So she wore dark glasses at nighttime, and she won. She won first place. All the Indian women liked her. She was accepted, you know. And she learned to sing Indian. One time we went to Nevada, Missouri. I met Archie Bunker [Carroll O'Connor] there. Nonie was just a little girl and she won first place there at the powwow. I showed them how to put up a teepee. I was involved in a lot of that kind of stuff. LaVeeda was a good shooter, too. She had a thirty-five-pound bow, just a little bow, but she was pretty good. When I lived in Wichita they had an archery club. Also, my dad used to make bows, so I was used to them. We took in all the contests. She would win all the time, but I never would hardly win. But I did win a couple of trophies.[38]

Anyway, getting back to the guy who didn't pay his taxes, one day LaVeeda said, "You know, that man is going to sell that house." "What's he want for it?" I had no idea myself, I never fooled around with money. "Twenty-two thousand dollars, but I think I can get him down to twenty," she said. It was a big house. In those days that was cheap. Well, it was a lot of money, but compared to now it's cheap. So he said he'd sell it to us. So we borrowed from her mother and dad, not much, then we borrowed from the bank, and I had my GI benefits. So we had a nice big house. Then I *had* to work. But I had a lot of things to do. Hollis D. was just at the right age. He played baseball. He was a good catcher. He liked to play basketball. That took up a lot of my time. And LaVeeda had two little ones. She decided to go back and get a degree in social work. Her mother babysat. Mrs. Alexander took care of the little ones. Hollis D. could take care of himself.[39]

I worked for Boeing fifteen years. One day they had a notice out. They needed an illustrator. I found two or three Indians working there in the Illustration Department, drawing. I got a job drawing a pilot's handbook. "Flip switch on toggle," that kind of stuff. Then I got working with a man; whenever they had a plane wreck he would take me out and we'd have a graph sheet. We'd graph the wreck. That was a good job. Then I took a job on the Saturn. That's when Russia was flying those Sputniks. My best job was working with engineers. They had so much to do. That was a good job, and I got a little extra money on that. My boss was a lady. No one wanted to work for her. She was kind of aggressive. I sure felt sorry for her. They treated her kind of bad. She'd be working out there, and some guy would say real loud, "Motel? Five dollars?" They were all white.[40]

One time we went to Lincoln. There was a big restaurant to the left of the football stadium, a pretty famous restaurant. Me and LaVeeda went in there and sat at the counter. We looked, and there was Elmer Blackbird, the descendant of the Omaha chief, and his wife in a booth. There was nobody there but us and a guy sitting at the counter, and he was looking right at me. Oh, he just looked daggers at me. He didn't like seeing an Indian with a white lady. LaVeeda was just having a good time, talking. She liked to talk, you know. When it started to get daylight, here came a black boy and a white girl walking in from the stadium. Oh, that guy got mad. You could see him slamming things, then he walked out.[41]

Anyway, Boeing is where I met Margaret, a half Cherokee, half white girl. She was an inspector. She was working on a college education, and she had a couple of children. I didn't know her real well. The way we got acquainted was, one day she came and stood by me. I said, "What's the matter?" "Oh, that guy is after me," she said. There was a guy, kind of hiding, looking at me. A couple days later he came up to me and said, "I didn't bother her, I didn't hit her or anything." Margaret would come to me to keep people away from her. I never did know what became of her. It would be cold out there and she'd have slippers on. I'd say, "Why don't you get some shoes on and put on a coat?" I don't know, maybe she didn't have the money. She was kind of like a little sister, I'd watch over her.[42]

There was another girl, Evelyn. Her mother was a cook at the institution. Evelyn was a friend of mine, but she couldn't talk to me. Her husband used to, he used to come around mad, like I had something going on with Evelyn. Domestic violence was kind of a secret thing then.[43]

There was one guy there, he got caught with a girl in a freight car. They called him Box Car Charlie. There were a lot of little things like that. And what gets me, they fired the girl and didn't fire him! I didn't have anything to do with that stuff. I worked there fifteen years. One day they called me to the office and said, "Do you want to go to Seattle?" I said, "No. Why?" "They're going to close this plant up. We went clear through the whole phase of B52s. We're out of work." They hadn't got the new contract. They said, "Do you want to go out East?" There was another place out there Boeing had. I said, "No, I don't care for Washington." I asked LaVeeda. She said, "No, let's stay around here." So that's how I got out of Boeing, fifteen years. They gave me a little check. That was a good job. I liked it, so many kinds of people around.[44]

So I got out, and I went back to Friends again, to get my teaching certificate. When I got back from school, I worked for the city a little bit, drafting for them. I liked that, but it didn't pay much. We collated pamphlets, just kind of a holdover job. I got acquainted with all those guys that worked for the city. In fact, I had been to high school with those guys, North High. After I got through school I got my teaching certificate, and I applied for a job with the public schools. They called me down to the office and they said, "We've got a job if you'd like it." I said, "Alright." They said, "It's an industrial arts job." I asked, "Which school?" Wichita had eighty-two elementary schools, fourteen junior highs, and seven high schools. A big place. They said, "It's by WU, Wichita University. It's called John Marshall School." That area used to be all white, and the blacks kept moving in. I didn't realize that because I never went down there.[45]

So they took me to a school called John Marshall. They said, "You can have anything you like here." They took me down to the industrial arts room. I checked out all of the machines. The only thing I didn't like was they had one wall there, nothing but wiring and tubes. You'd turn *on* something here, and something would go *off* over there. I told them, "Get that all straightened out," I told them like that. So they had men working on that. They had a surfacer, but it was all shot. I said, "I'd like to have a new one." They told me to go buy one. So I went and checked them out and got a new surfacer. I had everything I wanted. I was wondering why I was getting all that. I asked LaVeeda. She said, "Take the job. You can handle it." Turns out, the school was 99 percent black; I taught ninth graders, and these guys were great big guys. I had twenty-four desks and thirty people. Nobody told me what to do, how to do it. Turned out, I had three ninth-grade and two seventh-grade classes.[46]

I had nobody to ask what to do or how to do it. So I thought, what can I do to start? One thing I knew I could start them in was drafting. So I got everybody a piece of paper and showed them how to do the drafting. We had squares and different types of pencils. That I could do real good. I said I wanted everybody to write a letter home, and tell them that they have a new teacher and I want them to come up and visit. And I found out right away that they couldn't even write. They didn't know how to address their letters. First thing I did was get discipline. Like in the army, first thing when you go into a new outfit, some guys will like you and some won't. You have to sort them out. Next thing we did was learn how to address a letter. "I don't know what street I live on." "Well, go home and find out," I said.[47]

It turned out real good with those kids. The seventh-graders weren't hard, but the ninth-graders were great big old guys. Pretty soon I got acquainted with some of the boys. The best thing you can do is get somebody to back you up. Tom Moore was one of them, a handsome boy. All the girls, even the white girls, liked him. Him and Benny Sheely, and others, they backed me up. "Mr. Stablah, if this is how you want it done, we'll back you up." They didn't call me "Stabler." They called me "Stablah." Pretty soon their parents started coming in. I didn't have any problem with their parents at all. In those days I was full of energy. I could do a lot of things. Once, this boy came into my room, Benny Sheely, a good guy. "I want to arm wrestle with you," he told me. So I beat him, but every once in a while some guy would want to come in there and challenge me. I thought, what if I lose? But I never did. I guess I was just at the right age I could do that.[48]

We had a lot of fun with that. Then the superintendent said, "I want you to have a club." I couldn't think of a club. An Indian club? So I said, "Well, I'll take the High-Y." That's them Christian boys. So we decided we wanted a basketball team. We had to figure out a way to make some money, so we bought pickles, big old pickles, and we sold them. We got about twice what we paid for them. These kids were kind of ornery. We had a day, they called it a Style Show. Every month they had a Style Show. All the girls would dress up, and we'd have a dance. Of course, I liked to dance, so I danced with all those girls. Of all the kids I taught, the black girls were the friendliest. Frankly, when I walked down the hall, it would make me embarrassed. "Mr. Stablah! Mr. Stablah!" I didn't have any girls in my class because it was all boys. Then once when we had a dance, LaVeeda came. She said, "Why did you dance with those girls all that time?" [laughter] She couldn't figure out why I was so popular. There was a teacher upstairs, a black man. One day he came running into my room. "Mr. Stablah, something's gone wrong with my experiment." It was a stink bomb. We had to vacate the school! [laughter] Another time something exploded and he was all black all over his face! [laughter] Oh my, we had good times.[49]

One day I was working there, and here comes another teacher I knew, McCoy. And here comes a student running out. The school was built in an H shape. The teacher came running out there and his face was all bloody. I said, "What happened?" We went running through there and finally we got that kid cornered. The police came over. While we were talking, that kid hit McCoy again. I don't know what he was mad about. But that teacher, he was a real nice guy. He always wore golf clothes, or hunting clothes, or whatever kind of clothes that went with what he was doing.[50]

We decided we would take the boys out hunting. We said we'd take three guys from each class. That gave me nine boys to take, and he picked out some. And we had a couple teachers with us, too. He said, "I have a place where we can go rabbit hunting." Now this is the time when the blacks and the whites were fighting, in the 1960s. So one Saturday morning, here comes Benny, he had a yellow shirt on, a white T-shirt, black pants, white socks rolled up! I said, "Where are you going, to a dance? We're going hunting." [laughter] They had never been hunting.[51]

So we all got in the cars, about four cars. We got lost, way out in the country. [laughter] We said, "Well, let's see, we could stop and ask somebody." We stopped at a farmhouse. We got out, and these boys all had guns. I didn't think anything about it. But that lady opened that door, and, boy, she slammed that door shut so quick again! [laughter] We got back in the car and said, "We better get out of here!" We got out there into a nice valley. Not every one had guns, but a few of them had. We started down that path, and a little rabbit jumped up. It was just like Anzio! Everybody firing! I thought, "My God, we shouldn't shoot this rabbit like this!" But that little rabbit got out of that, I don't know how. Anyway, we kind of cut things back on the hunting trips a bit, later on. I thought the whole experiment was funny. Of course, those people didn't think like I did.[52]

Then another time we were selling pickles. Somebody told me, "Mr.

Stablah, somebody bit one of the pickles." I had about four guys there. "Alright!" I said, real stern. "Get in line here! Open your mouth!" One of the guys had a bulge in is mouth. "Pop that pickle," I told him. [laughter] I just did that for fun. But oh, those guys used to laugh about that. We had a lot of fun. My first three years I was there, I finally got them whipped into shape. I had a broken paddle. One swat, two swats, I'd swat them. One time Nonie came back from Lincoln and she said, "I met one of your former students. He's a black guy. He said, 'Mr. Stablah probably won't remember me because I was one of the good guys.'" [laughter].[53]

They were good after they got to know me. I'd holler at them if they needed it, but it didn't mean nothing. One Sunday it was raining, and dreary. We were returning from hunting. I came in, and they had a record player. They were playing a song the Beatles made famous. They were singing and dancing around. They had rhythm. They had several dances where they changed partners. I got out there with them; LaVeeda was with me and she got out there with them, too, but she didn't really get into it. [laughter] Anyway, that was my first three years there, and I thought we did real good. And then they had that busing, you know, making kids go to white schools, and that's what broke us up.[54]

The school district called me and said, "We want to give you the chance to have a nice school." They sent me out to Wilbur, a brand new junior high, nothing but white-collar and blue-collar children. It was nice, but they were way ahead of us, way ahead of me. They were way ahead of me, so I didn't care too much for the school. I remember, one of the boys committed suicide. He hung himself from a tree.[55]

Later they sent me to a junior high, Mayberry. Nonie was there. She had a locker next to a black girl. They were mean. They didn't like the white girls, or the Indian girls. But Nonie, boy, she's a tough girl when she wants to be. Boy, she stood up nose to nose with them once. They called me, and the principal came out and we separated them. Hollis D. was the same way. Anyway, I had a seventh-grade art class. One day they said, "Lock your door, Mr. Stabler. Don't let anyone out of the room. We have a streaker in the building." Here came that kid running, so I followed him. We got him in a room, and the assistant principal, a young man, had to tackle him. We used to tease that guy who tackled him all the time. Another time, a young teacher, a young woman, was getting a drink of water. Some guy came along and goosed her. Boy, she hollered out. I asked her, "Do you want me to get him?" She said, "No, I'll take care of him." Just ornery, those guys were. LaVeeda worked at another junior high, the nicest one in the system. The vice-principals use to ride little cars around. Hollis D. was working as a kind of police at the different schools. Anyway, they called me out to LaVeeda's school, and I went out into the hall, and there were two or three black families, and they were after one of the teachers. They came running out there. I held back a heavy-set girl. She was hitting me, cussing me. But they knocked that teacher down, and kicked him. It was a tough place to be. The kids, black and white, all ran outside and wouldn't come in. They joined hands in a circle all around the school.[56]

They had a new school, West High, and Hollis D was going there then. "Mr. Stabler, we want you to come and take the coach's place." One day I was standing there monitoring the halls. Somebody said, "Oh-Oh, Stabler and somebody else is going to have a big fight out here, a good one." They were talking about Hollis D. I went out there, and there was Hollis D. with the toughest guy in the school. Boy, they were out there. I walked out there, "Alright, break it up," I said. By that time we had other people out there. Later, I asked Hollis D. about it and he said, "Yeah, that guy has been after me for a long time. We were going to have it out." But it was an exciting job, I'll tell you that. I worked for them about nine or ten years. Eventually they put me in Human Relations.[57]

Everybody had a Masters and were working on their Doctorate. I was the only one who wasn't that educated. That's where I met Beverley Gutierrez, a black girl who didn't look like a black girl. There were six of us. Our boss was a Mexican boy who had married a white girl. Her father was a teacher at Friends, that's how I knew them. There was Horn—he was black—Funk, a white boy, me, Beverley, and another black woman, Mrs. Jones I think, very articulate. She knew a lot of things. Beverley did, too. So I got in with a bunch of smart and tough women. And that's when they were really having it out, the blacks and whites. I stayed there about two years.[58]

The increase in the number of urban Indians during the war years and after had led to the establishment of numerous urban Indian Centers in America's larger cities. Hollis would be instrumental in the founding of the Mid-America All-Indian Center in Wichita. For many Indians, these intertribal friendships offered their first opportunity to compare experiences with people from different reservations. Many found themselves called to radical political action that would eventually lead to a host of Native American civil rights, eventually culminating in the Indian Self-Determination Act of 1975. Others, like Hollis, found themselves called into multicultural exchange activity.[59]

★ I got a good pay raise. My job was to take care of the Indian students and their families. And we had a lot of them, because they worked for Boeing and Solar and Cessna. There were a lot of Indian families. I had workshops for how to get along with people. I had dances for them, Indian dances. It was a good job.

Later Hollis would claim,

Our children experienced the good part of being Indian in today's world. Their minds were not scarred by the dependent poverty that affected so many of our people. . . . Every month there would be a dance. There were Kiowa, Arapaho, Cheyenne, Osage, Ponca, Comanche, and many other tribes represented. It was amazing how they could sing together so well. It is a very satisfying thing to learn about people different from yourself. This is the answer to all peoples living together peacefully in the world today.[60]

Then we decided to come up here to Macy. In 1977, Edward "Eddie" Kline, the tribal chairman, came down to Wichita and said, "We want you to come back up to Macy." [It didn't hurt that Hollis D., a graduate of the University of Nebraska, was also the Community Planner for the Omaha tribe, although Hollis didn't mention this.] So I came up and worked my last five years here. I retired at sixty-five in Macy, in 1982.

Later, when asked why he gave up a comfortable job as the Director for Human Relations in the Wichita Public Schools to return to the reservation, Hollis replied, "It's a matter of pride. I'm proud to be an Omaha. If what I feel rubs off on some of our young folks, we all stand to gain."[61]

★ Kids up here were entirely different than the kids in the public school. I had to think of things for them to do. I tried to keep it on the Indian ways. We did frames for making rugs, and burlap, and we made all kinds of rugs and they liked that. One day a girl said, "Can we bring some music in?" So I let them bring music in. Then we did drawings. I got an ear of corn, put it on the table for a still life. The kids drew it from all different angles. They asked me, "How should we fill in the kernels?" I thought maybe they should put their names in the little kernels, one letter in each kernel. They still do that project today. [62]

I liked that, too. . . . But it was hard to get the Indian students motivated. We lived on the farm, in a brick house. Thirteen miles I drove everyday. It was good. When I was sixty-five I said, "I quit. I don't want to do it anymore." And I did. But we raised horses, and had cattle there on the reservation. Hollis D. and I bought fifty head of heifers and one bull. Next April, we had a hundred head of calves. We weren't ready for them. We had no experience, so we sold them. We made money. I like to try everything, you know. [63]

Hollis and LaVeeda led a full life following Hollis's retirement in 1982. As a tribal member, LaVeeda had worked hard to understand her family's culture. She learned to make and wear traditional regalia, and danced in powwows with Hollis and her children. The family was particularly active in Fremont Days in Fremont, Nebraska. LaVeeda's handmade shawls quickly became popular on the powwow circuit, and even today collectors eagerly snap up old dance shawls bearing LaVeeda Stabler's handmade label. [64]

When not participating in Native American cultural events, the Stablers often enjoyed traveling. LaVeeda and Hollis especially shared a love of hunting. Several times they hunted big game in northern Canada with their son Hollis D. "That's what I really liked about LaVeeda, you know. Anything I wanted to do, why, she'd do it with me," Hollis would later reminisce. [65]

Additionally, LaVeeda supported her husband's involvement with various veterans' associations. They often participated in reunions of the Second Armored Division Association and the Fourth Ranger Battalion Association. As recently as 2004, Hollis traveled to a reunion of the Bacone Indian College Forty-fifth Infantry Division in Muskogee, with whom he served in the National Guard in 1938 while studying art under Acee Blue Eagle. [66]

Unfortunately, the beautiful, lively, fun-loving LaVeeda Alexander Stabler passed away of a heart attack on January 3, 1999. Her obituary claims she was a member of The Order of the Eastern Star and the American Legion Auxiliary, and had been an ice skater and cheerleader at Wichita East High School. Her passing left an understandable void in the life of Hollis Stabler. [67] "LaVeeda had a heart attack and she left without talking to me and I know if she had been able to say something she would have because she liked to talk and visit with anyone. But I have no regrets, she changed my life for the better and no man could ask for more." [68]

Dr. Stephen Cobb, a professor from Messiah College in Grantham, Pennsylvania, had paid a visit to Hollis on the Omaha Reservation in the late 1980s. Dr. Cobb encouraged Hollis to write his war memoirs. He "suggested that my life in the army and family life as an Omaha should be written for future use in classes on culture. Dr. Cobb and I started with my mother's book, *How Beautiful the Land of My Forefathers*. We redid some pieces and added some items before reprinting it as *La-Ta-We-Sah, Woman of the Bird Clan*. That is how I got started writing. . . . My experiences in the army came along just at the right time for me. I got to do a lot of things and be part of the excitement. At least I made it back . . . with a lot of knowledge, good and bad." [69]

SEVEN

Conclusion

Few Native Americans who served in World War II could have been as prepared by their childhood experiences for life in the service as Hollis Dorion Stabler. Yet for all his early exposure to multiculturalism in his youth, even Hollis found himself in wonder of the world into which the U.S. Army sent him.

Hollis's parents, George and Eunice Woodhull Stabler, exerted a powerful influence on his early years, an influence that imparted to him a deep sense of cultural continuity and personal family history as an Omaha Indian, as well as a sense of well-being and independence, not to mention confidence in his own ability to negotiate the world. Eunice's education, her personal sense of adventure, her work ethic and her social connections to powerful people, such as Vice-President Charles Curtis, shielded her young children from much of the poverty, despair, and discrimination experienced by other Indian children, particularly those living on reservations in the early decades of the twentieth century.

Eunice's insistence that her children be raised off-reservation, even as they learned and carried forward the traditions of their Omaha elders, resulted in a childhood spent in Midwestern towns and cities— Sioux City, Wichita, Lawrence, Lawton, Pawhuska—large enough to contain diverse non-Indian populations—by the standards of the early twentieth century—yet near enough to Indian reservations to attract progressive Native Americans. And while other Native American children of his time may have been as familiar with as many cities on the Plains, it would be reasonable to presume that none but Hollis had also lived in both Washington DC and Hampton, Virginia. Before he had even graduated from high school, Hollis had been made aware that the world contained such diverse peoples as Omahas, Winnebagos, Osages, Cherokees, Apaches, Warm Springs Indians, Jews, Italians, Germans, Swedes, not to mention the dizzying swell of faces he would have been exposed to in Washington.

Although a quiet man, Hollis's father, George Stabler, left no less an imprint on his son's life. Though Hollis attributed his parents' marriage to Omaha clan custom, it is just as likely that they recognized in each other a determination to escape the dismal life that had become the Omaha Reservation. As Omaha in orientation as Eunice, George shared with his wife a work ethic inspired by his educational opportunities: his time at the Sherman Institute, his training in carpentry at the Indian school at Carlisle, Pennsylvania, his course in "automobilogy."

Moreover, George's friendship with such early twentieth-century athletic luminaries Jim Thorpe and John Levi must have further raised his stature in Hollis's eyes, and demonstrated to him the spectrum of achievement an Indian could attain. Additionally, George's part-time career in semi-pro baseball could only have enhanced Hollis's reputation with his childhood friends, such as Doody Green and the Big Hole Gang.

In many ways Hollis's childhood was ordinary, filled with "buddies," adventures, brushes with the law, and sports. Yet for all the progressivism of his family, Hollis could not escape the bigotry of those who were less familiar with the world than he. Where most boys of his generation would have recalled proudly their athletic achievements in high school, Hollis's recollections are colored by the racial prejudice of his teammates and their fathers (particularly), and his loss of self-respect over his own disrespectful treatment of the white girl, Ruby, whose worst offense had been to have a crush on an Indian boy.

It is, in fact, in regard to the girls of his youth that Hollis's memoirs contain their most palpable hint of regret. Almost seventy years later, Hollis expressed disappointment at his treatment of Ruby, and wished, even now, that all had turned out well for her. More importantly, his own reflections had brought him to the realization that his life experiences had not brought him in contact with many eligible Indian girls. His marriage to a white woman had happened almost by default. Had he stayed on the reservation, Hollis would no doubt have married an Omaha woman. Had he done so, particularly if his Omaha wife was not comfortable living off-reservation, his educational and employment opportunities would have been much more circumscribed than otherwise. Like many Indians, Hollis's destiny called for a choice between clinging to what remained of the homeland, or pursuing economic opportunity, although, as his family demonstrated, neither situation dictated a loss of culture. In the end, he would have his land, his tribe, and his education.

Once in the service, Hollis's life became much more comparable to that of his Indian peers. Like them, he became the ubiquitous "chief," presumed to have better hearing, better eyesight, more stamina, more courage, and better aim than his non-Indian soldier cohorts. Yet if his fellow soldiers were racially shortsighted, they could easily be forgiven, for most Indians brought with them into the service a naïveté regarding white people, as well.

Even Hollis, who had seen so much by twenty-one, made note of Red Dog Poland, the Alabama redneck who liked him, much to the confusion (one imagines) of Poland's own ingrained prejudices. Yet, despite their differences, they were all-American soldiers: Hollis and Poland and Zabel the Pole from Chicago and Delaney the Irishman from New York, Germaine the Germ's black soldiers, and hundreds of thousands of others—a class distinction that bonded them and overrode differences when confronted by "foreigners."

As an American Indian blessed with an outgoing personality, a good sense of humor, an education, and prior exposure to the world, Hollis was enabled to make the most of his new association with the Moroccans, Algerians, British, Scotch, Spaniards, Sicilians, Italians, and French who peopled his wartime world. With disarming charm, Hollis partook of the finest cultural experiences that North Africa, Sicily, Italy, and France could offer under the circumstances, and no doubt left more of value in his wake—in terms of memories and good will—than the helmet and tommy gun still hidden in some forgotten hotel in Nice.

In later years, Hollis would marvel that his love of horses had drawn him into the cavalry just in time to witness its transformation into an iron war machine. As one of the last mounted cavalrymen in the U.S. Army, Hollis could stake an historical claim to both the old mounted army of the American West and the most powerful, mechanized modern army on earth.

The accolades of war heaped upon those who served as part of "Hell on Wheels," Darby's Rangers, and the First Special Services Force fell on Hollis, as well. After the war he would maintain his relationship with these organizations through membership in veterans associations. But respect for Hollis as a veteran was expanded well beyond that of most non-Indian vets by virtue of his heritage. While other veterans officiated at association reunions and national holidays, Hollis also participated in Native American veterans affairs, and danced in many a powwow with other Indian veterans.

Hollis's experience with women punctuated his wartime experiences. They were in accord with those of many an American soldier who had dalliances on the front with foreign women, yet they held an additional layer of meaning for Native American men; for although Native women had historically been available to white men, Indian men had not had comparable access to white women. For many Native American soldiers, sexual relations with an African or European prostitute may have been their first experience with a non-Indian female, or, as with any number of young soldiers, with any woman at all.

But Hollis's gendered wartime experiences were not limited to girlfriends. Mothers, wives, and daughters played a role in his war, as well. Sixty-four years later, Hollis easily recalled Lowell Walstrom's hundred-year-old mother, and the breakfast that Red Dog Poland's mother cooked the morning the Japanese bombed Pearl Harbor. Most importantly, of course, Hollis was guided by his own mother, sustained by her love, bolstered by her courage, and influenced beyond measure by her example. Thanks in no small part to Eunice Woodhull Stabler, Hollis fought a human war rather than an impersonal one.

Wives and daughters made their way into Hollis's memories. The native Moroccans who sat him on a pillow and fed him the fruit of Africa; Diego's wife, the unnamed French woman who played the accordion and prepared a feast to please the American soldiers despite wartime shortages; the Sicilian woman and her daughter who rolled up their sleeves and made spaghetti for Hollis and his friends; the implacable French woman at Grasse, who with soup and bread fed the famished Force men marching through her property.

Some women in Hollis Stabler's war wielded power. The easy, indulgent girls of the Lone Star Hotel and the Villa de la Rosa; the French girl on the black horse, hair and banner flying, who had hailed them at Safi; the mysterious French woman in Casablanca who had paraded him before a room full of French men; the Army nurses who healed under the most stringent of circumstances; Eunice and her fight to bring Hollis home: all these, and more, would become part of the mosaic of war in Hollis Stabler's mind, a war in which both men and women participated.

Brotherhood also characterized Hollis's war. The sense of duty that compelled him to pull the wounded McCafferty (who had shot the hapless she-dog) into view of the ambulances; the compulsion to run to Pendarvis and reload the weapon of the rich man's son; the strength to take the pistol from a drunken fool—all bore witness to his bond with his fellow soldiers.

Furthermore, Hollis experienced a sense of relatedness to the Native American servicepeople, men and women, with whom he crossed paths: Sam One Skunk, whom the press chose as its "archetypal Indian soldier"; the nurse who sent him a gift of cognac; the Indian sailor who fed him bread and milk so he wouldn't have to eat horsemeat; Dave Walker, the Omaha man who brought news from home: with each of these Hollis identified above and beyond the status of fellow serviceperson. Each reminded the other of home and family in lands that offered no contextualization for Native American history. Not only were they far from home, they were far from the continent that defined their existence, unlike most soldiers—most obviously the Irish Delaney, the Polish Zabel, the French American soldier who owned a shop in Paris, and the black soldiers who rightfully persecuted the Germ, whose heritage traced back to Europe or Africa. To a Native American, to die in the war truly meant to be buried on foreign soil.

Most importantly, Hollis defined the war by what it meant to his brother, Bob, and to his family. Bob had died at Cisterna. Until 1948, he lay buried in Italy, far from those who mourned his passing. Eunice never healed from the grief of losing two children so young. Her attachment to Hollis, always strong, grew even stronger. For his part, Hollis remains grateful for having had the chance to see his little brother on the eve of his death. It was a good good-bye, befitting warriors.

As a veteran, Hollis took advantage of the educational opportunities available to him after the war. His education at Friends University, his career as a quality control inspector at Boeing, his subsequent years as an industrial arts teacher in Wichita, and his rise to Director of Human Relations in the Wichita Public Schools all had their genesis in the war years. But it was his "Omahaness," if there is such a word, that would qualify him as a teacher in the schools on the Omaha Reservation. His knowledge of Omaha culture, his sure position in the tribe—and the Black Shoulder clan—by birthright, his reputation as *hethúshka*—these qualified him to return home and take a position as a teacher on the reservation. Moreover, it was his wife LaVeeda's desire to be adopted into the Omaha Nation, her embrace of Omaha culture, her willingness to let Hollis *be* Omaha that enabled him to retire in peace to the beautiful land of his forefathers.

Some would say that Hollis Stabler's life was the stuff of which movies are made: Casablanca and Sicily, Anzio and the French Riviera, the Eleventh Cavalry, "Hell on Wheels," Darby's Rangers, the Special Forces, Sophia Loren, Jane Wyman, Mae West, Ginger Rogers, Jimmy Stewart, Ronald Reagan, the Roosevelts, Churchill, the Sultan of Morocco, Gen. Patton. But in the end, Hollis's story reminds us that war is a real experience, a human one that transcends analysis by race, class, gender, even celluloid. War is unrelenting hunger and thirst, fatigue, grime, noise, pain, anger, stench, fear, courage, death, homesickness, loneliness, vulnerability, valor, heartache . . . ingrown toenails. War is dropping your rifle and helmet in the ocean, fighting over toilet paper and relieving one's self on ancient aqueducts, shooting men in the name of your dead brother, and always, always, war means blisters. War means a proud limp and hard of hearing. War means war.

No, Hollis Stabler wasn't a hero in World War II, or a hero in the movies. He was just an Omaha Indian soldier who earned the European Theater of Operations Medal with four Bronze Stars—one each for his service in North Africa, Tunisia, Sicily, and at Anzio—and a Silver Star for his fifth campaign in southern France (his brother Bob got the Silver Star, posthumously, for his service at Anzio); a Purple Heart (but never the Oak Leaf Cluster he qualified for); the French Victory Medal; a European-African-Middle Eastern Campaign Medal; an American Defense Service Medal; a World War II Victory Medal; a Combat Infantryman's Badge (sharpshooter and pistol expert); a Bronze Arrowhead; a French Medal of Freedom; and the Honorable Service Lapel Button, World War II. Indeed, he *was* guarded by thunder.[1]

AFTERWORD

★ I wanted to dictate these stories for parents who have children in the service. The other day I was going through some old letters and cards my mother had saved. I found a card I had written to my mother. It said, "Hello Mother, how are you? I am well, your son, Hollis." I am ashamed to have written such a short letter. I am also ashamed because when my parents visited me in New York, they gave me a brand new wristwatch. When I got to Omaha, I sold it for drink. My mother died in 1963 and my father in 1971.

I never told these stories to my wife and my daughter (until much later) or to my mother, but I did tell them to my dad and sons. I felt the women wouldn't want to hear about the war. So I hope some mothers of soldiers will understand if their children don't say much about a war.

I also wanted to write this book to remember some old buddies and friends in the service. Most are not here any longer, but we played, talked, and fought a war together, and I *remember*—their names, even the cities they came from. I think of my sister, Marcella, and of my brother, Bob, who was killed in action in Italy in 1944. I'm glad we talked just before he was killed. As for me, I was no hero, but I knew what to do when things happened. It all seems like yesterday.

All horse troopers will have to go to Fiddler's Green to catch their mounts someday. We will saddle up and move out at the last bugle call. But old friends and buddies will ride together forever.

H.D.S.

APPENDIX

Hollis Stabler Genealogy

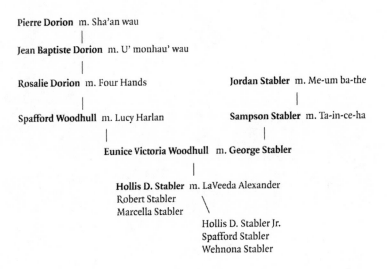

Pierre Dorion m. Sha'an wau

Jean **Baptiste Dorion** m. U' monhau' wau

Rosalie Dorion m. Four Hands

Spafford Woodhull m. Lucy Harlan

Eunice Victoria Woodhull m. **George Stabler**

Jordan Stabler m. Me-um ba-the

Sampson Stabler m. Ta-in-ce-ha

Hollis D. Stabler m. LaVeeda Alexander
Robert Stabler
Marcella Stabler

Hollis D. Stabler Jr.
Spafford Stabler
Wehnona Stabler

Source: Taken from Paul Brill, *Stabler Family Tree* (August 1983); and Hollis D. Stabler, "Family Tree, Chart" (1990), Stabler Family Papers, Walthill, Nebraska.

NOTES

Introduction

1. Elaine M. Nelson, "Eunice Woodhull Stabler, Omaha Indian Writer, 1885–1963" (master's thesis, University of Nebraska, Lincoln, 2004).

2. Theodore Rios and Kathleen Mullen Sands, *Telling a Good One: The Process of a Native American Collaborative Biography* (Lincoln: University of Nebraska Press, 2000), 3.

3. Rios and Sands, *Telling a Good One*, 4.

4. Rios and Sands, *Telling a Good One*, 79–110.

5. Rios and Sands, *Telling a Good One*, 196.

6. Rios and Sands, *Telling a Good One*, 49.

7. Rios and Sands, *Telling a Good One*, 156.

8. Rios and Sands, *Telling a Good One*, 140–41, 166, 217, 225.

9. Rios and Sands, *Telling a Good One*, 227.

10. Devon Abbott Mihesuah, ed., *First To Fight: Henry Mihesuah* (Lincoln: University of Nebraska Press, 2002), xvi, xvii, 17, 21–22, 25–26, 37, 41–42, 48, 70.

11. Mihesuah, *First to Fight*, 33–35.

12. Becky Matthews, ed., *Alma Hogan Snell Grandmother's Grandchild, My Crow Indian Life* (Lincoln: University of Nebraska Press, 2000); Frank Linderman, *Pretty-shield: Medicine Woman of the Crows* (Lincoln: University of Nebraska Press, 1974).

13. Tom Holm, "Fighting a White Man's War: The Extent and Legacy of American Indian Participation in World War II," *Journal of Ethnic Studies* 9, no. 2 (1981): 69–81.

14. William C. Meadows, *The Comanche Code Talkers of World War II* (Austin: University of Texas Press, 2002); Jeré Bishop Franco, *Crossing the Pond: The Native American Effort in World War II*, Vol. 7, War and the Southwest Series (Denton: University of North Texas Press, 1999); Alison Bernstein, *American Indians and World War II: Toward a New Era in Indian Affairs* (Norman: University of Oklahoma Press, 1991); Roderick Red Elk, "Comanche Code Talkers," *Prairie Lore* 27 (1): 113–14; Doris A. Paul, *The Navajo Code Talkers* (Pittsburgh: Dorrance, 1973).

15. Matthews, *Alma Hogan Snell*, 15.

1. *Wanoⁿshe*: Soldier

1. David J. Wishart, *An Unspeakable Sadness: The Dispossession of the Nebraska Indians* (Lincoln: University of Nebraska Press, 1994), 6–8; Hollis D. Stabler, "Hethúshka Warrior Society," Ms., Stabler Family Papers, Walthill NE; Stabler's personal song, as well as those of other Hethúshka Warrior Society members can be heard on *Four Hills of Life* (Whitetail Productions, 2003); Mark J. Awakuni-Swetland, *The Umoⁿhoⁿiye of Elizabeth Stabler: A Vocabulary of the Omaha Language* (Winnebago: Nebraska Indian Press, 1977). According to early documents, Hollis's mother originally gave his middle name as "Andrus." He claims it was changed later in life, and most documents reflect his middle initial as "D."

2. "Enlistment Record, Report of Separation, Honorable Discharge, Hollis D. Stabler, #6934103, Camp Shelby, Mississippi, February 4, 1946," Service Records, Stabler Family Papers, Walthill NE.

3. Information for Stabler family genealogy extracted from Nelson, "Eunice Woodhull Stabler," and Paul Brill, compiler, "Stabler Family Tree" (1983), Ms., Stabler Family Papers, Walthill NE [hereafter cited as Brill, "Family Tree"]. Paul Brill performed extensive Omaha Indian genealogies for enrollment purposes for the Bureau of Indian Affairs in the 1960s-1980s. Unattributed newspaper clipping [n.d.], "Lewis and Clark erred in not hiring Sioux interpreter;" unattributed newspaper clipping [n.d.], "Marker honors first French Yankton settler," September 4, 2002 (the article attributes the thesis to Ron Laycock, at an annual meeting of the Lewis and Clark Trail Heritage Foundation, Stabler Family Papers, Walthill NE. For an alternate account of the founding of Sioux City, see http://www.siouxcityhistory.org/people/more, under "Theophile Brugier." Lewis and Clark's encounter with Dorion can be found in their journals; for an easy reference, see Gary E. Moulton, *Lewis and Clark on the Middle Missouri* (U.S. Department of the Interior. National Park Service [Washington DC: Government Printing Office, 2001]); see also Wishart, *An Unspeakable Sadness*, 1–3.

4. Hollis Stabler, Omaha Indian Elder, interviewed by author, July 7, 2002, Walthill NE, tape recording and transcript, Stabler Family Papers, Walthill NE: 3. According to Nelson, "Eunice Woodhull Stabler," 17, Victoria Woodhull wanted to adopt Long Wing because he was the youngest in the class. His real mother, Rosalie, however, disapproved of the idea, and Woodhull simply sponsored him through the mission.

5. Francis D. La Flesche, *The Middle Five: Indian Schoolboys of the Omaha Tribe* (Lincoln: University of Nebraska Press, 1978.) Alice C. Fletcher and Francis D. La Flesche, *The Omaha Tribe* (Lincoln: University of Nebraska Press, 1911), 633.

6. See "Susan LaFlesche Picotte," http://www.usgennet.org/usa/ne/county/

thurston/susan.html, October 17, 2003; http://www.rootsweb.com/~nethurst/whowhotc.htm.

7. Hollis D. Stabler, interview, July 7, 2002, 2, 17.

8. Hollis D. Stabler, interview, July 7, 2002, 6–7. Hollis gives his mother's age as seven in the original, but subsequent facts place Eunice's age closer to eleven; see Nelson, "Eunice Woodhull Stabler," 1–2.

9. Hollis D. Stabler, interview, July 7, 2002, 9.

10. Hollis D. Stabler, interview, July 7, 2002, 14–15. See also Wishart, An Unspeakable Sadness, 161; for the Omaha's last buffalo hunt see Melvin R. Gilmore, "Methods of Indian Buffalo Hunts, With the Itinerary of the Last Tribal Hunt of the Omaha," in Eugene S. McCartney and Peter Okkelberg, eds., Papers of the Michigan Academy of Science Arts and Letters (Ann Arbor: University of Michigan Press, 1932): 17–32; Mark J. Awakuni-Swetland retraced this route in the late 1990s with Omaha schoolchildren and elders; see Awakuni-Swetland, "Omaha Buffalo Hunters in Wichita County, Kansas, 1876–1999," in History of Wichita County Kansas, Volume 2 (Leoti KS: Wichita County History Association, 2003) 132–38; Omaha World Herald, November 15, 1999; Franklin County [Kansas] Chronicle, November 23, 1999; Web 8 (2): 4–6.

11. Wishart, An Unspeakable Sadness, 230.

12. Hollis D. Stabler, interview, July 7, 2002, 14–15. See also Wishart, An Unspeakable Sadness, 19–20. Eunice's mentor was Susan La Flesche Picotte, an Omaha woman and the first Native American woman to become a physician; see also Valerie Sherer Mathes, "Susan La Flesche Picotte, MD: Nineteenth-Century Physician and Reformer," Great Plains Quarterly 13 (Summer 1993): 172–86, and Benson Tong, Susan La Flesche Picotte, MD: Omaha Indian Leader and Reformer (Norman: University of Oklahoma Press, 1999).

13. Hollis D. Stabler, interview, July 7, 2002, 11–12.

14. Hollis D. Stabler, interview, July 7, 2002, 7.

15. Unattributed newspaper clipping [n.d.], "Woodhull-Stabler," Stabler Family Files, Walthill NE; Woodhull-Stabler wedding invitation, Stabler Family Files, Walthill NE.

16. Hollis D. Stabler, interview, July 7, 2002, 4.

17. Hollis D. Stabler, interview, July 7, 2002, 7–9. Unattributed newspaper clipping [n.d.], "Mr. and Mrs. Geo. Stabler—A Son, born February 9, 1918."

18. W. Roger Buffalohead and Paulette Fairbanks Molin, "A Nucleus of Civilization: American Indian Families at Hampton Institute in the Late Nineteenth Century," Journal of American Indian Education 35, no. 3 (May 1996): 1–20, 10.

19. http://memory.loc.gov/cgi-bin/query/D?hawp: 15; "History of the American West, 1860–1920: Photographs from the Collection of the Denver Public Library," St. John's Church, Hampton, No. OCM40889592.

20. Brill, "Family Tree," Stabler Family Papers, Walthill NE. See also Wishart, *An Unspeakable Sadness*, 117–18, 230.

21. Hollis D. Stabler, interview, July 7, 2002, 29. Unattributed newspaper clipping [n.d.], "Wichita Man Knew Thorpe," Stabler Family Papers, Walthill NE; regarding Thorpe playing semi-pro baseball, and Thorpe returning to Haskell for a demonstration game, see Carter Revard, "Goal to Goal" (June 1998) and Clay Jones, "Thanksgiving" (October 1998) at http://home.epix.net/~landis/thorpe.html 03/29/00. Carlisle Indian School records at this site reflect George Stabler's enrollment there, and indicate the official records are in NARA RG, 75.

22. Hollis D. Stabler, interview, July 7, 2002, 19–20; Nelson, "Eunice Woodhull Stabler," 43, says George was employed at Hanford Hazlewood Cream Company.

23. Hollis D. Stabler, interview, July 7, 2002, 20–21; Nelson, "Eunice Woodhull Stabler," 49, claims the family lived on the corner of 2nd and Sioux Streets.

24. Hollis D. Stabler, interview, July 7, 2002, 21.

25. Hollis D. Stabler, interview, July 7, 2002, 21.

26. Hollis D. Stabler, "The Trolley Car," Ms., 1, January 25, 2003, Stabler Family Papers, Walthill NE.

27. Hollis D. Stabler, interview, July 7, 2002, 21.

28. Hollis D. Stabler, interview, July 7, 2002, 22.

29. Hollis D. Stabler, interview, July 7, 2002, 22.

30. Hollis D. Stabler, interview, July 7, 2002, 22.

31. Hollis D. Stabler, interview, July 7, 2002, 23.

32. Hollis D. Stabler, interview, July 7, 2002, 23.

33. Hollis D. Stabler, interview, July 7, 2002, 23–24.

34. Hollis D. Stabler, interview, July 7, 2002, 24–25.

35. Hollis D. Stabler, interview, July 7, 2002, 24; see also Hollis D. Stabler, Omaha Indian Elder, interviewed by author, July 8, 2002, Walthill NE, Stabler Family Papers, Walthill NE: 1.

36. This story is condensed from two sources: Hollis D. Stabler, interview, July 7, 2002, 26, and Hollis D. Stabler, "Halloween Story, Sioux City, 1925," Ms., Stabler Family Papers, Walthill NE.

37. Hollis D. Stabler, interview, July 7, 2002, 26.

38. Hollis D. Stabler, interview, July 7, 2002, 27.

39. Hollis D. Stabler, interview, July 7, 2002, 27.

40. Hollis D. Stabler, interview, July 7, 2002, 27.

41. Hollis D. Stabler, interview, July 7, 2002, 27; see also Hollis D. Stabler, Omaha Indian Elder, interviewed by author, September 11, 2003, Walthill NE, author's notes.

42. Hollis D. Stabler, interview, July 7, 2002, 28.

43. Hollis D. Stabler, interview, July 8, 2002, 4. Hollis had reversed the order of his father's employment at KU and Haskell in the original interview; it has been corrected here to reflect the facts. A forthcoming article by Benjamin Rader examines the history and implications of the 1926 Haskell powwow. For Haskell Stadium, see also http://www.ljworld.com/section/360/storypr/84876; for Kansas State Memorial Stadium, see http://www.kuathletics.com/facilities info/memorialstadium.

44. Hollis D. Stabler, interview, July 8, 2002, 29; Hollis D. Stabler, interview, September 11, 2003, author's notes.

45. Hollis D. Stabler, interview, July 7, 2002, 30.

46. Hollis D. Stabler, interview, July 7, 2002, 30–31.

47. Hollis D. Stabler, interview, July 7, 2002, 31.

48. Hollis D. Stabler, interview, July 7, 2002, 31–32; Hollis D. Stabler, "Coca-Cola—Bob and I Captured," Ms., Stabler Family Papers, Walthill NE.

49. Hollis D. Stabler, interview, July 7, 2002, 32.

50. Hollis D. Stabler, interview, July 7, 2002, 33.

51. Hollis D. Stabler, "Hethúshka Warrior Society," TMS, August 25, 2003, Stabler Family Papers, Walthill NE, 1.

52. Hollis D. Stabler, interview, July 8, 2002, 5. Nelson, "Eunice Woodhull Stabler," 54–56, 61; see also William E. Unrah, *Mixed-Bloods and Tribal Dissolution: Charles Curtis and the Quest for Indian Identity* (Lawrence: University of Kansas Press, 1989).

53. Hollis D. Stabler, interview, July 8, 2002, 2; Hollis D. Stabler, interview, September 11, 2003, author's notes. Quanah Parker was chief of the Kwahadi band of the Comanches, and the last Comanche leader to agree to reservation life. *Wazházhe* is an Omaha term for the Osage people.

54. Hollis D. Stabler, interview, July 8, 2002, 5.

55. For biography of *Ho-tah-moie*, see Stephen Cobb, Hollis D. Stabler, and Kathy Vander Werff, *La-ta-we-sah (Woman of the Bird Clan): Her Poetry and Prose* (Macy NE: Macy School Press, 1989), 37–48; see also John McKim and Charles Fletcher McComb, Osage Indian Elder, http://www.osage-ncoa.org/pages/john stink.shtml, under "John Stink," and Kenneth Jacob Jump, *The Legend of John Stink* (Pawhuska OK: n.p., 1977).

56. Hollis D. Stabler, interview, July 8, 2002: 5; as it turns out, Hollis's friend Morris Sunrise was one of the original Comanche code talkers and is featured in Meadows, *Comanche Code Talkers*.

57. Hollis D. Stabler, interview, September 11, 2003, author's notes.

58. Hollis D. Stabler, "My First Army Experience, 1937," TMS, Stabler Family Papers, Walthill NE.

59. National Portrait Gallery, *To Color America: Portraits by Weinold Reiss* (Washington DC: Smithsonian Institution Press, 1989), exhibition catalogue, with an

essay by John C. Ewers; Blue Eagle, Acee (1907–1959), Papers and Artwork, at http://www.nmnh.si.edu/naa/guide/_b2.htm#jrg9.

60. Bernstein, *American Indians and World War II*, 44.

61. Stabler, "My First Army Experience, 1937."

62. Hollis D. Stabler, interview, September 11, 2003, author's notes.

63. Hollis D. Stabler, interview, July 8, 2002, 8–9.

64. Hollis D. Stabler, interview, July 8, 2002, 9–10.

65. Hollis D. Stabler, interview, July 8, 2002, 10.

66. Hollis D. Stabler, interview, July 8, 2002, 10.

67. Hollis D. Stabler, interview, July 8, 2002, 10–11.

68. Hollis D. Stabler, interview, July 8, 2002, 12.

69. Hollis D. Stabler, interview, July 8, 2002, 6.

70. Hollis D. Stabler, interview, July 8, 2002, 6; Hollis is documented as having had three months of education at Bacone in a liberal arts program in 1938, "Army of the United States, Separation Qualification Record, February 4, 1946, Captain N. H. Senn, AGD," Stabler Family Papers, Walthill NE.

71. Hollis D. Stabler, interview, July 8, 2002, 6–7.

72. Hollis D. Stabler, interview, July 8, 2002, 7.

73. Hollis D. Stabler, interview, July 8, 2002, 7.

74. Hollis D. Stabler, interview, July 8, 2002, 8; Hollis D. Stabler, interview, September 11, 2003, author's notes.

75. Hollis D. Stabler, interview, July 8, 2002, 12.

76. Hollis D. Stabler, interview, July 8, 2002, 13.

77. Hollis D. Stabler, interview, July 8, 2002, 13.

78. Hollis D. Stabler, Omaha Indian Elder, interview, November 13, 2003, Walthill NE, Stabler Family Papers, Walthill NE: author's notes.

79. Hollis D. Stabler, interview, July 8, 2002, 13–14.

80. Hollis D. Stabler, interview, July 8, 2002, 14.

81. Hollis D. Stabler, interview, July 8, 2002, 15.

82. Hollis D. Stabler, interview, July 8, 2002, 16.

83. Hollis D. Stabler, interview, July 8, 2002, 16.

84. Hollis D. Stabler, interview, July 8, 2002, 17.

85. Hollis D. Stabler, interview, July 8, 2002, 17; see also, "Army of the United States, Separation Qualification Record, Hollis D. Stabler."

86. Hollis D. Stabler, interview, July 8, 2002, 17.

87. Hollis D. Stabler, interview, July 8, 2002, 17.

2. Operation Torch

1. Hollis D. Stabler, "In the Service, Being Indian," March 2003, Stabler Family Papers, Walthill NE.

2. Bernstein, *American Indians and World War II*, 40–43.

3. Bernstein, *American Indians and World War II*.

4. *Indians in the War* (U.S. Department of the Interior. Office of Indian Affairs [Washington DC: Government Printing Office, November 1945]). 1; Bernstein, *American Indians and World War II*, 40–43.

5. http://www.nebraskastudies.org/0800/stories/0801_0103.html, "Nebraskans on the Frontlines," May 22, 2003. U.S. Census Bureau, September 13, 2002; http://media.nara.gov/media/images/28/33/28-3276a.gif, under "The Honor List of Dead and Missing for the State of Nebraska," May 21, 2003.

6. Hollis D. Stabler, "Military Service Beginning in 1939," TMs, Stabler Family Papers, Walthill NE, 1.

7. Stabler, "Military Service," 1; see also, Hollis D. Stabler, Omaha Indian Elder, interviewed by author, August 11, 2002, Walthill NE, tape recording and typescript, Stabler Family Papers, Walthill NE: 14–15.

8. http://www.literature-web.net/stevenson, October 5, 2003.

9. http://www.lib.umd.edu.ARCH/honr219f/1939snfr.html; http://www.treasureislandmuseum.org/treasures/, October 5, 2003.

10. Stabler, "Military Service."

11. Stabler, "Military Service," 1; see also Stabler, "My First Army Experience, 1937," Stabler Family Papers, Walthill NE; Hollis D. Stabler, interview, August 11, 2002, 15–16. According to CTC Edward E. Nugent, USN (Ret.), in "The Forgotten Blimps of World War II," 1–6, blimps played a significant role in patrolling and destroying German submarines during the war. Their main base was in Tillamook, Oregon, several hundred miles north of Hollis's location in San Francisco in 1939, but it is not beyond possibility that a blimp was at March Field. Though it occurred after Hollis's time in the region, Treasure Island was the port of exit for a manned Navy blimp that returned without its crew in 1942. The fate of the crew remains a mystery today; http://www.bluejacket.com/usn_ww2_blimps.html, 9/29/03; see Richard Slotkin, *Gunfighter Nation: The Myth of the Frontier in Twentieth-Century America* (New York: Harper Perennial, 1992), 321, 336, for McLaglen's role in film history.

12. Stabler, "My First War Experiences," 2. Regarding Camp Ord, whose primary use was as an infantry training center, see "Fort Ord, California," 1–8, http://maps.yahoo.com/pdd?ed=4VM2keV.wineKOTnfCJSn.jke5MoYxK.sM2u fkBJZhsf, September 30, 2003.

13. http://www.nps.gov/prsf/history/Spanish_period.htm.

14. Gen. Lucien K. Truscott Jr., *The Twilight of the U.S. Cavalry: Life in the Old Army, 1917–1942* (Lawrence: University Press of Kansas, 1989), 47–48.

15. Truscott, *Twilight*, 47–48; see also "History of the 11th U.S. Cavalry," http://wildgun02.tripod.com/history.html, 1.

16. "History of the 11th U.S. Cavalry."

17. Hollis D. Stabler, "11th Cavalry (Campo)", Ms., Stabler Family Papers, Walthill NE: 2.

18. Stabler, "Campo," 2.

19. "Prayers for Stricken Jane Wyman," unattributed newspaper clipping [n.d.] Stabler Family Papers, Walthill NE.

20. "Ronald Reagan," http://www.wpafb.af.mil/museum/history/wwii/rr_htm, November 11, 2003.

21. Stabler, "Campo," 2–3.

22. Hollis D. Stabler, "11th Cavalry (Salinas)" unpublished manuscript, Stabler Family Papers, Walthill NE, 1.

23. Stabler, "Salinas," 3.

24. Stabler, "Salinas," 3.

25. Stabler, "Salinas," 3; see also Yukio Kawai, "M4A3 Sherman," 1/35 Military Miniature Series, U.S. Medium Tank: 75 mm Gun, Late Model, Tamiya, Inc., 3-Zondawara, Shuzuoka, Japan, Kit #MM-222A, 1.

26. Stabler, "Salinas," 2–3; see also Stabler, "Campo," 4.

27. Les Dershem, "Fiddler's Green," wysiwyg://27/http://hometown.aol.com/cavsgt2107, 1–3, October 17, 2003. Believed to be a sonnet composed by the U.S. Army's Sixth and Seventh Cavalries in the 1870s (original author unknown), it first saw print in *Cavalry Journal*, 1923.

28. Stabler, "Campo."

29. Stabler, "Campo."

30. Stabler, "Campo," 3; see also Stabler, "Salinas," 4.

31. Stabler, "Campo," 3.

32. Stabler, "Campo," 4–5.

33. Mary Lee Stubbs and Stanley Russell Conner, *Armor-Cavalry, Part I: Regular Army and Army Reserve*, Office of the Chief of Military History, Department of the Army (Washington DC: Government Printing Office, 1969), 70.

34. Stubbs and Conner, *Armor-Cavalry*, 70–71; http://jaie.asu.edu/v35/V35S3nuc.htm, under "11th Armored Cavalry (The Blackhorse Regiment): Lineage and Honors Information as of November 2001," September 30, 2003.

35. Hollis D. Stabler, "Bermuda's Train Trip," TMs, Stabler Family Papers, Walthill NE.

36. Stabler, "Bermuda's Train Trip."

37. Hollis D. Stabler, interview, September 11, 2003, author's notes.

38. Stabler, "Campo," 3.

39. Hollis D. Stabler, "Red Dog Poland," TMs by Mark J. Awakuni-Swetland, September 1, 2003, Stabler Family Papers, Walthill NE, 1.

40. Stabler, "Red Dog Poland," 8.

41. Hollis D. Stabler, "Operation Husky, World War II, European Theatre of

Operations, Gela, Italy, July 10, 1943," TMS, Stabler Family Papers, Walthill NE, 8–9.

42. Hollis Stabler, "Operation Torch," TMS by Mark J. Awakuni-Swetland, September 20, 2002, Stabler Family Papers, Walthill NE: 9.

43. Hollis D. Stabler, interview, September 11, 2003, author's notes.

44. Cobb, Stabler, and Vander Werff, La-ta-we-sah, 33–34.

45. Yukio Kawai, "U.S. Light Tank M3Stuart," 1/35 Military Miniature Series, Tamiya, Inc., 3-Zondawara, Shuzuoka, Japan, Item #35042, 1.

46. Hollis D. Stabler, Omaha Indian Elder, interviewed by author, November 20, 2002, tape recording and typescript, Walthill NE, Stabler Family Papers, Walthill NE: 7.

47. Stabler, "Operation Torch," 1; Hollis D. Stabler, interview, November 20, 2002, 7.

48. Donald E. Houston, Hell on Wheels: The 2nd Armored Division (San Raphael CA: Presidio Press, 1977): 131.

49. Houston, Hell on Wheels, 132.

50. Stabler, "Operation Torch," 2.

51. Stabler, "Operation Torch," 2.

52. Stabler, "Operation Torch," 2; unattributed newspaper clipping [n.d.], "Veteran's Memories of Comrade Lost at Sea," Stabler Family Papers, Walthill NE.

53. Stabler, "Operation Torch," 2.

54. Houston, Hell on Wheels, 131–33.

55. Stabler, "Operation Torch,", 2–3. The plane was shot down by antiaircraft fire from the USS Lakehurst; see Houston, Hell on Wheels, 133.

56. Stabler, "Operation Torch," 3. Houston, Hell on Wheels, 134, claims that when Harmon set up headquarters in Safi, it was under sniper fire.

57. Stabler, "Operation Torch," 2.

58. Stabler, "Operation Torch," 2.

59. Stabler, "Operation Torch," 4. Houston, Hell on Wheels, 135, documents this event—"Harmon listened to the old veteran explain that he had done his duty for the French republic"—as having occurred on the march to Casablanca.

60. Stabler, "Operation Torch," 4.

61. Stabler, "Operation Torch," 4.

62. Stabler, "Operation Torch," 4.

63. Houston, Hell on Wheels, 135.

64. Stabler, "Operation Torch," 4–5.

65. Stabler, "Operation Torch," 5.

66. Stabler, "Operation Torch," 5.

67. Stabler, "Operation Torch," 5; see also, Hollis D. Stabler, Omaha Indian Elder, interviewed by author, October 10, 2003, Walthill NE, author's notes.

68. *United States Army Air Forces in World War II: Landings at Fedela*, 1–2, http://www.usaaf.net/ww/vol6pg7.htm, September 29, 2003.

69. Stabler, "Operation Torch," 6.

70. Stabler, "Operation Torch," 6.

71. Stabler, "Operation Torch," 6.

72. Houston, *Hell on Wheels*, 136.

73. Stabler, "Operation Torch," 6.

74. Stabler, "Operation Torch," 6–7.

75. Albert N. Garland, *Sicily and the Surrender of Italy*, Office of the Chief of Military History, Department of the Army (Washington DC: Government Printing Office, 1965), 1–2.

76. Garland, *Sicily*, 1–2.

77. Stabler, "Operation Torch," 7.

78. Stabler, "Operation Torch," 7.

79. Stabler, "Operation Torch," 7–8.

80. Stabler, "Operation Torch," 8.

81. Stabler, "Operation Torch," 8–9.

82. Stabler, "Operation Torch," 9.

83. Stabler, "Operation Torch," 9.

84. Bernstein, *American Indians and World War II*, 40–63; Tom Holm, "Fighting a White Man's War: The Extent and Legacy of American Indian Participation in World War II," *Journal of Ethnic Studies* 9, no. 2 (1981): 69–81.

85. Holm, "Fighting," 71.

86. Houston, *Hell on Wheels*, 144.

87. *Sioux City [Iowa] Journal*, "Operation Torch—Closing the Vice," October 21, 2002.

3. Operation Husky

1. Houston, *Hell on Wheels*, 145; Daniel L. Dean, Untitled article, n.d. Stabler Family Papers, Walthill NE. Dean, the son of a Second Armored Division veteran, passed his article out at a division reunion.

2. Stabler, "Operation Torch," 9.

3. Hollis D. Stabler, Omaha Indian Elder, interviewed by author, December 5, 2002, Walthill NE, tape recording and typescript, Stabler Family Papers, Walthill NE: 2–3.

4. Stabler, "Operation Husky," 1.

5. Stabler, "Operation Torch," 9–10.

6. Hollis D. Stabler, interview, December 5, 2002: 4–5.

7. Stabler, "Operation Torch," 10–11.

8. Stabler, "Operation Torch," 11

9. Garland, *Sicily*, 49.

10. Garland, *Sicily*, 74–75.

11. Stabler, "Operation Husky," 11.

12. Stabler, "Operation Husky," 11.

13. Stabler, "Operation Husky," 11–12.

14. Hollis D. Stabler, interview, December 5, 2002, 10.

15. Hollis D. Stabler, interview, December 5, 2002, 10–11.

16. Hollis D. Stabler, interview, December 5, 2002, 12.

17. Hollis D. Stabler, interview, December 5, 2002, 12.

18. Stabler, "Operation Torch," 11.

19. Rex A. Knight, "Fighting Engineers on Sicily," *World War II* (September, 1999): 50–56.

20. Garland, *Sicily*, 78–79.

21. Garland, *Sicily*, 80–83.

22. Garland, *Sicily*, 82–83.

23. Garland, *Sicily*, 83–87.

24. Garland, *Sicily*, 88–89.

25. Garland, *Sicily*, 89–91.

26. Garland, *Sicily*, 96–97.

27. Stabler, "Operation Torch," 12; also Garland, *Sicily*, 77.

28. "Gela Beach," http://www.army.mil/cmh-pg/Brochures/72–16/72–16. htm, 1–2.

29. Garland, *Sicily*, 103–4.

30. Stabler, "Operation Husky," 1–2.

31. Knight, "Fighting Engineers," 50.

32. Garland, *Sicily*, 119–37.

33. Knight, "Fighting Engineers," 52.

34. Stabler, "Operation Husky," 1–2.

35. Stabler, "Operation Husky," 2.

36. Knight, "Fighting Engineers," 51.

37. Stabler, "Operation Husky," 2.

38. "Gela Beach," 3.

39. "Gela Beach," 3–5.

40. Gordon R. Sullivan, *The U.S. Army Campaigns of World War II: Sicily* (Washington DC: Government Printing Office, 1993), 14.

41. Sullivan, *Army Campaigns: Sicily*, 14–15.

42. "Gela Beach," 8–9.

43. "Gela Beach," 8–9.

44. Stabler, "Operation Husky," 3.

45. "Gela Beach," 5.

46. Garland, *Sicily*, 177.

47. Stabler, "Operation Husky," 4.

48. Stabler, "Operation Husky," 4.

49. Stabler, "Operation Husky," 4.

50. Stabler, "Operation Husky," 3–4.

51. Stabler, "Operation Husky," 4.

52. Stabler, "Operation Husky," 4.

53. Stabler, "Operation Husky," 4–5.

54. "Gela Beach," 13–18.

55. Stabler, "Operation Husky," 6–7.

56. Stabler, "Operation Husky," 6–7.

57. Stabler, "Operation Husky," 5.

58. Garland, Sicily, 168–69.

59. Stabler, "Operation Husky," 5.

60. Stabler, "Operation Husky," 5–6.

61. Stabler, "Operation Husky," 6.

62. Stabler, "Operation Husky," 6.

63. Sullivan, Army Campaigns: Sicily, 13–14.

64. Sullivan, Army Campaigns: Sicily, 14–15.

65. Sullivan, Army Campaigns: Sicily, 14–15.

66. Sullivan, Army Campaigns: Sicily, 16–17.

67. Sullivan, Army Campaigns: Sicily, 18–21.

68. Stabler, "Operation Husky," 6–7.

9. Stabler, "Operation Husky," 7.

70. Bernstein, American Indians and World War II, 58

71. Stabler, "The Recreation Incident," TMS, August 2003, Stabler Family Papers, Walthill NE.

72. Stabler, "Operation Husky," 7.

73. Stabler, "Operation Husky," 7.

74. Stabler, "Operation Husky," 7.

75. Sullivan, Army Campaigns: Sicily, 22–24.

76. Hollis D. Stabler, interview, December 10, 2002, 1.

77. "Gela Beach," 5–7; Sullivan, Army Campaigns: Sicily, 25–27.

78. Cobb, Stabler, and Vander Werff, La-ta-we-sah, 30; Eunice Woodhull Stabler's How Beautiful the Land of My Forefathers (Wichita KS: Wichita Eagle Press, 1943) is reprinted in full in Cobb, Stabler, and Vander Werff, La-ta-we-sah.

4. Operation Shingle

1. Portions of Hollis Stabler's Anzio memoirs have been previously published in Hollis D. Stabler et al., We Remember World War II: A Collection of U.S. Army Ranger Stories (Elk River MN: Meadowlark, 2003); Hollis heard about Nero while stationed in Italy (see Hollis D. Stabler, Omaha Indian Elder, Walthill

NE, interviewed by author, April, 2, 2003, tape recording and transcript, Stabler Family Papers, Walthill NE: 4); as to the truth of Nero's actions, it lies beyond the scope of this book to determine.

2. "Anzio Beachhead: The Anzio Landing (January 22–29)" http://www.army.mil/cmh-pg/books/wwii/anziobeach/anzio-landing.htm, 1, October 10, 2003.

3. Hollis D. Stabler, "Anzio, Italy, 1944," TMS, Stabler Family Papers, Walthill NE: 1.

4. Stabler, "Anzio," 1; for information on World War II uniforms, see Philip Katcher, The U.S. Army, 1941–45, with color plates by C. L. Doughty. Men at Arms Series, ed. Martin Windrow (London: Osprey, 1977), as well as other titles by Katcher.

5. Hollis D. Stabler, interview, December 10, 2002, 2.

6. Hollis D. Stabler, interview, December 10, 2002, 2; see also, "Sam One Skunk, 4th H.Q., 4th Ranger Battalion . . ." (Handwritten note on cover), file compiled from unattributed collection of One Skunk clippings, Stabler Family Papers, Walthill NE.

7. "Sam One Skunk." One Skunk passed away January 29, 1979, at the Fort Meade Veteran's Hospital in Sturgis, South Dakota; his pallbearers included World War II Indian and Ranger veterans. The topic of Indians as portrayed by journalists of the era is long overdue for scholarly study.

8. Hollis D. Stabler, interview, December 10, 2002, 2; Stabler, "Anzio," 1.

9. "Anzio Beachhead," http://www.army.mil/cmh-pg/books/wwii/anzio-landing.htm, 8.

10. "Anzio Beachhead," 8–9.

11. Hollis D. Stabler, interview, December 10, 2002, 2–3; Stabler, "Anzio," 1; Hollis D. Stabler, interview, October 10, 2002, author's notes.

12. Hollis D. Stabler, interview, December 10, 2002; Stabler, "Anzio," 1.

13. Hollis D. Stabler, interview, December 10, 2002, 4.

14. Hollis D. Stabler, interview, December 10, 2002, 4–5.

15. Hollis D. Stabler, interview, December 10, 2002, 5–6.

16. Hollis D. Stabler, interview, December 10, 2002, 5–6.

17. "Anzio Beachhead," 9–10.

18. Hollis D. Stabler, interview, December 10, 2002, 6.

19. Hollis D. Stabler, interview, December 10, 2002, 6.

20. Hollis D. Stabler, interview, December 10, 2002, 7.

21. Hollis D. Stabler, interview, December 10, 2002, 7.

22. Stabler, "Anzio," 2.

23. Stabler, "Anzio," 3.

24. U.S. Army Ranger Association, Inc., "Ranger Roy Murray, 1910–1998," 1–4, http://www.ranger.org.usara/s1/memoriam/murray_memoriam.htm, October 13, 2003.

25. Hollis D. Stabler, interview, December 10, 2002, 8.

26. Hollis D. Stabler, interview, December 10, 2002, 8.

27. Stabler, "Anzio," 3; Hollis D. Stabler, interview, December 10, 2002, 8–9.

28. Stabler, "Anzio," 3.

29. Stabler, "Anzio," 3; Hollis D. Stabler, interview, December 10, 2002, 8–10.

30. Stabler, "Anzio," 3–4. Robert D. Stabler, Cavalry Third Reconnaissance Troop, Third Infantry Division, killed in action at Cisterna, Italy, January 31, 1944, buried at Nettano, Italy, and later returned to Pawhuska, Oklahoma on July 30, 1948; from various unattributed newspaper clippings [n.d.], Stabler Family Papers, Walthill NE.

31. "Obituary: Robert D. Stabler," unattributed newspaper clipping [n.d.], Stabler Family Papers, Walthill NE; "Wichita Brothers Reported Killed, Wounded in Fighting," *Wichita Beacon*, April 4, 1944, Stabler Family Papers, Walthill NE.

32. Stabler, "Anzio," 4; "Wichita Brothers Reported Killed."

33. "Wichita Brothers Reported Killed."

34. Stabler, "Anzio," 4; Hollis D. Stabler, interview, December 10, 2002, 13–14.

35. Stabler, "Anzio," 5; Hollis D. Stabler, interview, December 10, 2002, 14.

36. Hollis D. Stabler, "Bayonet Charge" (handwritten addendum to Stabler, "Anzio").

37. Stabler, "Bayonet Charge"; Hollis D. Stabler, interview, December 10, 2002, 15.

38. Stabler, "Anzio," 5.

39. Hollis D. Stabler, interview, December 10, 2002, 17–18.

40. Hollis D. Stabler, interview, December 10, 2002, 17–18.

41. Hollis D. Stabler, interview, December 10, 2002, 18.

42. Hollis D. Stabler, interview, December 10, 2002, 18.

43. Hollis D. Stabler, interview, December 10, 2002, 18–19.

44. Hollis D. Stabler, interview, December 10, 2002, 19.

45. Hollis D. Stabler, interview, December 10, 2002, 19.

46. Hollis D. Stabler, interview, December 10, 2002, 20.

47. Hollis D. Stabler, interview, December 10, 2002, 20.

48. Hollis D. Stabler, interview, December 10, 2002, 21.

49. Hollis D. Stabler, interview, December 10, 2002, 21.

50. Hollis D. Stabler, interview, December 10, 2002, 21; see also, Bob Barnard, "A Busy Night in Italy, 1944" (addendum to Stabler, "Anzio,"), 9–10. Hollis's friend Barnard had enlisted at the same time as Hollis, and they shared the train ride to Hamilton Field together. They later reunited and correspond regularly.

51. Stabler, "Anzio," 10; Hollis D. Stabler, interview, December 10, 2002, 21–22.

52. Stabler, "Anzio," 10; Hollis D. Stabler, interview, December 10, 2002, 22.

53. Stabler, "Anzio," 10; Hollis D. Stabler, interview, December 10, 2002, 23.

54. Hollis D. Stabler, interview, December 10, 2002, 24.

55. Hollis D. Stabler, interview, December 10, 2002, 24.

56. Hollis D. Stabler, interview, December 10, 2002, 25.

57. Stabler, "Anzio," 5; Hollis D. Stabler, interview, December 10, 2002, 25–26.

58. Stabler, "Anzio," 6.

59. Stabler, "Anzio," 6; Hollis D. Stabler, interview, December 10, 2002, 26–27.

60. Stabler, "Anzio," 6; Hollis D. Stabler, interview, December 10, 2002, 27.

61. Stabler, "Anzio," 6–7.

62. Stabler, "Anzio," 7; Hollis D. Stabler, interview, December 10, 2002, 27.

63. Stabler, "Anzio," 7.

64. Stabler, "Anzio," 7; Hollis D. Stabler, interview, December 10, 2002, 30.

65. Stabler, "Anzio," 7–8.

66. "Citation for Indian Service Nurse," unattributed news clipping [n.d.], Stabler Family Papers, Walthill NE; it is not clear from the evidence whether Wood was Indian or white.

67. Stabler, "Anzio," 8.

68. Stabler, "Anzio," 8.

69. Stabler, "Anzio," 8.

70. Stabler, "Anzio," 8; Hollis D. Stabler, Omaha Indian Elder, interviewed by author, November 13, 2003, Walthill NE, author's notes.

71. Stabler, "Anzio," 9.

72. Stabler, "Anzio," 9.

73. Hollis D. Stabler to Eunice Woodhull Stabler, January 16, 1944, Stabler Family Papers, Walthill NE. Eunice kept records of both of her sons' wartime experiences.

74. Hollis D. Stabler to Eunice Woodhull Stabler, April 25, 1944, Stabler Family Papers, Walthill NE.

75. Brigadier General Robert H. Dunlop, Acting Adjutant General, Washington DC, May 29, 1944, to Eunice Woodhull Stabler; Brig. Gen. Dunlop to Eunice Woodhull Stabler, April 29, 1944; Brig. Gen. Dunlop to Senator Hugh Butler, May 2, 1944; all Stabler Family Papers, Walthill NE.

76. Hollis D. Stabler to Eunice Woodhull Stabler, May 4, 1944, Stabler Family Papers, Walthill NE.

77. Brig. Gen. Dunlop to Eunice Woodhull Stabler, May 29, 1944.

78. Hollis D. Stabler to Victoria Smith, phone interview, May 2004.

79. "What Went Wrong at Anzio?," unattributed contemporary newspaper clipping [n.d., though apparently clipped during the early months of 1944], Stabler Family Papers, Walthill N E: "Heavy, gooey mud has clamped our tanks and other armored vehicles into inactivity . . . and Nazi troop and artillery concentrations operate in efficient fashion."

5. Operation Anvil/Dragoon

1. "Operation Anvil," http:www.multimanpublishing.com//pp/anvil.html., 2, October 17, 2003.

2. Wayne M. Dzwonchyk, "Coastline's Quiet Shattered," *World War II* (May 1986): 1–2, 16–25.

3. Dzwonchyk, "Coastline's Quiet Shattered," 1–2, 16–25.

4. Alan F. Wilt, *The French Riviera Campaign of August 1944* (Carbondale: Southern Illinois University Press, 1981): 46–50; Hollis D. Stabler, "Anvil, World War II, European Theatre of Operations, August 15, 1944," TMs by Mark J. Awakuni-Swetland, March 14, 2003, Stabler Family Papers, Walthill N E: 3.

5. Wilt, *French Riviera Campaign*, 56.

6. Dzwonchyk, "Coastline's Quiet Shattered," 18–19; Wilt, *French Riviera Campaign*, 60, contends that the name was changed for security purposes.

7. Dzywonchyk, "Coastline's Quiet Shattered," 19; Wilt, *French Riviera Campaign*, 70.

8. Hollis D. Stabler, "Anvil," 1. Hollis Stabler, Omaha Indian Elder, Walthill N E, interviewed by author, April 1, 2003, No. 1, tape recording and typescript, Stabler Family Papers, Walthill N E: 30.

9. Hollis D. Stabler, interview, April 1, 2003, No. 1, 31.

10. Hollis D. Stabler, interview, April 1, 2003, No. 1, 31.

11. Stabler, "Anvil," 2.

12. Stabler, "Anvil," 2; Hollis D. Stabler, interview, April 1, 2003, No. 1, 31–32.

13. Stabler, "Anvil," 2; Hollis D. Stabler, interview, April 1, 2003, No. 1, 31–32.

14. Wilt, *French Riviera Campaign*, 70; Dzwonchyk, "Coastline's Quiet Shattered," 18.

15. Stabler, "Anvil," 2; Hollis D. Stabler, interview, April 1, 2003, No. 1, 31–32; see also Tom Holm, "Fighting a White Man's War: The Extent and Legacy of American Indian Participation in World War II," *Journal of Ethnic Studies* 9, no. 2 (1981): 69–81, 71, 80n16. Holm can be credited with one of the first analyses of Indians in World War II written by an Indian veteran and scholar.

16. Dzwonchyk, "Coastline's Quiet Shattered," 19; Wilt, *French Riviera Campaign*, 89.

17. Stabler, "Anvil," 31–32.

18. Stabler, "Anvil," 31–32.

19. Stabler, "Anvil," 31–32; Hollis D. Stabler, interview, April 1, 2003, No. 1, 33.

20. Stabler, "Anvil," 2–3; Hollis D. Stabler, interview, April 1, 2003, No. 1, 34.

21. Stabler, "Anvil," 3; Hollis D. Stabler, interview, April 1, 2003, No. 1, 34.

22. Stabler, "Anvil," 3.

23. Hollis D. Stabler, interview, April 1, 2003, No. 1, 34.

24. Stabler, "Anvil," 3.

25. Dzwonchyk, "Coastline's Quiet Shattered," 19.

26. Stabler, "Anvil," 3; Hollis D. Stabler, interview, April 1, 2003, No. 1, 34–35.

27. Stabler, "Anvil," 3.

28. Stabler, "Anvil," 3.

29. Stabler, "Anvil," 3–4.

30. Stabler, "Anvil," 4.

31. Stabler, "Anvil," 4.

32. Stabler, "Anvil," 4.

33. Stabler, "Anvil," 4.

34. Stabler, "Anvil," 4; Hollis Stabler, Omaha Indian Elder, interviewed by author, April 1, 2003, No. 2, tape recording and typescript, Stabler Family Papers, Walthill NE: 1.

35. Hollis D. Stabler, interview, December 10, 2002, 39.

36. Stabler, "Anvil," 4–5.

37. "Côte d'Azur-Îles D'Hyères-Porquerolles," http://www.jack-travel.com/CoteAzur, 1–4, October 17, 2003; Jacques Robichon, The Second D-Day, translated from the French by Barbara Shuey (New York: Walker and Company, 1962), 254.

38. Dzwonchyk, "Coastline's Quiet Shattered," 23.

39. Dzwonchyk, "Coastline's Quiet Shattered," 21.

40. Dzwonchyk, "Coastline's Quiet Shattered," 21.

41. Dzwonchyk, "Coastline's Quiet Shattered," 19–21.

42. Dzwonchyk, "Coastline's Quiet Shattered," 22.

43. Hollis D. Stabler, interview, December 10, 2003, 41–42.

44. Wilt, French Riviera Campaign, 89.

45. "Grasse—Arriving in the City," http://www.jack-travel.com/CoteAzur, 1–3, October 17, 2003.

46. Stabler, "Anvil," 5; Hollis D. Stabler, interview, December 10, 2003, 42.

47. Stabler, "Anvil," 5; Hollis D. Stabler, interview, April 1, 2003, No. 2, 2–3; Hollis D. Stabler, interview, December 10, 2003, 43.

48. Stabler, "Anvil," 5; Hollis D. Stabler, interview, April 1, 2003, No. 2, 2–3; Hollis D. Stabler, interview, December 10, 2003, 43; "de Gaulle, Charles (-André-Marie-Joseph) 1890–1970," http://search.biography.com, 18, November 2003.

49. Hollis D. Stabler, interview, April 1, 2003, No. 2, 3; Hollis D. Stabler, interview, December 10, 2002, 43.

50. Stabler, "Anvil," 5; Hollis D. Stabler, interview, December 10, 2002, 43.

51. Hollis D. Stabler, interview, April 1, 2003, No. 2, 3.

52. Dzwonchyk, "Coastline's Quiet Shattered," 24.

53. Dzwonchyk, "Coastline's Quiet Shattered," 24–25.

54. Stabler, "Anvil," 5–6; Hollis D. Stabler, interview, April 1, 2003, No. 2, 4.

55. Hollis D. Stabler, interview, April 1, 2003, No. 2, 4.

56. Stabler, "Anvil," 6; Hollis D. Stabler, interview, April 1, 2003, No. 2, 4.

57. Stabler, "Anvil," 6; Hollis D. Stabler, interview, April 1, 2003, No. 2, 5.

58. Stabler, "Anvil," 6; Hollis D. Stabler, interview, April 1, 2003, No. 2, 5.

59. Hollis D. Stabler, interview, December 10, 2002, 45.

60. Stabler, "Anvil," 6.

61. Stabler, "Anvil," 6; Hollis D. Stabler, interview, December 10, 2002, 46.

62. Hollis D. Stabler, interview, April 1, 2003, No. 2, 5–6; Hollis D. Stabler, interview, December 10, 2002, 46.

63. Wilt, French Riviera Campaign, 144.

64. Stabler, "Anvil," 6–7; Hollis D. Stabler, interview, April 1, 2003, No. 2, 6.

65. Stabler, "Anvil," 7; Hollis D. Stabler, interview, December 10, 2002, 46–47.

66. Stabler, "Anvil," 7.

67. Stabler, "Anvil," 7.

68. Stabler, "Anvil," 7.

69. Stabler, "Anvil," 7; Hollis D. Stabler, interview, December 10, 2002, 48.

70. Stabler, "Anvil," 7; Hollis D. Stabler, interview, December 10, 2002, 48.

71. Hollis D. Stabler, interview, April 1, 2003, No. 2, 8.

72. Hollis D. Stabler, interview, December 10, 2002, 49; an extensive search of the Internet fails to reveal a Hotel Plesene in Nice (through December 2004).

73. Stabler, "Anvil," 7; Hollis D. Stabler, interview, December 10, 2002, 48–49; Hollis D. Stabler, interview, April 1, 2003, No. 2, 8.

74. Hollis D. Stabler, interview, December 10, 2002, 50–51.

75. Hollis D. Stabler, interview, December 10, 2002, 49–50.

76. Hollis D. Stabler, interview, April 1, 2003, No. 2, 8–9; "Overview of Grenoble," http://www.fromme . . . m/destinations/grenoble, November 19, 2003.

77. Wilt, French Riviera Campaign, 159.

78. Wilt, French Riviera Campaign, 160; Robichon, Second D-Day, 296.

79. Sen. Hugh Butler to Eunice Woodhull Stabler, October 31, 1944, Stabler Family Papers, Walthill NE.

80. Brig. Gen. Edward F. Witsell, Acting Adjutant General, to Senator Hugh Butler, November 16, 1944, Stabler Family Papers, Walthill NE.

81. Stabler, "Anvil," 7–8; Hollis D. Stabler, interview, October 10, 2003, author's notes.

82. Stabler, "Anvil," 8.

6. *Tígthe*: Home

1. Hollis Stabler, Omaha Indian Elder, interviewed by author, October 9, 2003, Walthill NE, Stabler Family Papers, Walthill NE: 1.

2. Hollis D. Stabler, interview, November 14, 2003, author's notes.

3. Hollis D. Stabler to Eunice Woodhull Stabler, December 26, 1944 (Monte Carlo), Stabler Family Papers, Walthill NE.

4. Hollis D. Stabler, interview, October 9, 2003, 1; Hollis D. Stabler, interview, August 12, 2003, author's notes.

5. Hollis D. Stabler, interview, October 9, 2003, 1.

6. Hollis D. Stabler, interview, October 9, 2003, 1.

7. Hollis D. Stabler, interview, October 9, 2003, 1–2.

8. Beth Bailey and David Farber, "Hotel Street: Prostitution and the Politics of War," *Radical History Review* 52 (1992): 54–77; while this article specifically discusses prostitution in Hawaii in World War II, it can be presumed, in many respects, to be representative of situation over the entire theater of operations.

9. Bailey and Farber, "Hotel Street," 66, 77n13.

10. Bailey and Farber, "Hotel Street," 66, 77n13.

11. Bailey and Farber, "Hotel Street," 54, 58, 60, 66, 77n13.

12. Hollis D. Stabler, interview, October 9, 2003, 2; see also unattributed newspaper clipping [n.d.], James Denney, "Omaha Indian Hollis Stabler: He Hears the Indians' Call," 10–12; and unattributed typescript biography [n.d.], "In 1942 Hollis landed in North Africa . . . ," both in Stabler Family Papers, Walthill NE.

13. Jeré Bishop Franco, *Crossing the Pond: The Native American Effort in World War II* (Denton: University of North Texas Press, 1999) 194–99; Bernstein, *American Indians and World War II*, 136.

14. Hollis D. Stabler, interview, October 9, 2003, 2.

15. Hollis D. Stabler, interview, October 9, 2003, 2.

16. Hollis D. Stabler, interview, October 9, 2003, 2–3.

17. Hollis D. Stabler, interview, October 9, 2003, 3.

18. Hollis D. Stabler, interview, October 9, 2003, 3; Hollis D. Stabler, interview, August 12, 2003, author's notes.

19. Hollis D. Stabler, interview, October 9, 2003, 3.

20. Hollis D. Stabler, interview, November 13, 2003, author's notes.

21. Hollis D. Stabler, interview, October 9, 2003, 3–4.

22. Hollis D. Stabler, interview, October 9, 2003, 4; regarding substandard housing and Indians in the city, see Bernstein, *American Indians and World War II*, 79.

23. For Indians and the postwar economy, see Bernstein, *American Indians and World War II*, 132–58.

24. Hollis D. Stabler, interview, October 9, 2003, 4.

25. Bernstein, *American Indians and World War II*, 75.

26. Hollis D. Stabler, interview, October 9, 2003, 4.

27. Hollis D. Stabler, interview, October 9, 2003, 4–5.

28. Hollis D. Stabler, interview, October 9, 2003, 5.

29. Hollis D. Stabler, interview, October 9, 2003, 5.

30. Hollis D. Stabler, interview, October 9, 2003, 5.

31. Hollis D. Stabler, interview, October 9, 2003, 5.

32. Hollis D. Stabler, interview, October 9, 2003, 5.

33. Hollis D. Stabler, interview, October 9, 2003, 6.

34. Franco, *Crossing the Pond*, 199.

35. Bernstein, *American Indians and World War II*, 142–44.

36. Hollis D. Stabler, interview, October 9, 2003, 6.

37. Hollis D. Stabler, Omaha Indian Elder, interviewed by author, November 21, 2002, Walthill NE, Stabler Family Papers, Walthill NE: 18–19.

38. Hollis D. Stabler, interview, November 21, 2002, 19, 21.

39. Hollis D. Stabler, interview, October 9, 2002, 6.

40. Hollis D. Stabler, interview, October 9, 2003, 6–7.

41. Hollis D. Stabler, interview, November 21, 2002, 23.

42. Hollis D. Stabler, interview, November 21, 2002, 7.

43. Hollis D. Stabler, interview, November 21, 2002, 22.

44. Hollis D. Stabler, interview, November 21, 2002, 22.

45. Hollis D. Stabler, interview, November 21, 2002, 22.

46. Hollis D. Stabler, interview, November 21, 2002, 7–8.

47. Hollis D. Stabler, interview, November 21, 2002, 8.

48. Hollis D. Stabler, interview, November 21, 2002, 8.

49. Hollis D. Stabler, interview, November 21, 2002, 8.

50. Hollis D. Stabler, interview, November 21, 2002, 8–9.

51. Hollis D. Stabler, interview, November 21, 2002, 9.

52. Hollis D. Stabler, interview, November 21, 2002, 9.

53. Hollis D. Stabler, interview, November 21, 2002, 9.

54. Hollis D. Stabler, interview, November 21, 2002, 9.

55. Hollis D. Stabler, interview, November 21, 2002, 9–10.

56. Hollis D. Stabler, interview, November 21, 2002, 10.

57. Hollis D. Stabler, interview, November 21, 2002, 10.

58. Hollis D. Stabler, interview, November 21, 2002, 10.

59. The standard reference for postwar urban Indian experiences is Donald Fixico, *Termination and Relocation* (Albuquerque: University of New Mexico Press, 1986); see also Bernstein, *American Indians and World War II*, 158; see also, the unattributed biography [n.d.] of Hollis Stabler, "In 1942 Hollis landed in North Africa . . . ," typescript, Stabler Family Papers, Walthill NE: 1.

60. "In 1942 Hollis landed in North Africa . . . ," 2.

61. Hollis D. Stabler, interview, October 9, 2003, 10; "In 1942 Hollis landed in North Africa . . . ," 2; Denney, "Omaha Indian Hollis Stabler," 2.

62. Hollis D. Stabler, interview, October 9, 2003, 10.

63. Hollis D. Stabler, interview, October 9, 2003, 10.

64. Colleen Flores, Omaha tribal member, May 1–2, 2003, interviewed by author, Lincoln NE, author's notes; LaVeeda was adopted by Ted Morris, a member of the Hó[n]ga clan; see "In 1942 Hollis landed in North Africa . . . ," 1.

65. Hollis D. Stabler, interview, November 13, 2003, author's notes.

66. Hollis is still active in the Second Armored Division Association and the Fourth Ranger Battalion Association.

67. Unattributed obituary [n.d.], "LaVeeda Stabler," Stabler Family Papers, Walthill NE.

68. Hollis D. Stabler to Ellis Whitley, February 8, 2000, Stabler Family Papers, Walthill NE.

69. Hollis D. Stabler, "Biography," February 2003, TMs, Stabler Family Papers, Walthill NE: 2.

7. Conclusion

1. Authorization for Issuance of Awards, National Personnel Records Center to Hollis D. Stabler, Service Number 6-934-103, October 9, 2001; Hollis D. Stabler, interview, November 13, 2003, author's notes; Hollis's and Bob's awards are among Hollis's extensive material collections at his home in Walthill NE.

BIBLIOGRAPHY

Primary Sources

Stabler Family Papers, Walthill, Nebraska

Unpublished Manuscripts

Barnard, Bob. "A Busy Night in Italy, 1944." TMS.

Stabler, Hollis D. "11th Cavalry (Campo)." Ms.

———. "11th Cavalry (Salinas)." Ms.

———. "Anvil, World War II, European Theatre of Operations, August 15, 1944." TMS.

———. "Anzio, Italy, 1944." TMS.

———. "Bayonet Charge." Ms.

———. "Bermuda's Train Trip." TMS.

———. "Coca-Cola Bob and I Captured." Ms.

———. "Halloween Story, Sioux City, 1925." Ms.

———. "Hethúshka." TMS.

———. "Hethúshka Warrior Society." Ms.

———. "In the Service, Being Indian." Ms.

———. "Military Service, Beginning in 1939." TMS.

———. "My First Army Experience, 1937." TMS.

———. "Operation Husky, World War II, European Theatre of Operations: Gela, Sicily, July 10, 1943." TMS.

———. "Operation Torch." TMS.

———. "Red Dog Poland." TMS.

———. "The Recreation Incident." TMS.

———. "Sam One Skunk, 4th H.Q., 4th Ranger Battalion . . ." File.

———. "The Trolley Car." Ms.

Interviews

All interviews were conducted by the author at Walthill, Nebraska, unless otherwise indicated.

Stabler, Hollis D., Omaha Indian Elder. Interview by Victoria Smith, 7 July 2002. Tape recording and typescript.

———. August 11, 2002.

———. November 20, 2002.

———. November 21, 2002.

———. December 5, 2002.

———. December 10, 2002

———. April 1, 2003, No. 1.

———. April 1, 2003, No. 2.

———. September 11, 2003 (*by telephone*).

———. May 2, 2003 (*by telephone*).

———. August 12, 2003 (*by telephone*).

———. October 10, 2003 (*by telephone*).

———. November 13, 2003 (*by telephone*).

———. November 14, 2003 (*by telephone*).

Flores, Colleen. Omaha Tribal Member. Lincoln, Nebraska. Interviewed by the author, May 12, 2003.

Miscellaneous

Brill, Paul. "Stabler Family Tree." (August 1983).

Dean, Daniel L. Untitled Article distributed at Second Armored Division reunion, date unknown.

Four Hills of Life. Whitetail Productions. 2003. Compact disc.

Kawai, Yukio. "U.S. Light Tank M3Stuart: 1/35 Military Miniature Series." Tamiya, Inc. 3-Zondawar, Shzuoka, Japan, Item # 35042, 1.

"M4A3 Sherman," 1/35 Military Miniature Series, U.S. Medium Tank: 75mm Gun. Late Model, Tamiya,Inc., Kit No. MM-222A, 1.

Sam One Skunk. File.

Service Records. File.

Enlistment Record, Report of Separation, Honorable Discharge, Hollis D. Stabler Service No. 6934103, Camp Shelby, Mississippi, 4 February 1946.

Army of the United States, Separation Qualification Record, February 4, 1946.

Authorization for Issuance of Awards, National Personnel Records Center to Hollis D. Stabler, October 9, 2001.

Stabler, Hollis D. "Omaha Tribal Circle." Sketch with text.

———. "Stabler Family Tree." Compiled June 22, 1990. Pender, Nebraska.

Unattributed [n.d.]. "Biography of Hollis Stabler: In 1942 Hollis landed in North Africa . . ."

Secondary Sources

Awakuni-Swetland, Mark J. "Omaha Buffalo Hunters in Wichita County Kansas, 1876–1999." History of Wichita County Kansas 2, Leoti KS: Wichita County Historical Association, 132–38.

Awakuni-Swetland, Mark J., Compiler, and Elizabeth Stabler. The Umonhoniye of Elizabeth Stabler: A Vocabulary of the Omaha Language. Winnebago: Nebraska Indian Press, 1977.

Bailey, Beth, and David Farber. "Hotel Street: Prostitution and the Politics of War." Radical History Review 52 (1992): 54–77.

Bernstein, Alison R. American Indians and World War II: Toward a New Era in Indian Affairs. Norman: University of Oklahoma Press, 1991.

Buffalohead, W. Roger, and Paulette Fairbanks Molin. "A Nucleus of Civilization: American Indian Families at Hampton Institute in the Late Nineteenth Century." Journal of American Indian Education 35, no. 3 (May 1996): 1–20.

Cobb, Stephen, Hollis D. Stabler, and Kathy Vander Werff. La-ta-we-sah (Woman of the Bird Clan): Her Poetry and Prose. Macy NE: Macy School Press, 1989.

Dzwonchyk, Wayne M. "Coastline's Quiet Shattered." World War II (May 1986): 16–25.

Fletcher, Alice C., and Francis La Flesche. The Omaha Tribe. Lincoln: University of Nebraska Press, 1911.

Franco, Jeré Bishop. Crossing the Pond: The Native American Effort in World War II. Denton: University of North Texas Press, 1999.

Fixico, Donald. Termination and Relocation. Albuquerque: University of New Mexico Press, 1986.

Garland, Albert N. Sicily and the Surrender of Italy. Office of the Chief of Military History, Department of the Army. Washington DC: Government Printing Office, 1965.

Gilmore, Melvin R. Methods of Indian Buffalo Hunts, with the Itinerary of the Last Tribal Hunt of the Omaha. Papers of the Michigan Academy of Science, Arts and Letters, ed. Eugene S. McCartney and Peter Okkelberg. Ann Arbor: University of Michigan Press, 1932.

Griffo, Pietro, and Leonard von Matt. Gela: The Ancient Greeks in Sicily. Greenwich CT: New York Graphic Society, 1968.

Holm, Tom. "Fighting a White Man's War: The Extent and Legacy of American Indian Participation in World War II." Journal of Ethnic Studies 9, no. 2 (1981): 69–81.

Huston, Donald E. Hell on Wheels: The 2nd Armored Division. San Raphael CA: Presidio Press, 1977.

Jump, Kenneth Jacob. *The Legend of John Stink*. Pawhuska OK: n.p., 1977.

Katcher, Philip R. N. *The U.S. Army 1941–45*. Text by Philip Kather; color plates by C. L. Doughty. London: Osprey, 1977.

Knight, Rex A. "Fighting Engineers in Sicily." *World War II* (September 1999).

Kredel, Fritz, and Todd, Frederick P. *Soldiers of the American Army, 1775–1941*. Text by Frederick P. Todd, drawings by Fritz Kredel, with a foreword by Brig. Gen. Oliver L. Spaulding. New York: H. Bittner and Company, 1941 [reprinted as *Soldiers of the American Army, 1775–1954*. Chicago: H. Regnery Co., 1954].

La Flesche, Frances D. *The Middle Five: Indian Schoolboys of the Omaha Tribe*. Foreword by David A. Baerris. Lincoln: University of Nebraska Press, 1978.

Linderman, Frank. *Pretty-shield: Medicine Woman of the Crows*. Lincoln: University of Nebraska Press, 1974.

Mathes, Valerie Sherer. "Susan La Flesche Picotte, MD: Nineteenth-Century Physician and Reformer." *Great Plains Quarterly* 13 (Summer 1993): 172–86.

Moulton, Gary S. *Lewis and Clark on the Middle Missouri*. U.S. Department of the Interior. National Park Service. Washington DC: 2001.

Matthews, Becky, Ed. *Alma Hogan Snell: Grandmother's Grandchild, My Crow Indian Life*. Lincoln: University of Nebraska Press, 2000.

Meadows, William C. *The Comanche Code Talkers of World War II*. Austin: University of Texas Press, 2002.

Mihesuah, Devon Abbott, Ed. *First to Fight: Henry Mihesuah*. Lincoln: University of Nebraska Press, 2002.

Nelson, Elaine M. "Eunice Woodhull Stabler, Omaha Indian Writer, 1885–1963." Master's Thesis. University of Nebraska, Lincoln, 2004.

National Portrait Gallery. *To Color America: Portraits by Weinold Reiss*. Exhibition catalogue, with an essay by John C. Ewers. Washington DC: Smithsonian Institution Press, 1989.

Paul Doris A. *The Navajo Code Talkers*. Pittsburgh: Dorrance, 1973.

Red Elk, Roderick. "Comanche Code Talkers." *Prairie Lore* 27, no. 1 (1991): 113–14.

———. "Comanche Code Talkers." *Prairie Lore* 28, no. 1 (1992): 1–10.

Rios, Theodore, and Kathleen Mullen Sands. *Telling a Good One: The Process of a Native American Collaborative Biography*. Lincoln: University of Nebraska Press, 2000.

Robichon, Jacques. *The Second D-Day*. Translated from the French by Barbara Shuey. New York: Walker, 1969.

Slotkin, Richard. *Gunfighter Nation: The Myth of the Frontier in Twentieth-Century America*. New York: Harper Perennial, 1992.

Stabler, Eunice Woodhull. *How Beautiful The Land of My Forefathers*. Wichita: Wichita Eagle Press, 1943.

Stabler, Hollis D., et al. *We Remember World War II: A Collection of U.S. Army Ranger Stories*. Elk River MN: Meadowlark Publishing, 2003.

Stubbs, Mary Lee, and Stanley Russell. *Armor-Cavalry, Pt. 1: Regular Army and Army Reserve*. Office of the Chief of Military History, Department of the Army. Washington DC: Government Printing Office, 1969.

Sullivan, Gordon R. *The U.S. Army Campaigns of World War II: Sicily*. Washington DC: Government Printing Office, 1993.

Tong, Benson. *Susan La Flesche Picotte, M.D.: Omaha Indian Leader and Reformer*. Norman: University of Oklahoma Press, 1999.

Truscott, General Lucien K. *The Twilight of the U.S. Cavalry: Life in the Old Army, 1917–1942*. Lawrence: University Press of Kansas, 1989.

Unrah, William E. *Mixed-Bloods and Tribal Dissolution: Charles Curtis and the Quest for Indian Identity*. Lawrence: University Press of Kansas, 1989.

Wilt, Alan F. *The French Riviera Campaign of August 1944*. Carbondale: Southern Illinois University Press, 1981.

INDEX

In the American Indian Lives series: